The Long 2020

Richard Grusin, *Series Editor*

The Long 2020

RICHARD GRUSIN AND
MAUREEN RYAN, EDITORS

Center for 21st Century Studies

UNIVERSITY OF MINNESOTA PRESS

MINNEAPOLIS • LONDON

Portions of chapter 11 are adapted from David Gissen, "Disabling Environments: Human Physiology and Its Architectural Conditions," in *The Architecture of Disability: Buildings, Cities, and Landscapes beyond Access* (Minneapolis: University of Minnesota Press, 2022). Portions of chapter 12 are adapted from conversations on *Platform* in the "Ventopenings: Conditioning in Pandemic Times" series, with Daniel A. Barber, Dorit Aviv, and Ahu Aydogan, edited by Marta Gutman. Portions of chapter 14 are adapted from Dehlia Hannah, "Inversion Layer," in *BREATHLESS*, edited by Ala Roushan, The Power Plant Contemporary Art Gallery, Toronto, 2021.

In chapter 16, excerpt from "Long time ago" from *Storyteller*, Leslie Marmon Silko, copyright 1981, 2012 by Leslie Marmon Silko. Used by permission of Viking Books, an imprint of Penguin Publishing Group, a division of Penguin Random House LLC. All rights reserved.

Published by the University of Minnesota Press
111 Third Avenue South, Suite 290
Minneapolis, MN 55401-2520
http://www.upress.umn.edu

ISBN 978-1-5179-1470-7 (hc)
ISBN 978-1-5179-1471-4 (pb)

Library of Congress record available at https://lccn.loc.gov/2022039091

Printed in the United States of America on acid-free paper

The University of Minnesota is an equal-opportunity educator and employer.

UMP BmB 2022

Contents

Introduction

By many accounts, 2020 was the longest year in recent memory. From the early days of the year, people in the United States and across the globe careened from one unfolding catastrophe to another. The novel coronavirus that emerged in December 2019 in China reached full-blown pandemic status in March 2020. Everywhere, shortages of hospital beds, ventilators for Covid-19 patients, and basic supplies became urgent concerns. In the United States, every state declared a state of emergency and some form of shelter-in-place mandate to stave off a collapse of the health care system; panic and paranoia were everywhere, seen in the empty store shelves and shuttered schools, felt among those who were catapulted into unemployment and those service workers suddenly deemed "essential" and thrust onto the front lines. The bottom dropped out of the global economy; hundreds of thousands of Americans lost their jobs, and an eviction crisis loomed. A new experience of time characterized daily life under the stay-at-home orders; weeks and months seemed interminably long and undifferentiated without the rituals of social gatherings, birthdays, or events to mark the changing of days. For people thrust into the roles of at-home teachers and caregivers on top of their work-from-home duties, time was too short.

But time was marked in other ways. In late May 2020, George Floyd was murdered by Minneapolis police officer Derek Chauvin, suffocated by an interminable nine-minute choke hold that was captured on video by a young bystander. By June, the video had kindled more than forty-seven hundred demonstrations nationwide, in nearly every major city.[1] President Donald Trump, hoping to consolidate the (white) law-and-order vote for his reelection, called on local and federal forces to violently suppress these protests, warning in a tweet that "when the looting starts, the shooting starts."[2] In June, two hundred U.S. cities were under curfew to curb protests, and seventeen thousand National Guard troops were activated.[3] As the summer dragged on, deaths from Covid-19 mounted, and wildfires consumed 8.9 million acres of land in the United States, blanketing most of the West Coast in apocalyptic ash and red haze.[4] On the other side of the country, the Atlantic raged in a record-breaking hurricane season with thirty named storms, the most on record.[5]

These social and ecological crises were flanked by mounting political crises in the United States too. As the presidential election approached, Donald Trump began actively discrediting the election process and claiming rampant voter fraud (in anticipation, many observed, of his likely electoral loss). By November, fears that he would attempt a coup were palpable.[6] Although Trump indeed lost the popular vote by 7 million and the electoral vote by 74, his incessant months-long Twitter and media campaign to invalidate the election had its desired effect, sowing chaos and fueling his cult of personality, leading thousands of Trump loyalists to stage an attempted coup at the nation's Capitol on January 6, 2021.

What makes something feel long? Is it the consequence of compounding uncertainty that makes time seem to hang in the balance? Is it the registering of effects both somatic and psychological on the body? Sleeplessness, chronic pain (including long-haul Covid-19 symptoms), generalized anxiety, acute depression: all of these warp time and upend our rhythms. But there is also the experience of exposure and vulnerability—to climate catastrophe, to viral infiltration and immunocompromisation, to racial violence and other emergent threats—that has shaped many people's experiences of 2020, although as Nirmala Erevelles points out in this volume, shelter from these threats has always been an unevenly distributed privilege. The ruptures of these overlapping catastrophes felt like a shock to the populace of the privileged West, so much so that many took to declaring 2020 the "worst year ever." *Time* magazine's December 14, 2020, cover story declared it to be so, as did a podcast called *Worst Year Ever* and a panoply of internet memes.[7]

But while the experience of living through the calendar year 2020 felt interminably long, 2020 has proven even longer than its 366 days. It would not be incorrect to say that 2020 began well before the calendar changed on January 1. Indeed, 2020's political crisis, which scholars have argued is a crisis of democracy, goes back at least to 2015 and the nomination of Donald J. Trump as the Republican candidate for the 2016 presidency. Perhaps it goes back to the emergence of social media. But broadly speaking, many of the catastrophes of 2020 have much deeper roots than that. The long 2020 could be traced back to the European fascism of the 1930s; to past pandemics like the Spanish Flu of 1918; to the unfinished business of the civil rights movement or the failed Reconstruction after the Civil War; to 1619 or 1492; to wherever one might want to place the "golden spike" marking the beginning of the Anthropocene. The potential origins of the long 2020 are manifold.

Nor, despite the fervent hopes of U.S. and global social media, did 2020 end when the calendar turned to 2021, as the January 6 insurrection at the U.S. Capitol attested. The consequences of 2020's devastating events are sure to impact the planet for decades, if not centuries, to come. Even with widespread, if uneven, global vaccination, social interaction will be changed for the foreseeable future. The fight for racial justice will go on until it is won. The economic fortunes of global capitalism will be buffeted by the shocks of 2020 for decades. Climate change; trust in government, democratic process, and the media; the belief in science and truth; higher education; architecture; public space—all of these will bear the imprint of the catastrophic events of 2020.

In the first months of 2021, the Center for 21st Century Studies (C21) invited a diverse array of scholars and public intellectuals for a series of online conversations on what we had begun to call "The Long 2020." This volume is the product of those conversations. In naming our project, we play on a now-familiar academic trope of long years, wars, decades, and particularly centuries—such as Fernand Braudel's idea of the "long sixteenth century" or Eric Hobsbawm's "long nineteenth century," both of which paved the way for Giovanni Arrighi's highly influential economic history *The Long 20th Century*.[8] Like these earlier works, which are committed to various notions of the *longue durée*, this volume puts pressure on easy periodizations, reflecting our commitment to historical and disciplinary complexity. Closer to home, we are remediating an earlier C21 project from 2008, "Since 1968," which culminated in an edited 2013 volume titled *The Long 1968*.[9] In scaling down centuries to years, C21 could be seen to be reflecting the more recent notion that the internet has sped up time, reflected in the techie trope that the ratio of human years to internet years is equivalent to that of dog years to human years, 1:7. On internet time, our years had already lengthened before 2020, a process that has only been exacerbated by the intensities of the long 2020.

Our intent in assembling these online fora was to think together across disciplinary and institutional boundaries about this seemingly endless year. These conversations form the basis of the edited volume you have in your hand (or on your screen). As has been true of the Center's work for most of its fifty-plus years of existence, the short essays in the volume are wide-ranging in discipline, methodology, and format. What unites them is their participation in C21's mission to focus on the intersection of the humanities, arts, and sciences (social and natural) with issues of compelling concern. We asked our contributors to consider the question of the long 2020 from the perspective of their own expertise, to think either about the lived experience of this year, its long and deep roots in various human and nonhuman pasts, or its transformation of post-2020 futures. This volume represents the fruit of these conversations, which are only a beginning to what we expect will be an ongoing series of evaluations of the roots and consequences of the long 2020.

Although each essay is wide-ranging and interdisciplinary in its own way, we have arranged them in three loose categories: "Kronos," "Oikos," and "Demos." Under the heading of "Kronos," we have grouped essays that take up questions of time, history, and scale as they have played out, and continue to play out, in the long 2020. These essays are personal, philosophical, political, and historical in their approaches to temporality, often moving back and forth between personal experience of the long 2020 and the much slower and longer temporality of pandemic events in the past, present, and future. The section titled "Oikos" is held together by the term's original Greek meaning, "home," which etymologically grounds our modern sense of "ecology" as wisdom about our planetary home. These pieces dramatize the relationship between home and environment, focusing variously on architecture, breathing, and human–nonhuman relations. Our final grouping, "Demos," brings together essays concerned with the experience of cultural, political, and social life in the long 2020. The pieces in this section deploy cultural and political theory to explore questions of race, gender/sexuality, and democracy. As this brief characterization of our structure already reveals, our groupings are in many ways arbitrary, as almost every essay deals with relations between two or more of our organizing categories. But in arranging the volume this way, we have also sought to group together within the categories essays that resonate with others in that grouping.

KRONOS

The first three essays of the volume take personal experience as a jumping-off point for more philosophical reflections on time. Having moved to Oregon shortly before the Covid-19 pandemic began, Stacy Alaimo uses the feeling of "epistemological rupture" in her own personal life to explain the "deeper sense in which the events were simultaneously surprising and expected, novel and yet deeply sedimented in social, political, and environmental realities." For Alaimo, the experience of living through the pandemic "illustrates the most basic ecological notion of interrelation, the Indigenous ideas of profound relationality, and the recognition that mastery of the world as dead resource must give way to material agencies and multispecies liveliness." In an effort to think about "the pandemic before the pandemic," Levi R. Bryant similarly moves between personal reflections of living through the pandemic in Texas and philosophical speculation about temporality and capitalism. In Bryant's eyes, the pandemic had already happened in a variety of decisions made by global capitalism: to limit numbers of hospital beds; to foster global travel networks that allowed easy transmission of the virus; to favor just-in-time production; to tie health care to employment status; and to create a socially mediated network of information that encouraged "people to become enclosed in television, radio, and internet information bubbles." Megan Craig also takes up her personal experience of mothering during the pandemic to explore what she describes as two conflicting temporalities: "(1) the human time of the immediate present that became over the last year slow, intense, and unyielding and (2) the inhuman time of nature in its unforgiving but lifesaving flux." Like Bryant, she uses the idea of "two times" as a launching pad for philosophical speculation about the strange temporality of the long 2020.

The next three essays take up historical antecedents of the events of 2020. Wai Chee Dimock explores how two historically disparate pandemics, smallpox and Covid-19, differently impacted Native Americans. Dimock contrasts how smallpox decimated Cherokee peoples in the mid-eighteenth century with how the Navajo Nation has responded to Covid-19 by attaining a higher rate of vaccination than any U.S. state, helping "to make the future thinkable, actionable, and meaningful." Like Dimock, Frédéric Keck pairs the Covid-19 pandemic with an earlier historical moment, 1962, when the "coexistence between orders of living beings was described and when warning signals of its disruption were sent." To make sense of the long history of the Covid-19 pandemic, Keck excavates "what was known in ecology, microbiology, and anthropology in three important works published in 1962": Rachel Carson's *Silent Spring*, Frank Macfarlane Burnet's *Natural History of Infectious Diseases*, and Claude Lévi-Strauss's *La pensée sauvage*. Roderick A. Ferguson turns a historical eye to a different kind of pandemic rampant in 2020, focusing on "the backdrop of post-truth." Ferguson traces the history of a post-truth sensibility and political discourse in the United States to the 1980s, emphasizing how intersectionality was engaged in the struggle against this dangerous discourse.

The final essays in the first section take up questions of futurity. Nirmala Erevelles seeks to reimagine the idea of "crip futurity" in light of the repeated trope by media and politicians that what people most ardently desire is to return to normal after the pandemic. Erevelles uses two different historical events from 2014—the birth of the Black Lives Matter (BLM) movement and the "racist response to the Ebola outbreak in West Africa that same year"—to demonstrate the undesirability of going back to a normal "rooted in acts of brutal violence that preceded this pandemic." She urges a crip futurity to counter normal "visions of a neoliberal ableist future." Rebecca Wanzo takes up a different media trope, the popular framing of 2020 as the "worst year" ever, a trope that has, she reminds us, been applied to other years before it. Wanzo deploys Lauren Berlant's powerful concept of cruel optimism to argue that while the trope of the worst year implies a kind of hope to some, we need to put such "annum narratives to bed" in "solidarity with all those whose perpetual precarity places them out of sync with wished-for futures." William E. Connolly analyzes what he calls the "obduracy of events" by thinking through the contrast between linear time and multiple, intersecting temporalities. While recognizing that "a society sharply divided by hierarchies of class, race, sexuality, and creed" is impacted unevenly by obdurate events like those that have dominated the long 2020, Connolly calls on his fellow intellectuals to "follow the event where it cascades." We need, he urges, to forge a future in which we "work on our operative spiritualities so that we periodically overflow professional confinements, are presumptively more receptive to unfamiliar orientations and experiences, and become more worthy of the events that keep rolling in."

OIKOS

The book's second section takes up the transformation of ideas and practices of home and dwelling in the long 2020, beginning with three essays by architecture historians on relations between inner and outer, built and unbuilt, space. Beatriz Colomina contends that the ongoing Covid-19 pandemic has laid bare a truth often concealed or erased—that "illnesses and architecture are inseparable." Colomina traces the "intimate" relationship "between architecture and the human body," arguing that modern architecture was developed as "sick architecture." The client was idealized as healthy, athletic, and vertical but was in fact sick, weak, and horizontal, as exemplified by the tuberculosis patient. Sanitoria became the model for all architecture. Where Colomina claims that modern architecture defines "the human species itself as weak, fragile, vulnerable, and immersed in bacteria," David Gissen draws another conclusion: "the events of 2020 demonstrate the need for a form of disability rights that is relevant to the architectural environment." Gissen takes up the normalized notion of comfort in designing ventilation systems, arguing that "the study and engineering of heat, coolth, ventilation, and light" pictures the human as "a diagram of a standing able-bodied man shown in the manner of a medical journal." Writing with "the lens of disability," Gissen calls not only for accommodation of the needs of the disabled but for a more fundamental rethinking of how "spaces predetermine the character of human-ness." Daniel A. Barber also looks at how mechanical ventilation and HVAC mediate between our internal and external homes, drawing from the experience of the pandemic the lesson that such systems are necessary for inhabiting buildings in the twenty-first century and have significant ecological consequences. Like Gissen, Barber sees the current pandemic as offering architects a creative opportunity to rethink notions of designing for comfort not only in terms of diverse and varied human abilities but also in terms of its ecological cost.

To rethink design in relation to ventilation is to rethink how the atmosphere inside buildings remediates the air outside. Jennifer Gabrys approaches this question in terms of breathability, focusing on the air less inside our homes and workplaces than on the outside. Gabrys considers "different ways of breathing in the long 2020 through three particle stories that sift from the debris of this moment: an airborne virus, particulate matter, and wildfire smoke." Drawing on her decade-long Citizen Sense research project, which aims to guide us "toward more breathable worlds,"

Gabrys details the different kinds of particulate matter generated by three crises of 2020: Covid-19, the George Floyd murder, and the wildfires in the western United States. Dehlia Hannah also considers the ways in which "the act of breathing became newly fraught" in 2020, noting that air can no longer be taken as an invisible medium for human and nonhuman life. Hannah offers an eco-philosophical meditation on air that addresses the question, "Why did the pandemic become such a captivating analogy for climate change?" Among her answers is that Covid-19 forces us to address the relationship between bodily vulnerability and the air we breathe, creating what she calls "virally induced inversions within the concepts of air, climate, atmosphere, and related terms."

The final three essays of this section perform their own conceptual inversions, taking up in very different ways the agency and point of view of the SARS-CoV-2 virus. Stephanie Fishel understands this virus as a "microscopic actor," "born from humankind's disregard for ecosystems and the murder, enslavement, and trade of nonhuman animals." Thinking about this microbial actor leads her to ask, "How might we understand the body politic through the flesh and viscera of the human body?" This question leads her to the one that is at the heart of her essay: "What does—or could—freedom mean in a pandemic?" One answer she provides is that "freedom, from both a microbial and an immunological viewpoint, is less about individuality and more about finding connections between human and nonhuman worlds; freedom is about being *more connected*, not cut free from our bonds to others." Bernard C. Perley depicts both the costs and possibilities from these connections between humans and nonhumans in a delightful and incisive graphic novella that tries to imagine how the global pandemic of the long 2020 might look from the point of view of the SARS-CoV-2 virus. Perley explores how object-oriented ontology could "decenter the human from the pandemic and imagine pluriverse relations across living entities." Eben Kirksey offers a complementary strategy for decentering the human, focusing on microscopic, viral agency through the lens of multispecies ethnography. His essay draws on emergent biological knowledge to make sense of how the coronavirus was one among a number of multispecies agents in ongoing necropolitical wars. Kirksey explains how viruses are agential beings "involved in the coproduction of worlds—from microcosms in cells to the macrocosms of ecosystems and human social institutions." Because microbes like SARS-CoV-2 are only "just starting to reveal their disruptive potential," the disturbance of "global systems sustaining human life" that began in March 2020 is certain to extend that long year almost indefinitely.

DEMOS

The final section is concerned with our shared fates: what it means to live and work alongside one another; how we work to make a nation, or a world, hold together; and what happens when it doesn't. Protest, bitter and sometimes violent, was a defining feature of the long 2020, and several authors take up protests explicitly. In her essay, Elisabeth Anker looks at two moments of protest in 2020—BLM protesting and those against government mask mandates—as a way of thinking about two starkly different conceptualizations of freedom in the United States and the "political stakes of democratic possibility emerging out of the long 2020." Anker argues that the antimaskers and Capitol insurrectionists of January 6, 2021, share an investment in "masculinized, white freedom"—that is, the notion that government should work only for white people, and if it doesn't, it should be dismantled. Jonathan Flatley reflects on his experience of protesting this summer and the foment of antipolice sentiment among BLM protesters and others protesting oppressive regimes across the world. Building on his work as an affect theorist, he argues that the hatred of the police, which united protesters in the United States with antiracist protesting all over the world, was a vital political affect that built among protesters "the imagination of a vast unending solidarity." In that sense, he argues, "hatred for the police is hopeful." Policing is also the subject of Adia Benton's anthropological "mixtape" that draws strong parallels between the public health work of contact tracing (in the 2015 Ebola outbreak in Sierra Leone and the coronavirus pandemic) and the police work of prosecuting BLM protesters. The parallels go both ways: epidemiology and public health are underfunded, feminized, and often carceral in their approaches to tracking and containing victims of the Ebola virus. Conversely, policing is like "fieldwork" in an anthropological and epidemiological sense, where police collect evidence in the field. It is, she muses, "biopolitics all the way down."

Other chapters confront the biopolitical through an examination of how bodies have been policed during 2020. Cary Gabriel Costello outlines the many ways in which the Trump administration and its loyalists persecuted trans and nonbinary people, while claiming themselves to be a persecuted minority. This inversion is a strategy common to sexual assaulters and rapists—deny, attack, and reverse the victim and offender (DARVO)—and, he argues, it further frays our fragile shared reality. Relatedly, McKenzie Wark considers our shared language for "sex," "gender," and the concept of "the norm" in the long 2020. Wark challenges the widespread social desire to "return to normal" after the pandemic, arguing that in the context of trans lives, the "normal"—and, along with it, even liberal ideas about what constitutes sex and gender—might have always been too limiting. "To escape the norm is an art, a kind of labor that willfully or experimentally makes things otherwise," she notes, reflecting that the labor of trans collective care and community building operates as a praxis in and around and against the norm.

Labor and praxis are central to Tom Rademacher and Bonnie Honig as well. Middle school teacher Tom Rademacher reflects on his work in a Minneapolis middle school after George Floyd was murdered not ten miles away and the slow-motion tragedy of pandemic-era schooling. Rademacher explores how his students' grief (and his own) about overlapping traumas was handled in the everyday practices of caring for students as individuals and as a school community. Against the crushing failures of policing, the education system, and the entrenched poverty that leads to diminished lives among his pupils, Rademacher highlights how students nonetheless show up for themselves and one another in ways that astonish. In her chapter on the 2020 election, Honig pays close attention to the ordinary and vital labors of poll workers and ballot counters. Honig writes that the dangers of the 2020 election—including the virus and the physical, bodily harm threatened by angry "stop the steal" protesters—did not prevail over workers running the election. Indeed these dangers remind us how "much *work* is involved in elections and, by extension, in the larger functioning of democracy; and we saw how essential, and hands-on, such work indispensably is." The work of finding astonishment amid devastation is both theme and analytical method for the Slough Sayers collective, a group of women of color "working and writing against Anthropocene devastation." In our final chapter, they highlight several communities of practice in Puerto Rico and Alberta, Canada, that in various ways "design[ed] collaborative research that gathered communities to bear witness to devastation and wonder." Although the work that these organizations did was disrupted by the pandemic, the Slough Sayers show that "to appreciate making wonder within devastation, we need close attention to more-than-human lives and livelihoods in the making of community."

In bringing together this diverse group of authors, we have not attempted to offer a comprehensive history of, or set of reflections on, the ongoing long 2020. Instead, we offer a variety of perspectives on the impacts of that fraught year, the effects of which are still ongoing. Nonetheless, crucial through lines have emerged across the organizational boundaries of our book's three sections, which could serve to provide pointers for future observations and speculations on the continuing effects of this *annus horribilis*. One of these through lines is the relationality of action: the recognition emphasized by the long 2020 that humans, technologies, and nonhuman nature cannot be thought in isolation from one another but must be understood as always already acting in assemblages and collectivities made up of human and nonhuman actants. Essays across each of the three sections also demonstrate how the long 2020 has intensified and laid bare the economic, social, and political inequality of U.S. and global capitalism, with particular attention to the BLM protests and the injustices and systematic violence committed both by capital and by the state against people of color and LGBTQ+ communities. And of course, most of the essays, as the year itself, situate themselves in the context of the ongoing Covid-19 pandemic, not only in terms of the medical and public health crises created by the SARS-CoV-2 virus but also in terms of the way the pandemic has exacerbated existing geopolitical fractures. These truths—of our relationality, of the deep racial and economic inequality of our age, and of the pandemic's ongoing reverberations through space and time—will by necessity shape the intellectual work that must be done if we hope to survive the future.

NOTES

1. Heather Cox Richardson, *Letters from an American*, May 25, 2021, https://heathercoxrichardson.substack.com/.

2. Michael S. Rosenwald, "'When the Looting Starts, the Shooting Starts': Trump Quotes Miami Police Chief's Notorious 1967 Warning," *Washington Post*, May 29, 2020, https://www.washingtonpost.com/history/2020/05/29/when-the-looting-starts-the-shooting-starts-trump-walter-headley/.

3. Michael S. Rosenwald, Rachel Chason, Marissa J. Lang, and Perry Stein, "Thousands Descend on D.C. Protests to Push Back against Trump's Show of Federal Force," *Washington Post*, June 3, 2020, https://www.washingtonpost.com/local/new-fencing-encircles-white-house-continued-federal-forces-on-day-5-of-dc-protests/2020/06/02/d323e112-a4e8-11ea-b473-04905b1af82b_story.html.

4. Center for Disaster Philanthropy, "2020 North American Wildfire Season," December 7, 2020, https://disasterphilanthropy.org/disaster/2020-california-wild fires/.

5. National Oceanic and Atmospheric Administration, "Record-Breaking Atlantic Hurricane Season Draws to an End," November 4, 2020, https://www.noaa.gov/media-release/record-breaking-atlantic-hurricane-season-draws-to-end.

6. Barton Gellman, "How Trump Could Attempt a Coup," *The Atlantic*, November 2, 2020, https://www.theatlantic.com/politics/archive/2020/11/how-trump-could-attempt-coup/616954/.

7. Michael S. Rosenwald, "Was 2020 the Worst Year Ever? Historians Weigh In," *Washington Post*, December 30, 2020, https://www.washingtonpost.com/history/2020/12/30/ranking-2020-worst-year-history/.

8. Fernand Braudel, *Civilization and Capitalism, 15th–18th Century: Vol. I. The Structure of Everyday Life*, trans. Siân Reynold (Berkeley: University of California Press, 1992); Eric Hobsbawm, *The Age of Revolution: 1789–1848* (New York: New American Library, 1962); Giovanni Arrighi, *The Long 20th Century* (London: Verso, 1994).

9. Daniel J. Sherman, Ruud van Dijk, Jasmine Alinder, and A. Aneesh, eds., *The Long 1968: Revisions and New Perspectives* (Bloomington: Indiana University Press, 2013).

KRONOS

1 The Portal Was Already Here

Epistemological Rupture, Speculation, and Design in the Long 2020

STACY ALAIMO

When news of the impending pandemic hit, the most mundane daily activities suddenly epitomized life in what Ulrich Beck termed "risk society" and what this volume characterizes as "the long 2020."[1] We required scientific data to assess the most basic activities, such as buying groceries or getting the mail. We feared the virus itself but also suffered from the "double shock" of the loss of sovereignty, the inability to determine how to keep ourselves and our loved ones safe without adequate information. Should we mask outside? Do we dare to eat takeout? As an environmentalist who avoids toxins, I was unprepared for the initial frenzy of disinfecting—there was not one drop of hand sanitizer, disinfectant, bleach, or other such chemical concoction in my possession. And yet, even as I resisted the coming isolation, heartbroken at having to cancel personal and professional travel, fearing the isolation of living in a new city without being able to see my people, I was strangely prepared for this event, in the sense of having long inhabited environmental conceptions of living as an embodied being inextricably interconnected with larger material, economic, and political forces. Feminist, environmentalist, and new materialist theories all shift us toward onto-epistemologies in which knowing and being are not divided. Vivid onto-epistemological moments particular to this pandemic included the way my hands learned, early on, to remember whether I had touched something that could be contaminated; they tingled with uncertainty and apprehension until they were scrubbed. And when I

3

walked the dogs up and down the block, my body stiffened up at the sight of people heading toward us, before I could remember what it was that was so frightening about a small family taking a stroll.

The pandemic seemed both novel and utterly familiar, as it epitomized my theory of transcorporeality, which draws on Beck but also Karen Barad's feminist new materialism, underscoring the need for scientific disclosures to assess invisible risks while insisting that such seemingly abstract assessments shift the epistemological into the ontological, interweaving knowing and being while expanding ethical and political terrains through the practice of speculating about geographically and temporally long chains of interconnection. Transcorporeality emerged from environmental justice and environmental health movements, which are primarily anthropocentric, but it dissolves the boundaries of the human by tracing embodied interconnection with the material world, interconnections that all species inhabit. Though my book *Bodily Natures: Science, Environment, and the Material Self* focused on xenobiotic chemicals, not viruses, the parallels to the Covid-19 crisis have felt a bit eerie, especially for those of us who are chemically sensitive, who must assess the risks of invisible hazards, such as air fresheners or cleaning chemicals in public spaces.[2] Todd Haynes's film *Safe*, for example, an eerie melodrama of environmental illness, dramatizes how something as ostensibly inert as a newly delivered couch could become a monstrous antagonist for the placid heroine. *Safe* also dramatized the racial and class disparities of chemical exposures as well as the "privilege" of having the time and resources to trace and identify an illness that, in Joseph Dumit's terms, you have to "fight" to get.[3] This unnerving onto-epistemology of immersion is vital, I believe, for living through the Anthropocene, where nothing—not the air, the climate, populations of birds and insects, or consumer products, and certainly not "nature"— can be presumed to be a background or resource for the exploits of the human. As we rush back to "normal," in the "aftertimes," will we maintain a sense of the onto-epistemologies that the pandemic made vivid? Can we turn away from the possessive individualist, consumerist, and humanist notion of the bounded immaterial self and learn from environmental justice movements that have long demonstrated that health is not an individual matter but that racial and class inequities, with their long histories and effects, forge landscapes where culture and nature, body and place, cannot be disentangled? Such a sense of the world demands that academic disciplines and political movements delve into the messy places where social justice and environmental concern are enmeshed, where ethics and politics require speculative engagement with scientific captures of radically, rapidly transforming material realities.

EPISTEMOLOGICAL RUPTURE:
SEDIMENTED AND SURPRISING

In the before times, it was normal for privileged peoples to live with a comforting disconnect between knowing and being. In capitalist consumerism a conventional sense of well-being depends on ignorance, denial, and the presumption of impermeability. Things are supposed to do what you bought them to do; they appear with their extractive, harmful origins and polluting futures erased. Best not to think about how the shiny new cell phone has harmed (and will harm once it is tossed away) ecologies, wildlife, and various groups of people. Tracing such harms requires both information and speculation across geographical and temporal distances, a practice that transforms present, immediate realities into ethical and political expanses. Extractivism, objectification, and division are naturalized in the basic routines of everyday life and the conception of the separate self. The domestic realm is literally walled off from the long trail of interconnected harms to local and distant peoples and ecologies that maintain it. Covid-19 both ruptured that norm and reinforced it. It interrupted expectations that constant streams of consumer goods would flow into our homes, as toilet paper and flour disappeared and people had to consider supply chains. When meat was not abundantly available, perhaps some people reckoned with the many hardships endured by workers in that industry, if not the suffering of the animals themselves. But the pandemic also necessitated barrier methods, including the production of a great many disposable face masks, polypropylene and polystyrene food containers, and plastic packaging, granting individual protection through the amped-up production of materials that, after a brief moment of use, become nearly eternal pollution, killing sea turtles, whales, and other creatures in their wake. While romanticized, delusional, and often ecofascist visions of how animals were "coming back"—frolicking across cities or relaxing in quieter seas—spread across social media during the early pandemic, such fantasies evaporated with the obvious realization that the lockdown would not last forever. Not only would global shipping, airline flights, and auto traffic resume but the drive to isolate individuals from the virus would itself result in the production of garbage and toxic chemicals that inadvertently harm nonhuman life, not to mention (almost no one does mention it) that Covid-19 would increase animal testing. In a compelling essay, Bjørn Kristensen notes the tragic irony that "rhesus macaques, the same species of monkey that activists are rescuing from starvation on one side of the planet, are also a common species being used in animal testing," including research related to Covid-19.[4] The pandemic witnessed not only a shortage of toilet paper but a shortage of a strategic "resource"—the rhesus macaques.[5] Reckoning with the dissonance between the romanticized spectacles of imagined animal freedom and the overlooked objectification of nonhuman beings as "resources" for medical experimentation requires a more incisive, connected, and ethical formulation of what Lucinda Cole has aptly termed the "medical posthumanities," as does grappling with the zoonotic origins of this and other pandemics.[6]

Even though the pandemic sparked a sense of epistemological rupture or the loss of intellectual sovereignty, there is a deeper sense in which the events were simultaneously surprising and expected, novel and yet deeply sedimented in social, political, and environmental realities. News of how BIPOC peoples have suffered higher rates of infection and mortality from the virus underscores the impossibility of separating human health from historical and contemporary structures of inequality, oppression, and violence. As environmental justice movements reveal, racism is not a free-floating ideology but instead something sedimented into embodied geographies of harm that are enmeshed with, but not reducible to, class disparities. Environmental justice movements manifest how new materialist onto-epistemologies can be deeply political matters, sedimentations permeating bodies and places.[7] Even if the summer of racial reckoning after the killing of George Floyd was considered separate from the pandemic, the simultaneity of another horrific police killing of a Black person with the brutal racial inequalities in terms of Covid-19 outcomes raises crucial questions about the interrelations between intentional violence, structural violence, the long material histories of racism, and its present effects. Even the popular television series *Gray's Anatomy* included scenes during the 2020–21 season that suggested these parallels, raising viewers' consciousness and encouraging further inquiry into their relations. At the same time that some seek to scientifically, philosophically, and politically understand and attempt to ameliorate racialized health disparities, others launched an onto-epistemological backlash marked by aggressive posturing and violence. It was all too predictable that the masked face of

Covid-19, a symbol of vulnerability, interconnection, and social responsibility, would trigger a masculinist, aggressive, white supremacist, hyper-individualist panic. The anti-maskers, like the climate deniers, and most vividly the "rolling coal" movement that epitomizes "carbon-heavy white masculinity,"[8] refuse risk society, science, corporeal vulnerability, and interconnection, in brutal and often racist displays.

Michael Taussig writes that the "fantastic power of catastrophe is the new normal," resulting in a crisis of representation. "It is a dangerous moment. You feel the world tremble."[9] Arguing for the "mastery of non-mastery" and the "reenchantment of nature," he contends that "the phantom illness is the sickness of the planet, a sickness that causes cancer and strange fatal viruses and is itself caused by the sickness of human society fouling its nest, trapped in a toxic economic system bound to 'growth' at any cost."[10] Although I agree with his arguments for cultivating non-mastery and the reenchantment of nature, ideas with long roots in feminist science studies, environmental studies, and new materialism, I think his dramatic statement "we seem stuck in a nightmare we cannot express" misses something.[11] Being "stuck" does not capture the more disturbing sense that life as we have known it is shifting under our feet—the "we" here being privileged settler colonialists, rather than Indigenous peoples, who, as Kyle Powys Whyte argues, have been experiencing cataclysmic, genocidal change since colonization, making climate change and the Anthropocene nothing new.[12] Furthermore, while it may be difficult to "express" this nightmarish moment, there is a more paradoxical sense in which each disturbing event of 2020, from the killing of unarmed Black people by police to the unequal distribution of pandemic harm to the devastation of the wildfires in the West and the apocalyptic winter in Texas, is something we already knew. As countless social media skirmishes illustrate, the long 2020 has been punctuated by people posting about some horrific event, followed by a flash of realization and an expression of outrage, and then a paradoxical lament that this is but can't be reality, only to be met with a chorus of exasperated, weary, and sometimes virtue-signaling people yelling "but we already know this, we've known this, we knew this, why didn't you know this, why doesn't anyone know anything?" The frustrated cries of contemporary Cassandras underscore the pervasiveness of denial and the "resilience" demonstrated by the repeated returns to an already dystopian "normal." While phrases like "the new normal" try to tame the devastation of the epistemological rupture of the long 2020 with acceptance, normalizing settles into complacency. Such fragmented, fleeting, and dis-connected moments of "knowing" cannot sustain change. Coming to terms with the long 2020 means that we know and we don't know; we expected it, yet are shocked. We pivot back and forth between these recognitions, scale shifting, connecting, speculating about what is, what has long been, and what could be. What is demands as much speculation as what could be, because the portal is already here.

STRANGE FACTS AND SPECULATIVE FUTURES

Now what? The antidote to the postfact era, populated by climate deniers, conspiracy theorists, and presidentially endorsed wackos, should not be a return to a simplistic notion of "facts" as things uncovered by a scientific practice that is untainted by economic, ideological, and social structures. Robert Proctor's title *Cancer Wars: Why Politics Shapes What We Know and Don't Know about Cancer* succinctly states why we cannot just return to a simplistic notion of scientific fact as separate from political and eco-nomic forces. Isabelle Stengers, in "Science Fiction to Science Studies," writing about climate science, states, "As for how the peoples of this earth will be able to address the coming disorders, it is certainly not a matter of 'accepting scientific authority.' Climate science is mute about that. Instead it is a question which diffracts, or should diffract, across all our habits of thinking and imagining."[13] She argues that many of her concepts "are meant to activate the speculative imagination—at once an appetite for what may be possible and resistance against the normalcy of what is considered self-evident," proposing that science fiction (SF) writers "be understood as researchers, the authors of particular thought experiments."[14] Such thought experiments may transform habits of thinking and being through their perceived immediacy. Despite its engagement with ecological science and climate change, Charlotte McConaghy's recent novel *Migra-tions,* which follows someone who is following the last of the Arctic terns, does not feel like SF. It is written in an unremarkable style and flat tone, devoid of weirdness or world building or postapocalyptic urgency. It is not only the flat affect that makes it profoundly unsettling, however, but its temporal intimacy; the ostensible "future" in which nearly all species have already gone extinct feels immediate, already present, requiring no imaginative speculation.[15] Indeed, there is little to visualize when there is nothing left to see. The novel quietly amplifies the Sixth Great Extinc-tion, placing the reader just a bit up the road, perhaps following Stengers's provocations for "resistance against the normalcy of what is considered self-evident."

If you are paying attention to such things as climate change, extinction, wildfires, water shortages, famines, climate refugees, mammoth mountains of garbage, the collapse of ocean ecologies, and intensifying racism, misogyny, transphobia, and fascism, you may feel like we are living in an SF novel, one that demands constant speculation about futures that have already arrived. The practice of speculation, taking scientific knowledge and extrapolating it in imaginative ways, is vital for developing ethical, political, and practical responses to the Anthropocene, a time when nothing can be presumed to be a stable background. Scientific disclosures are necessary for the practices of daily life as well as for the construction of compelling critiques, ethicopolitical mapping, and visions of less diminished futures. As ashes from the wildfires fell in my yard, including my vegetable gardens, during the long, dark week, I wondered what they consisted of. What exactly was this ash, and what risks might it pose?[16] A poetic social media post suggested that people in Oregon envision the burned bodies of wild animals in the ashes falling around us, inviting us to grieve their deaths along with the deaths of people. Because so many houses, mobile homes, vehicles, and consumer goods went up in flames, the ashes must have consisted of a slew of toxic chemicals, along with trees and bodies. Despite masks and air filters, we—I, my dogs, my neighbors, the birds and other wildlife—breathed it all in, a dystopian, transcorporeal intimacy with plants, animals, and, presumably, toxic, xenobiotic substances.

Felicia Luna Lemus, in her poetic work *Particulate Matter*, suggests the strange temporalities and material intimacies of living through wildfires. The ominous line commanding an entire page, "I smell fire again," is followed by a description of the packing up of valuables (including, ironically, three urns of ashes), followed by a solitary phrase, an isolated update that hovers on the next page—"Five thousand acres and growing"—followed by a more intimate bodily sensing of the ash: "Ash falls like light snow, caught in my lashes, in my breath, the sun gray."[17] The predominance of blank space on each of the pages underscores the sense of urgency of each moment as it unfolds, but it can also invite scale-shifting speculations about vast anthropocene geographies, temporalities, and futurities for which we may not have the words. The last page of this prose poem expresses the need for an ending but can only hold the present moment in brackets, as if admitting the impossibility of defining or delimiting the expansive catastrophes: "[There is no end in sight.]."[18]

The intimacy with futures already in process resonates with Arundhati Roy's inspiring idea of the pandemic as a portal. In her early and searing account of Covid-19, focused on India, she writes that "the tragedy is immediate, real, epic and unfolding before our eyes. But it isn't new. It is the wreckage of a train that has been careening down the track for years."[19] Indeed, in so many ways that Roy describes and that the authors in this collection analyze, the tracks leading to the wreckage of the long 2020 are long and multiple. Roy's conclusion, however, severs the imagination from material realities. Yes, nothing "could be worse than a return to normality," but to "imagine the world anew," by seeing the pandemic as "a portal, a gateway between one world and the next," invites a dreamy transcendence rather than a painful reckoning with present realities that cannot simply be left behind: "We can choose to walk through it, dragging the carcasses of our prejudice and hatred, our avarice, our data banks and dead ideas, our dead rivers and smoky skies behind us. Or we can walk through lightly, with little luggage, ready to imagine another world. And ready to fight for it." If only prejudice and hatred and avarice were mere carcasses. If only we could leave the dead rivers and smoky skies behind. This vision offers the most privileged among us an ethereal, idealist escape clause, when the messier, more mundane matters require attention. Having lived through my first summer of wildfires in Oregon, I can say that it is not so easy to leave the smoky skies behind—every day, I checked the maps to see in which direction we should flee if the nearby fires got too close, only to find that there were no good directions. No exit. Readers will object that I am taking Roy's poetic conclusion too literally—but that is exactly my point. We can't escape the material world through metaphor; we can't travel through tropes. Social and environmental visions and aesthetic representations can, of course, inspire change through their visions of what is possible, but the danger is that we are all so well trained to compartmentalize these flights of fancy—indulging in them even as we routinely live in profoundly destructive ways. To rewrite Stengers, it is not only climate change but also the Sixth Great Extinction, and the continuing violences of racism, colonialism, extractivism, and capitalism, that we need to diffract across "all our habits of thinking and imagining." But it is not enough to think and imagine; intellectual and creative work must also inform our daily practices in the here and now, within the rusty, decomposing portal that has long been present. Such onto-epistemologies, as orientations toward both social justice and multispecies perspectives, can refuse the elevation of disconnected reason or transcendent imagination, which is part of a Western, Enlightenment humanism at the root of so many of the crises that confront us. Thinking with the provocation of the long 2020, in the wake of debates about the Anthropocene, new materialism, and posthumanism, means that we need to reckon with the delusional figure of the separate, bounded, and transcendent human, the unmarked white, ableist Man of Western capitalism, that floating apparition of reason and spirit, untethered to the earth, unrelated to any other form of life. Instead, the long 2020 sharply illustrates the most basic ecological notion of interrelation, the Indigenous ideas of profound relationality, and the recognition that mastery of the world as dead resource must give way to material agencies and multispecies liveliness.

EPIGRAPH: PRACTICING MULTISPECIES DESIGN

Before the pandemic began, I already felt isolated, having recently moved to Oregon with only my dog, Felix, but I was lucky to have family and friends visit. Once the pandemic began, like most people, I read and listened to the news, constantly, putting the emerging bits of expert advice into practice as soon as possible. But I complemented these practices with a more positive obsession, that of transforming empty lawns, devoid of much life, to places where native plants support birds, bees, butterflies, and other critters. Learning about native plants; speculating about how the plants, insects, and birds interact; creating stone piles and stick piles for critters to hide; letting the leaves, pine needles, falling branches, and pine cones pile up to create a more natural ground; and relishing the many aesthetic pleasures and the palpable companionship of multispecies communities has been the onto-epistemological environmental practice that sustained me through the long 2020. Owning a house and yard, as a white settler colonialist, in a region where many people live without a home of any kind, is certainly a privileged and fraught position, without innocence, and yet it can also offer a way of modestly doing some small positive thing. Arturo Escobar, in *Designs for the Pluriverse*, asks, "For those of us without an ancestral mandate to help our worlds persevere, the question becomes, how do we recreate and recommunalize our worlds? How do we develop forms of knowing that do not take words and beings and things out of the flow of life—that is, forms of knowing and being that do not recompose nature as external to us, as dead or unsentient matter? What kinds of ritu-als might we develop to this end?"[20] Escobar's sense of multispecies design is a vital practice for the long 2020, not as a portal to someplace else, but as an invitation to make space, here—wherever that here may be—for other creatures, however we can. As Escobar states, "design can thus become an open invitation for us all to become mindful and effective weavers of the mesh of life."[21]

NOTES

1. See Ulrich Beck, *Risk Society: Towards a New Modernity,* trans. Mark Ritter (London: Sage, 1992). My thanks to Maureen Ryan, Richard Grusin, and C21 for inviting me to think with the long 2020. I am grateful to Priscilla Solis Ybarra for early conversations about understanding the pandemic through our work.

2. Stacy Alaimo, *Bodily Natures: Science, Environment, and the Material Self* (Bloomington: Indiana University Press, 2010). For more on transcorporeality as exposure, domestic enclosure, the Anthropocene, and the agencies of plastic pollution, see Alaimo, *Exposed: Environmental Politics and Pleasures in Posthuman Times* (Minneapolis: University of Minnesota Press, 2016).

3. J. Dumit, "Illnesses You Have to Fight to Get: Facts as Forces in Uncertain, Emergent Illnesses," *Social Sciences and Medicine* 62, no. 3 (2006): 477–590.

4. Bjørn Kristensen, "Welcome to the Viralocene: Transcorporeality and Peripheral Justice in an Age of Pandemics," *Medium,* May 19, 2020, https://medium.com/@bjornkristensen/viralocene-66a954260487.

5. Sarah Zhang, "America Is Running Low on a Crucial Resource for COVID-19 Vaccines: The Country Is Facing a Monkey Shortage," *The Atlantic,* August 31, 2020, https://www.theatlantic.com/science/archive/2020/08/america-facing-monkey-shortage/615799/. I write this on the very day I am scheduled for my second Covid-19 vaccine, painfully aware of my own implications in the suffering of the animals used to manufacture these vaccines.

6. Lucinda Cole, "Zoonotic Shakespeare: Animals, Plagues, and the Medical Post-humanities," in *The Routledge Handbook of Shakespeare and Animals,* ed. Karen Raber and Holly Dugan, 104–15 (London: Taylor and Francis, 2020).

7. See also Zakiyyah Iman Jackson's brilliant book *Becoming Human: Matter and Meaning in an Antiblack World* (New York: New York University Press, 2020). While Jackson's argument is too complex to be represented in this short essay, it makes many arguments that bear upon larger questions of onto-epistemologies, posthu-manisms, animal studies, and race, including the idea that "'race' and 'species' have co-evolved and are *mutually reinforcing terms*" (12, emphasis original). She also argues that many "critics of anthropocentrism have mistakenly perceived that the problem of our time is anthropocentrism rather than a failed praxis of being" (15). Jackson's articulation of a "failed praxis of being" is precise and provocative.

8. For more on rolling coal, see Alaimo, *Exposed,* 95–98.

9. Michael Taussig, *Mastery of Non-mastery in the Age of Meltdown* (Chicago: University of Chicago Press, 2020), 29, 32.

10. Taussig, 105.

11. Taussig, 29.

12. See, e.g., Kyle Powys Whyte, "Our Ancestors' Dystopia Now: Indigenous Conservation and the Anthropocene," in *The Routledge Companion to the Environmental Humanities,* ed. Ursula K. Heise, Jon Christensen, and Michelle Niemann, 206–15 (New York: Routledge, 2017).

13. Isabelle Stengers, "Science Fiction to Science Studies," in *The Cambridge Companion to Literature and Science,* ed. Steven Myer (New York: Cambridge University Press, 2017), 35.

14. Stengers, 26, 32.

15. Charlotte McConaghy, *Migrations* (New York: Flat Iron Books, 2020).

16. Farmworkers and other people who work outdoors may be disproportionately at risk from wildfire smoke and ash. Xiaoming Wan, Chongyang Li, and Sanjai J. Parikh conclude in one study, for example, "Based on these data, it is proposed that the potential health risks of farmworkers caused by fire ash during fire recovery work should be carefully considered, especially for sites with a history of multiple fires and ash located close to buildings." Wan, Li, and Parikh, "Chemical Composition of Soil-Associated Ash from the Southern California Thomas Fire and Its Potential Inhalation Risks to Farmworkers," *Journal of Environmental Management* 278, part 2 (2021).

17. Felicia Luna Lemus, *Particulate Matter* (New York: Akashic Books, 2020), 120–23.

18. Luna Lemus, 130.

19. Arundhati Roy, "The Pandemic Is a Portal," *Financial Times,* April 3, 2020, https://www.ft.com/content/10d8f5e8-74eb-11ea-95fe-fcd274e920ca.

20. Arturo Escobar, *Designs for the Pluriverse* (Durham, N.C.: Duke University Press, 2017), 200.

21. Escobar, 215.

2 The Pandemic before the Pandemic

LEVI R. BRYANT

It is April 2021, yet we are still somehow in the year 2020. Somehow we have been plunged into a perpetual present, a time that refuses to pass. For now, 2020 has become the horizon in which our lived time unfolds, even if days on the calendar nonetheless appear to pass. It is as if we have all awoken in the film *Groundhog Day,* or a version of Zeno's paradoxes demonstrating that the passage of time and change are illusions. So much has happened during this horizon in which we live in the perpetual long 2020, yet it also seems as if nothing has happened at all. Perhaps the vaccine will allow time to resume again, yet only if a critical mass of people take it and it is distributed throughout the world. It is right to worry about whether that will happen. Will we be beset by endless waves of new variants of the virus?

I write in fragments because that is the style proper to this time. I cannot synthesize it into a coherent narrative. Imagine a photo album arranged in a linear order, recording traces of a life. One day you drop it, and all of the photographs fall out, mixing chaotically. That is what the long 2020 is like. It is a jumbled mass of images and intensities whose order of occurrence I do not know; it is a disordered montage of events I cannot order. It is fragments of a whole that perhaps does not exist or whose secret I cannot decipher. This is a time of fragments.

Every day is the same, yet so much happens every day, especially in the months leading up to the U.S. presidential election and its aftermath. Will I ever remember it all? When you predominantly teach online, there is no longer any inside or outside to labor. Labor is everywhere, and you never really leave it. Work becomes a hamster wheel, an eternal return of the same. As of today, 3,013,818 people are dead from the virus globally, with 567,032 people dead in the United States. I cannot comprehend these numbers. I have been vaccinated and feel both guilt and relief: relief for the temporary safety it has given my wife and me, guilt that others have not yet been able to get vaccinated. Is there a world for us to return to now that we are immeasurably safer? Her car sits in the garage, its battery dead from lack of use. There are cobwebs about the tires, and it is covered with dried and canned goods. Is this not what our lives have become during the long 2020?

The time of which I speak is a deep and structural time. It is ordinal, not cardinal. Ordinality is positional: first, second, third, like bases in baseball. Cardinality is serial: 1, 2, 3 . . . There is an ordinality of time from the standpoint of lived experience. The past, present, and future are positions that structure our way of living time. To claim that 2020 is the horizon of the present is to cite, not a date, but a horizon or structure of time. Past and present are dimensions of this deep, structural present. There was a before time that had a different horizon. I worry whether there will be an after this time.

Let us recall a fundamental Deleuzian distinction. In *Difference and Repetition*, Deleuze is careful to point out that the virtual is not the same as the possible, nor is the virtual opposed to the real.[1] On one hand, there is the couplet of the possible and the real that proceeds by way of what he calls "realization." This is the logic of the metaphysics of identity. The possible, says Deleuze, resembles the real.[2] The real is identical to the possible, differing only in existence. The possible is that which does not yet exist but rather must be realized. Somewhere in God's intellect, Leibniz would say, is a concept of me that contains every predicate or feature of my being—past, present, and future—down to the length of the hairs on my beard, the number of gray hairs I have, and the various moles I have.[3] God's concept of me is identical to me in all respects—including the experiences I will have throughout my life—and in creating me, he merely realizes in existence what was already present in this infinite analytic concept. If Kant, in *Critique of Pure Reason*, will say that "being is obviously not a real predicate," if he will say that there is no more in a hundred imagined dollars than a hundred real dollars, then this is because the possible is identical to the real conceptually.[4] Consequently, he will say that we cannot deduce existence from a concept. There is no genuine creation where realization is concerned.

Matters are quite different with the virtual and the actual. When we hear the word *virtuality*, we should not think of virtual reality such as is depicted in *The Matrix*. Rather, the virtual refers to the conditions of real existence. Of the virtual, Deleuze will say that it is real without being actual, ideal without being abstract.[5] It is by virtue of the virtual that beings become the unique beings they are through a process of actualization. Above all, Deleuze will be careful to emphasize that the virtual does not *resemble* the actual. The virtual is not like God's concept of me, which is identical to me in all respects minus existence or actuality. It shares no resemblance to the actuality that will come to be out of it. The actualization of the virtual is a genuine creation that brings something new into existence.

The trees that surround the parking lot where I like to skate have tops that all grow in a northerly dimension. These trees are actualities. They are actually existing beings. Leibniz would say that prior to the creation of the universe, there was a concept of each of these trees in the intellect of God identical to them in all respects, down to the smallest possible detail, and that their existence was merely realized in and through God's creation. The concept of the tree in God's intellect maximally resembles its existence.

The virtual, by contrast, does not resemble the actual. Actualization is a creative process. The virtuality of the trees is that out of which the trees come to be in their uniqueness. Why is it that the trees grow in a northerly direction? Is this some strange peculiarity of their genetics? Certainly the genes of the trees are an element in the virtual dimension of their being. Deleuze himself makes this connection. Those genes, of course, do not resemble the actualized trees. The nutrients in the soil, annual rainfall, insects, and other plant and animal wildlife in the area are also virtual elements out of which the trees are actualized. If the treetops grow in a northerly direction, then this is because there is a persistent wind that blows in that direction from the south. These trees are wind that has become wood. As they developed and grew, they folded or pleated wind into themselves, taking on that form and shape as a consequence. In navigating the virtual field out of which they grew, they became these unique beings. These are the virtual conditions for the possibility of these singular trees.

To speak of a pandemic before the pandemic is not to speak of a chronology where one pandemic followed another. Rather, it is to speak of a virtual pandemic contemporaneous with the actual pandemic. Deleuze associates the virtual with the past and memory, yet it is a strange sort of ontological past, not the past of specific recollections. Following Bergson, Deleuze argues that the past is always present with the present.[6] It is not that there is *first* the past, *then* the present. Nor is it that there was *first* the present that *then* became the past. Rather, the past is right there with the present. To be sure, there was a virtual pandemic that preceded the actual pandemic, yet it is also entirely present with the actual pandemic. The pandemic had already happened; it just had not yet taken place.

I would like to ask the question, What were the conditions for the possibility of the pandemic? In doing so, I risk exposing myself to ridicule. Do we not all already know how the pandemic happened? Have we not all heard about the virus mutating in bats and being exposed to humans in Chinese wet markets that serve up exotic foods? Was not the pandemic simply the result of a particularly contagious and deadly virus?

On February 14, 2021, my wife and I were celebrating Valentine's Day and mourning the passing of her mother years ago by making Greek spaghetti, a decadent and simple dish her mother made for her every year on her birthday. We were filled with joy and giddy excitement by the heavy snow that was falling—an exceedingly rare event that hardy ever happens in Texas. When such a snow blankets the earth, the world is filled with a comforting silence and a paradoxical warmth that fills me with a strange affective warmth as well. I was overwhelmed with excitement and could not keep a silly, childlike grin from my face all evening. This was wondrous.

After an evening of lovely conversation, sometimes sad as we remembered her amazing mother, at other times filled with laughter as she told me stories of all the amusing things her mother would do, we went to sleep and slept the sleep that is only possible when the world is muffled and aglow from freshly fallen snow. How we had missed this sort of snow we had regularly experienced during the years we had lived in the northern states.

Around two in the morning, we awoke to a frigid house without electricity. We had expected this, as we were told that there would be short rolling electric blackouts to reduce demand on the electric system. I got up to shut off the loud, beeping alerts from the computer backup battery and promptly fell back to sleep. When we awoke hours later, the power was still out. Despite the fact that we had opened the faucets to drip, the pipes had all frozen, and we were now at the beginning of an ordeal where we would be completely without electricity or running water for thirty hours. Our home got down to the low thirties. Fortunately, we have a gas fireplace that allowed us to get a minimal amount of heat and had plenty of sweaters and heavy blankets from our years up north. At one point I began gathering snow in every container I could find and melting it by the fire to provide water for the toilet tanks. Many Texans were not as fortunate as us. People had pipes burst, destroying their homes. A number of people died from hypothermia and carbon monoxide poisoning resulting from bringing grills inside for warmth. Many simply did not have the sort of clothing necessary for the weather. We were wearing three sweaters each and were under heavy down blankets. Many in this region of the country just don't have these sorts of things, as they're not necessary. We have experienced a number of serious winter storms throughout our lives. We had never experienced anything like this. There were moments I worried we would die.

When I returned to the classroom a week or so later, I asked my students whether this was a natural disaster or a human-made disaster. They unanimously said that it was a natural disaster. I am not so sure. There are a number of now well-documented reasons this storm was so severe. First, the electric plants throughout the state were not properly regulated and winterized to render them capable of withstanding these sorts of low temperatures. Second, housing regulations allowed builders to place water pipes on exposed walls in housing and apartments, with very little in the way of insulation. It was this, in part, that led pipes to freeze and burst. Third, because of regional average temperature throughout Texas, many people simply did not have the clothing necessary for this sort of weather. Moreover, rather than concluding that this was a once-in-a-generation storm, Winter Storm Uri can arguably be seen as the result of climate change in the age of the Anthropocene. We will see more of these "freak" weather events. There were semiotic components functioning as necessary conditions for the possibility of Winter Storm Uri, such as the regulations pertaining to how houses are built and electric power plants are maintained, along with a free market ideology that holds that markets best regulate themselves. There were also material components pertaining to the physical actualities of homes, power plants, available clothing, and all the rest. These were the storm before the storm took place. Such are the virtual conditions for the possibility of the storm. There was a storm before the storm.

We should speak of the "before" in "the storm before the storm" and "the pandemic before the pandemic" in the sense of Foucault's historical a priori. It is not a chronological before, though it was indeed here prior to these events taking place, but rather a set of virtual conditions for the possibility of certain enunciations, certain statements and historical events.[7] Under Deleuze's reading of Foucault, assemblages all have one face pointing to the plane of enunciation or the semiotic field of statements governing what is sayable and another face pointing to the plane of content or how material beings are organized, rendering what is visible visible.[8] This is the historical a priori that is the before or condition out of which these events are actualized or come to be. They are like the wind, rain, sunshine, and soil out of which the trees grow.

We need to learn how to stop saying nature and culture, or rather, we need to learn to write and think ~~nature~~ and ~~culture~~ under erasure. This is a true challenge, for this distinction, along with the closely related distinctions of form (intellect) and matter (body), is a fundamental distinction that pervades every aspect of the semiosphere of our thought or the plane of enunciation, functioning as a historical a priori governing what is thinkable and sayable for us. So deep are these distinctions within our thought, so thoroughly do they determine what we can think and say, that we cannot even discern that they function in this way for us. Rather, we must learn to say that there is *only* the wilderness or that the wilderness is *all* there is. If the wilderness is *all* there is, then this entails, by simple syllogistic deduction, that even in the city of Dallas, we are in the midst of the wilderness. The wilderness is no longer what is outside. It is no longer that which is outside culture and society. It no longer refers to that which is yet to be domesticated. Being, whether in the domain of ~~culture~~ or of ~~society~~, or the domain of ~~nature~~, is the wilderness through and through.

If both the pandemic and Winter Storm Uri have been apocalypses to varying degrees, then this is not due merely to their terrifying destructiveness;
they have been revelations, the true meaning of apocalypse. These events
have uncovered or revealed something. They have been forms of *aletheia*
in Heidegger's sense of the term. Above all, they have revealed the manner
in which the essence of being—or, at least, our historical a priori—is the
wilderness. No doubt the term *wilderness* invites confusion. One will mistakenly think I am referring to remote forests and jungles, to that which
has not yet been domesticated. It is always a dangerous exercise, usually
doomed to fail, to resignify the meanings of familiar terms. One keeps hearing old meanings in the new that is being proposed. And, of course, in striving to resignify terms within the semiosphere within which we all think,
one always strives to preserve and shelter some of those old resonances.

Wilderness names the collapse of the distinction between ~~nature~~ and
~~culture~~ or the way in which this distinction is no longer variable in the age
of the Anthropocene. "Anthropocene" names that age in which humanity,
through its agriculture and technology, has completely transformed the
entire fabric of the planet—at least, the planet's surface—becoming the
dominant vector of geological and environmental change across the earth.
We can no longer disambiguate which is which, what share each contributes, what causes what, and therefore the distinction has been rendered
null. There is no nature, nor is there culture. There is just the wilderness.

We think of the wilderness as that which is undomesticated and unpredictable. As compared to our fine cities with their neatly planned roads,
where we believe all is largely predictable and within the orbit of our mastery, the wilderness is thought as that which is unruly and filled with mys-
tery, where the unexpected might happen at any moment, such as in the
case of a sudden bear or hippo attack. Yet this is how it is with the Anthropocene. Like escaped golems created by sorcerers who then go on rampage,
as depicted in Jewish folklore, our own agriculture and technology have
become a set of golems behaving in unruly ways we can no longer anticipate and control or master. The wilderness is a place where one gets lost,
and we are today lost even in the heart of the city or suburb where we feel
most at home. Wilderness signifies that we will no longer speak and think
within the framework of nature or culture but only of ~~nature~~ and ~~culture~~,
because we still aren't entirely sure how to dispense with these words. To
evoke the name "wilderness" is to say that there is *only* being. We will be
accused of trying to think without binaries and reminded that for any

coherent thought to be possible, there must be a complementary opposite. We will be told that a term becomes meaningless when this semio-
logical law is not at work. I will respond by throwing up my hands in the
air, pleading that this is true and that the opposite of wilderness thought
is that form of thought based on the nature–culture binary. I know of no
other way to proceed.

Following his former teacher Michel Serres, time, says the archaeologist
Christopher Witmore, percolates.[9] In this way he contests the conception
of time as a linear sequence, where the past is what is gone, the present
is what is here now, and the future is what is yet to come. A percolating
liquid is incredibly turbulent. If we think of time as a sort of percolating
liquid, then we can conceptualize it as a sort of fluid in which sometimes
the future is in the past, the past is in the future, the present is in the past,
and the past is in the present. We cannot order it in a neat sequence. In a
discussion with Latour, Serres gives the metaphor of a crumpled napkin.[10]
When the napkin is crumpled, various points that would not be adjacent
touch. This is how it is, he says, with time. We think of the Roman Empire
under Caesar as no longer touching us today, yet Witmore and Serres
would argue that it persists in all sorts of ways in the present and not simply as a recollection or an influence.

  Witmore's thesis does not simply come out of a perverse desire to provide a perverse conception of time that violates our commonsense assumptions. Rather, his reflections on time arise directly out of his fieldwork as
an archaeologist. Contrast the historian with the archaeologist. Historians
often divide things into periods as if they could be smoothly demarcated
such that one period begins after another ends. Of course, they will concede that there are transitions. The archaeological dig reveals something
quite different. A dig cannot be divided into easily delineated periods. Why?
Because objects—especially architectural objects—persist from one period
to another. They are like time machines or shards of memory. The corner
wall of a building built in ancient Greece lives on, continues to exist, during the Middle Ages and even up to the present. It makes up the corner
wall of a barn or home that someone lives in now. People still live about
and among these things, making it difficult to determine what the essence
of a time period might be.

  Two conclusions follow from this. First, there is a very real sense in
which the past and memory are material. By this I do not mean to say that

memory is lodged in the brain, though that is probably true as well. Rather, I mean to say that memory is there in the things themselves or the physically existing objects out there in the world. Memory is not merely something that is recollected and recorded in history books. It is here, in the present, in the very things we live among. We are constantly navigating these material memories, making decisions in the present based on these memories that are present in the present. The street design and layout of a city decided in the 1920s is still here in the present, raising all sorts of challenging questions about how to put in a public train system or fit a new building into the existing layout. The past isn't simply remembered. It exists here now.

Second, we can think of things, objects, and events as assemblages of different durations. That building in the present is not merely of that time. It is an assemblage composed of the duration of ancient Greece, intervening periods, and the present, supposing we can cleanly delineate what the present is. This is true at the levels of both form and matter. At the level of form, for example, there are all sorts of techniques for molding matter and producing materials that come from different periods. The humble bicycle percolates with all sorts of different times, hearkening back to the invention of the wheel as a form that has migrated into the present, albeit in modified form due to new technologies for producing metals, unheard of substances, and so on, along with that period in which were found the secrets of how to manufacture rubber and make use of gears. The bike is an intersection of all sorts of temporalities that all affect and are affected by one another. It is this that Witmore once taught me when I went on an archaeological expedition with him.

What, then, are the conditions for the possibility of the pandemic? It is not as simple as a mutation that took place in a virus, producing a particularly infectious and deadly disease. Time percolates. We live in the wilderness. There are virtual conditions for the actualization of every event that presides over why it takes the unique form it takes in no other form. Here we cannot generalize to all countries because those virtual conditions will be different in each case. I will restrict myself to the United States.

There was a pandemic before the pandemic, a historical a priori. The pandemic had happened before it took place. It happened at the level of an infrastructure that limited the number of beds in hospitals for economic reasons and similarly limited the number of ventilators. It had happened as a result of a global air travel system that allowed the disease to travel very easily. It had already happened at the level of an economic philosophy that favored just-in-time production that ensured there were no wasteful surpluses of goods lying about, leading the system of production to be overwhelmed when far more ventilators, masks, bleach wipes, surgical gloves, and toilet paper were needed. It had already happened at the level of an economic system that tied people's health insurance to their employment status and that had different levels of health care coverage according to how much they were willing to pay. And, perhaps above all, it had already happened at the level of a polluted semiosphere, allowing people to become enclosed in television, radio, and internet information bubbles that perpetually reinforced the idea that government is the problem, not the solution, and that the pandemic is a hoax that is of little to no danger. There was an entirely material past in the present, a percolating time that persists in the present, a series of decisions that had been made well before 2020, that were all the virtual pandemic before the actual pandemic.

NOTES

1. Gilles Deleuze, *Difference and Repetition* (New York: Columbia University Press, 1995), 208–9.

2. Deleuze, 208–9.

3. G. W. Leibniz, *Discourse on Metaphysics and Other Essays* (New York: Hackett, 1991), 41.

4. Immanuel Kant, *Critique of Pure Reason* (Cambridge: Cambridge University Press, 1999), 567.

5. Deleuze, *Difference and Repetition,* 208.

6. Deleuze, 81.

7. Michel Foucault, *The Archaeology of Knowledge: And the Discourse on Knowledge* (New York: Vintage, 1982), xxi.

8. Gilles Deleuze, *Foucault* (Minneapolis: University of Minnesota Press, 1988), 43.

9. Christopher L. Witmore, "Landscape, Time, Topology: An Archaeological Account of the Southern Argolid, Greece," in *Envisioning Landscape: Situations and Standpoints in Archaeology and Heritage,* ed. Dan Hicks, Laura McAtackney, and Graham Fairclough (New York: Routledge, 2007), 205.

10. Bruno Latour and Michel Serres, *Conversations on Science, Culture, and Time: Michel Serres with Bruno Latour* (Ann Arbor: University of Michigan Press, 1995), 60.

3 The Present, Tense

MEGAN CRAIG

WAITING

Over the last year, I have written two short opinion pieces for the *New York Times* that relate to time in the long 2020 pandemic. The first one, called "The Courage to Be Alone," detailed a walk I took with my then six-year-old daughter in March 2020, just a few days after the first shutdown in the United States.[1] It was freezing, and we were walking every day, trying to find some measure of freedom and calm despite the feelings of isolation and global panic. My daughter was not always enthusiastic about heading off for a walk or a hike, but I motivated her with the promise of an extended pretend game in which she could be anyone she wanted. She would choose a character and walk to the rhythm of her own chatting, stopping to pick up crystals and sticks along the way. On one of our first pandemic walks, she decided to be the mother of three babies, the youngest of whom, her beloved Annabelle, had coronavirus.

In those early weeks and months of the pandemic, my children were a source of constant, welcome distraction. They knew less, and they were alive to their own realities. I tried to write about what it feels like to be present to them in this time: the tug between the intensity of my daughter's world of dolls, rocks, and make-believe and the intensities of the wider world—illness, deaths, numbers of hospital beds, infection rates . . . an onslaught of metrics and numbers.

I had wanted to write about Emmanuel Levinas's short essay "Nameless," written twenty-five years after the Second World War, in which he talks about lessons a new generation will need to survive. It's an essay I kept thinking about as I read about Covid-19 patients in Italy and New York

dying alone in spring 2020. Levinas writes that the new generation will
have to learn the courage to be alone in order to have the psychic resources
required for a future time when the world might fall apart or abandon
them.[2] It seemed like such an urgent lesson for this time of profound and
unevenly distributed isolation. But every time I tried to write about Levinas, to write philosophically, I was interrupted. My children needed me.
The dishes needed washing. The seminar I was teaching on John Dewey
needed preparing. I couldn't think straight. And I didn't want to try to teach
anyone a philosophy lesson anyhow. So I wrote about the things closest to
me and the feeling of starting to think, only to be pulled relentlessly back
into the world of pretend or the world of distance learning—listening in
one ear to the sounds of my girls, listening in the other to the news; listening, in vain, for a train of thought that seems forever derailed.

My second piece for the *Times* was written to appear on the winter
solstice, December 21, 2020—the shortest day of the longest year. I had
hoped to title it "The Present Tense," but editors at the *Times* were more
pragmatic and wanted a title with viable search words—and so it appeared
as "Time Isn't Supposed to Last This Long."[3] This essay, like the first one,
follows the mundane arc of my family's life, this time from summer through
fall. Rather than the rhythm of a single walk in the woods, I was thinking
about the changing rhythm of seasons syncopated against the monotonous
rhythm of laundry and meals, the infinite loop of our chores and routines.

I tried, in this piece, to express the tension between two times, or between
two rates of time that seem jarringly at odds with each other. One is the
hyperintense time of being together in our small family unit at home. This
time can have the feeling of being endless and infinitely slow, not because
nothing is happening, but because there is so much repetition and waiting
for something to begin and for something else to end. Someone is waiting for breakfast, waiting to log on to Zoom, waiting for the Lego house
to be complete, waiting for a playdate, waiting for a vaccine. Initially, if the
girls asked to see their friends, we would say "just wait." But the time of
"social distancing" has dragged on longer than anyone anticipated, and
waiting is no longer something to exert special effort about; it is just how
things are.

In waiting, time feels so long that sometimes minutes can feel like hours.
I associate this kind of time with early childhood and the various experiences of being at the mercy of events out of your control. The eternal waiting for a birthday, for dessert, for Christmas morning. But I also associate

this time with the feeling of illness, a condensation of time into the shallow space of a fever or pain. Pandemic time feels like that: slow, dragged, stalled. A lifetime ago, it was early March 2020 and life had its variable pace and flow, and then it was as if someone changed the speed on a record player and everything seemed suddenly warped, suspended, stuck. We came up with new meals to cook. We learned to play new board games. We found new walks to take. But nothing felt new. It felt like the same things over and over, a never-ending day.

The sense of being stalled is also, for better or worse, tied for me to the *Hamilton* soundtrack, to which we were subjected on repeat from July through November, after letting our daughters watch the movie on TV on the Fourth of July. The girls immediately memorized the whole thing and spent hours reenacting scenes.[4] It provided a source of distraction for them as they disappeared into their rooms for "rehearsals." It also provided some form of sublimation as they sang at the tops of their lungs about time and heartbreak and history. Every day brought a new iteration of the same refrain: "You hold your child as tight as you can and push away the unimaginable."[5]

Hamilton pits the frenetic man of action (Alexander Hamilton) against the man in waiting (Aaron Burr). It is almost exactly the difference William James imagined between two essential character types: one whom James saw as the typically impulsive, American "man of action and realization," the other a Rousseau-like European dreamer who never musters the energy to do anything substantial.[6] James thought both extremes were tempting and dangerous, and he spent his own life literally and figuratively casting between shores. As the time of the pandemic stretched on, I couldn't help feeling that Burr's song "Wait for It" had become the soundtrack of Pandemic Life, more so in those months when we were also waiting for the election, waiting for the results to be counted, waiting for the Georgia Senate runoff, and then, after the violence of January 6, waiting for the inauguration. Somehow we had been collectively cast as Burr: helpless, lying in wait. The repetition of *Hamilton* songs merged with the deadening repetition of the numbers of new cases, hospitalization rates, and deaths. The same soundtrack over and over with each new wave of the pandemic.

But against this time of waiting, I was also aware of a different time: the time of spring, summer, fall, and winter, tracking the days in the weather and the budding of new plants, the early spring haze of green that seemed

so indifferent to and at odds with a grim reality. I could only think of the
first stanza of Seamus Heaney's poem:

Sheer, bright-shining spring, spring as it used to be,
Cold in the morning, but as broad daylight
Swings open, the everlasting sky
Is a marvel to survivors.[7]

Nature wasn't waiting. It didn't care about the numbers or the protocols
or masks or insurrections. This was the time of birds at the feeder, snow
blanketing the apple blossoms, tulip trees in fits of gold. All of it seemed
impossible to reconcile with the feeling of the pandemic, the *centrality* of
the pandemic for human consciousness.

Nature's time moving forward with steady, disinterested regularity made
me feel hopeful in the fact that human beings are at the center of so many
calamities, but not at the center of everything. This other dimension of
time relates to the deep time of geology Hugh Raffles has written about
in *The Book of Unconformities: Speculations on Lost Time,* explaining that
"even the most solid, ancient, and elemental materials are as lively, capri-
cious, willful, and indifferent as time itself."[8] It is the time to which Oliver
Sacks turned near the end of his life, in his essays collected in the slim
volume called *Gratitude,* writing about the bit of eternity in every element
of his beloved periodic table. Describing one of his last views of the sky
"powdered with stars," Sacks wrote, "It was this celestial splendor that suddenly made me realize how little time, how little life, I had left."[9]

HOPING

Two times: (1) the human time of the immediate present that became
over the last year slow, intense, and unyielding and (2) the inhuman time
of nature in its unforgiving but lifesaving flux. These two times have made
me think about Henri Bergson's descriptions of *durée* and *élan vital,* duration and vital impetus. Bergson, the beloved nineteenth- and twentieth-
century philosopher of vitalism, described *durée* in his 1913 text *Time and
Free Will.* There, *durée* is tied to the intensity of psychic states, to time as
it is lived rather than how it is measured or quantified by calendars or
clocks. To give us a sense of *durée,* Bergson famously invoked the example of waiting for a sugar cube to dissolve in a glass of water, time that
takes only two or three minutes by your watch but feels like forever as you

intently wait.[10] He also says this is the time of memory and dreams, time that refuses to organize or cohere in a linear timeline or to spread out neatly like an open fan. *Durée* is also the time of sickness or pain, time when the discomfort or sheer agony of embodiment makes one wonder how or whether it is possible to endure from one moment to the next.[11]

In *Time and Free Will*, Bergson is worried that all our mechanisms for dividing, counting, and measuring time have altered and obscured *durée*, making us forget something essential about what it is to be alive. He's worried that we are becoming more and more like our machines: "more and more lifeless, more and more impersonal."[12] And so, *Time and Free Will* is a plea for us to find some ways of reclaiming lived time, of deliberately experiencing *durée*, as a means of reconnecting to the emotional depth and complexity of ourselves, each other, and life itself.

But such intense involution is not without risks, and this has been a part of what interests me in connecting Bergson with our own historical time. On one hand, *durée* seems to allow for individuality and idiosyncrasy, for freedom and a heightened sensitivity to life. For Bergson, *durée* is the only *real* time, and to the degree that we can feel *durée*, we feel ourselves to be alive. Toward the end of *Time and Free Will*, Bergson describes the ways in which we are all suspended between "two selves": a practical, social, surface self who meets the demands of the day and a deeper, original self who dreams and feels and is tied to the unspeakable but vibrant current of life.[13] He describes various ways that the deep self might be awakened through hypnosis or dreams, through trancelike, transient episodes that crack and shed the veneer of the social self.

Such episodes are paradigmatically instructive for Bergson, because they show the possibility of connecting to an inner reservoir of inarticulate feeling and deep-seated emotion, accessing something we might call our soul.[14] Life becomes vivid in the intensity of *durée*. But Bergson also cautions against a life lived entirely at the pitch of *durée*, acknowledging that "the self has everything to gain by not bringing back confusion where order reigns."[15] A person submerged in her deep self would be profoundly awake to the multiplicity and intensity of her own life and profoundly asleep to other lives. For the deep self has no means of social connection, no language, no signs, no way back up to the surface. We might say that the person subjected to prolonged or indefinite *durée* risks becoming permanently or pathologically asocial.[16] So while Bergson was worried that human beings were losing time and beginning to merge with their impersonal machines, he also worried that in reclaiming personal time and *durée,* we might go mad and be forever stranded apart from one another in some unending hypnosis or nightmarish dreamscape.

These feel like risks we are navigating today. We have, for instance, decided in America that the risks of Covid-19 are greater than the risks of isolation for children who have been out of school for over a year. We have accepted that the risks of Covid-19 outweigh the risks of isolation for those in long-term care facilities, for the chronically ill, and for so many others. Perhaps that's right and necessary. History will have to decide. People with the privilege, resources, and occupations amenable to it have stayed home and stayed apart to slow the spread of infection and to protect those especially vulnerable to the virus (the elderly, the sick, smokers, those with diabetes or heart disease, the obese, and those living at or below the poverty line—often overlapping and historically marginalized populations). We have worn masks and washed our hands. But Bergson reminds us of the double edge of *durée* that is relevant as we continue our vast experiment with "social distancing." The virus is still spreading despite best-laid plans.[17] Many of us have grown closer than ever to the members of our own households and perhaps even more in tune with the intensity of our own psychic states. But we have also grown away from each other. Some, especially those already battling different degrees of isolation, have turned drastically in on themselves.[18] And it's not at all clear what "return" means or will entail for those most abandoned to the prolonged *durée* of this time, for those who have had to wait and endure more, and especially for the youngest children in the most precarious situations who have known little else.

Another aspect of time, nature and seasonal change, appears in Bergson's later, Nobel Prize–winning text *Creative Evolution.* There Bergson is thinking, not about the deepening of consciousness for a single person, as he was in *Time and Free Will,* but about the array of consciousness over the whole of animate life, a kind of glistening field of life-forms asleep and awake to varying degrees. Reacting to the various evolutionary trends of his own time, Bergson tells an evolutionary story that is not regulated by any determinate mechanism or governed by the grand design of any finalism (religious or otherwise). Instead, he describes the ways in which life subtly and unpredictably implicates itself in matter, like water seeping into the cracks of a parched field. He gives us an account of life rife with detours, circles, and abandoned routes. It's messy and tangled, nothing like an elegant arc or neat design.

In *Creative Evolution*, Bergson is thinking about *durée* not only in terms of individual, human, psychic time but together with what he calls *élan vital*, time considered at the scale of all life, a movement inherent in life itself that breaks up with explosive force into different tendencies.[19] In *Time and Free Will*, Bergson had argued that psychic states are not discrete objects with definite outlines. Sadness, for example, shades imperceptibly into depression, which colors everything else. In *Creative Evolution*, he argues that life-forms likewise blur and blend into one another. Furthermore, he argues that by focusing on the "fringed" interconnections of life across multiple species, we might "derive the impetus necessary to lift us above ourselves."[20] *Creative Evolution* gives us a picture of life in the making and never fully made, a story in which human beings are the culmination of only *one* of life's multiple tendencies.

While *durée* bears down in its individuating insistence, *élan vital* spins outward in a dizzying multiplicity of life-forms: orchids and mushrooms, mollusks, wasps, and ants. *Élan vital* reminds us that we, as human beings, are not the only or the final story, reminding us of our contingent and tiny place in a vaster composition in which our own consciousness, this time, and *this* pandemic, are barely blips. Maybe that's all we need to remind ourselves that the tense present of *durée* need not be the ultimate register of time. It is as if time itself can roll up into a ball or splatter like a jar of paint tipped off the table. Time is dense or diffuse, repetitive and new all at once. The audacity of the daffodils to bloom again as if nothing happened. The saving grace of every one of them. The pandemic has exacerbated the differential speeds of time lived by different populations—speeds that are also exposed in daily instances of brutality and joy lived out by different creatures in different measures all the time, not only in pandemic time. We congeal inward in our individual experiences of *durée,* and we are drawn onward and outward into the future by the anonymous tide of *élan vital.*

While I find in Bergsonian *durée* reasons to be cautious about the long-term effects of "social distancing," isolation, and the feelings of stasis and blur, I also find in *élan vital* a reason to hope for more time, for recovery and ongoing transformations. Annabelle, my daughter's baby doll, has recovered from the coronavirus and now has a broken leg. Our walks continue in rain and sun. Some days we are sisters living in Hawai'i. Other days we are competitors on a baking show or gymnasts in the Olympics vying for gold medals. We are planning an eighth birthday with a scavenger hunt and lemon cake. One person at home is partially vaccinated. The light shifts and the days elongate as the redbuds push fuchsia blooms from their bark.

Thank goodness for my children, who have made it impossible for me to turn fully inward on myself in this time. They have their own *durée*, but they are also tiny instances of *élan vital* exploding in unpredictable ways day after day, calling me off-center, interrupting my philosophy, my sleep, my gloom. I'm writing about time now, just as earlier I boiled water for tea and folded the sheets, to the tune of the *Hamilton* finale building in the background. Bergson has helped a bit in my own effort to understand the complex feeling of this long 2020, a sense of immobilization and an unyielding present that have coalesced with the prolonged anxiety and isolation of this time. He has helped me to appreciate what might be gained by *durée* as well as what might be lost if, becoming enamored with or just accustomed to "social distance," we leave each other alone in our own times, forgetting to connect or to go outside. We are caught in our own time at the same moment that we are entangled in time that outpaces us— caught in the tension between the before and the after, hyphens elongated in the present tense.

It is April 2021 now. Unbelievably, time passes, even if it feels as if we have been standing still. As Bergson reminds us, there is no way backward. There is only the snowballing accumulation of time in living beings, time that registers whether or not we mark it down or pay attention to it. Meanwhile, the bland minutiae of the day-to-day ricochets against the blare of daffodils dabbing the field: a pile of books, mismatched socks, Bergson's sugar, Seamus Heaney's "everlasting sky," Sack's stars, my girls singing, and the dog barking at a robin on the lawn.

NOTES

1. Megan Craig, "The Courage to Be Alone," *New York Times,* May 3, 2020.

2. Emmanuel Levinas, "Nameless," in *Proper Names,* trans. Michael Smith, 119–23 (Stanford, Calif.: Stanford University Press, 1996).

3. Megan Craig, "Time Isn't Supposed to Last This Long," *New York Times,* December 21, 2020.

4. With my girls playing all the parts, I joked that we should launch a feminist retelling of *Hamilton* (with better and more parts for women) titled "The Womb Where It Happened."

5. Lin-Manuel Miranda, "It's Quiet Uptown," *Hamilton* (Broadway Music ASCAP, Atlantic Recording Corporation, 2015).

6. James writes, "There is no more contemptible type of human character than that of the nerveless sentimentalist and dreamer, who spends his life in a weltering sea of sensibility and emotion, but who never does a manly concrete deed. Rousseau, inflaming all the mothers of France, by his eloquence, to follow Nature and nurse their babies themselves, while he sends his own children to the foundling hospital, is the classical example of what I mean." William James, *The Principles of Psychology* (Cambridge, Mass.: Harvard University Press, 1981), 1:129.

7. Seamus Heaney, "To a Dutch Potter in Ireland," in *The Spirit Level* (New York: Farrar, Straus, and Giroux, 1996), 6.

8. Hugh Raffles, *The Book of Unconformities: Speculations on Lost Time* (New York: Pantheon, 2020), 6.

9. Oliver Sacks, "Oliver Sacks: My Periodic Table," *New York Times*, July 24, 2015.

10. Henri Bergson, *Creative Evolution,* trans. Keith Ansell Pearson (New York: Palgrave Macmillan, 2007), 6.

11. This is the eternity of isolation in the last moments of life for Covid-19 patients across the globe as well as the eternity of the nine minutes and twenty-nine seconds Derek Chauvin knelt on George Floyd's neck on May 25, 2020.

12. Henri Bergson, *Time and Free Will,* trans. F. L. Pogson (New York: Dover, 2001), 136.

13. Bergson writes, "As the self thus refracted, and thereby broken into pieces, is much better adapted to the requirements of social life in general and language in particular, consciousness prefers it, and gradually loses sight of the fundamental self" (128).

14. By treating our own psychic states as discrete objects, Bergson thinks "we have caused . . . feeling to lose its life and colour. Hence we are now standing before our own shadow" (133).

15. Bergson, 139.

16. Bergson ties *durée* to freedom and an ability to break out of habitual, automated patterns of selfhood. But he also insists that such interruptions of the socialized self are "rare," writing that "free acts are exceptional" (167) and "the moments at which we thus grasp ourselves are rare, and that is just why we are rarely free. The greater part of the time we live outside ourselves, hardly perceiving anything of ourselves but our own ghost" (231).

17. I am writing this on April 14, 2021, the day after the Centers for Disease Control and Prevention suspended the use of the Johnson and Johnson vaccine in the United States. New cases are up by 8 percent nationwide, and the risk of infection by Covid-19 is listed as "very high" in my county.

18. Carol Graham documents "evidence of spillover effects of COVID-19 among populations already vulnerable to deaths of despair" in her article "The Human Costs of the Pandemic: Is It Time to Prioritize Well-Being?," Brookings Institution, November 17, 2020, https://www.brookings.edu/research/the-human-costs-of-the-pandemic-is-it-time-to-prioritize-well-being/. See also Abby Goodnough, "Overdose Deaths Have Surged during the Pandemic, CDC Data Shows," *New York Times*, April 14, 2021.

19. Bergson describes elementary tendencies toward stasis (plant life) or movement (vertebrate life) as residual marks of *élan vital* that can be understood "like psychic states, each of which, although it be itself to begin with, yet partakes of others, and virtually includes in itself the whole personality to which it belongs. There is no real manifestation of life, we said, that does not show us, in a rudimentary or latent state, the characters of other manifestation." Bergson, *Creative Evolution*, 77.

20. Bergson, 32.

4 A Long History of Pandemics

WAI CHEE DIMOCK

Where we begin makes a world of difference to what kind of narrative follows, where it is likely to go, and who the protagonists are. Covid-19 is a case in point. While it sometimes feels like an eternity, with no before and no after, most of us in fact assign to it a start date that is quite recent: New Year's Eve 2019, when a cluster of severe pneumonia cases was detected in Wuhan, China. To begin with the pneumonia—a symptom caused by a pathogen—is to tell a story initiated by the virus, an outsize actor responsible for all our ills. This invisible enemy has come out of nowhere, unprovoked, unprepared for, going after us for no reason that we can see, bringing untold suffering both to those infected and to everyone else who happens to be alive.

Is there another start date to consider? The World Health Organization (WHO) investigative team had several. Their report, released on March 30, 2020, was criticized by the United States and thirteen other countries for having no new findings and no recommendations for a path forward, but it did have something specific to say—about the "evolutionary process" by which SARS-CoV-2, the virus responsible for the disease, became not just any virus but one with "pandemic potential." To become this kind of world-class virus, "SARS-CoV-2 progenitor strains" must have gone through a few hoops. Starting out "in an animal reservoir," they had somehow managed to make a quantum leap, throwing up a game-changing variant, one that can infect humans. Because the "evolutionary distance" between this variant and its progenitors is "estimated to be decades," the jump from animals to humans probably didn't happen all at once but in stages, through intermediate hosts. It was a multiparty relay, decades in the making. This

34

long evolutionary time frame suggests that December 2019 was just the last leg of the journey. The story probably began much earlier, not in Wuhan at all, but in a place where the virus would have plenty of time to circulate and mutate and produce variants while being hosted by "coronavirus-susceptible animals." The wildlife farms in Yunnan province would have been such a place.[1]

These farms, suppliers for the Huanan Market, were part of a rural revival project the Chinese government had been promoting for more than twenty years. Wild animals like civet cats, porcupines, pangolins, raccoon dogs, and bamboo rats, prized in traditional Chinese medicine and as gourmet food items, were bred here in captivity. The revenue generated would lift rural populations out of poverty and close the urban–rural income gap, a perennial ambition for the Chinese government. In 2017, the industry was valued at 520 billion yuan, or US$77 billion, and employed 14 million people.[2]

All that came to an end on February 24, 2020. In an abrupt about-face, the Chinese government ordered the shutdown of some twenty thousand wildlife farms. It sent out instructions about how to dispose of the animals—kill, burn, and bury them—in the speediest way possible.[3] It was the clearest acknowledgment that these farms were a public health hazard. Three-quarters of the world's emerging infectious diseases are zoonotic diseases, jumping from animals to humans. As David Quammen warned some time ago, these spillovers typically arise when habitats are lost, when species otherwise living apart are thrown into close proximity, allowing viruses to jump easily from host to host.[4] Zoonotic viruses are the proverbial canary in the coal mine, bearing witness to the degradation of entire ecosystems. Previous coronaviruses like SARS and MERS have emerged in this way; SARS-CoV-2 seems to be no exception. The discovery of its closest relatives in Laos, bordering Yunnan, coupled with other relatives also known to exist in nearby Cambodia, shows that this region is a zoonotic hot spot.[5]

Not everyone bought this theory, of course. In fact, the WHO's own director-general, Tedros Adhanom Ghebreyesus, was blunt about the lack of transparency on the part of the Chinese government.[6] He called for a full investigation both of the Huanan Market and the Wuhan Institute of Virology, now known to be conducting gain-of-function research, which is to say, working with highly adapted viruses. A lab leak could have released one with a unique "furin cleavage," maximizing human transmissibility.[7]

Molecular biologist Alina Chan, who first sounded the alarm, has laid out
a full argument in *Viral: The Search for the Origin of COVID-19*, coauthored
with science writer Matt Ripley.[8]

Wildlife farms, animal markets, virology labs—these different candidates
line up with different politics as well as different evolutionary theories.
But the three aren't so far apart after all. They all point to the nontrivial
presence of human institutions in the emergence of pandemics. The virus
didn't show up on its own, in a vacuum. It did so in multispecies environments created by humans. Thanks to these, it was able to make that
final, fatal jump. Human agency, seen through this lens, is at once pivotal
and maddeningly diffused, with many of its effects not intended and not
materializing until far into the future. Not limited to a single outcome, it
is also not the work of a single species. Developed over the long haul, it
is shaped at every turn by nonhuman actors both large and small, some
of them created by us but not always under our control, bringing about
epochal changes we never see coming.

Anthropogenic is a word we have learned to use, in the context of climate change, to think about this kind of slow-emerging, time-delayed,
often obliquely manifested form of human agency. It is equally helpful in
bringing into focus the nontrivial but also nonlocalized human input into
the history of diseases. In what follows, I map these delayed effects on a
longitudinal axis spanning centuries, centered on Native Americans and
encompassing two pandemics, smallpox and Covid-19, the better to study
time as a medium for a volatile, elongated form of human causation, featuring evolutionary ruptures as well as continuities, elemental loss, and
incremental restitution.

In early 1760, in the midst of the French and Indian War, Lord Jeffrey
Amherst, commander in chief of the British forces in North America,
wanted the Cherokee Nation destroyed and knew a way to do it. The
Cherokees had been allies for almost a century, fighting alongside the
British against the French. The alliance fell apart, however, when at least
thirty Cherokee warriors were murdered during spring and summer 1758.
The Anglo-Cherokee War (1759–61) followed, as a smallpox epidemic raged
among the colonists and Indigenous populations. At this juncture, Amherst instructed Colonel Archibald Montgomery to "punish the Indians . . .
in such manner that His Majesty's subject may hereafter enjoy their pos-
sessions without any dread of these barbarous and inhuman savages."[9]

He spelled things out three years later, at the onset of Pontiac's War, as the Ottawas, Lenapes, and Shawnees lay siege to Fort Pitt. When Colonel Henry Bouquet requested help, Amherst made this now-infamous suggestion on July 7, 1763: "Could it not be contrived to send the smallpox among these disaffected tribes of Indians? We must, on this occasion, use every stratagem in our power to reduce them."[10] Bouquet wrote back on July 13, promising to do his best, "taking care however not to get the disease myself."[11] But perhaps there was no need for him to exert himself, because William Trent, trader, land speculator, and militia captain stationed at Fort Pitt, had already taken the initiative. Two weeks earlier, on June 24, 1763, Trent had confided to his journal, "We gave them two blankets and an handkerchief out of the smallpox hospital. I hope it will have the desired effect."[12]

The smallpox blankets, first reported by nineteenth-century historian Francis Parkman, have gone viral again in the twenty-first century. And Lord Amherst, from being a military genius transforming an island nation into the world's greatest colonial power, has evolved into a scoundrel of global proportions, a champion of biological warfare. The shock waves have ricocheted across North America. Montreal no longer has an Amherst Street; it is now Atateken Street.[13] Amherst, Massachusetts, named after the British general, had even more to contend with. As local residents weighed in, Amherst College scrambled to rename its historic Lord Jeffry Inn and Lord Jeff mascot, a development reported with some disapproval by the *New York Times*.[14]

And yet, as historian Paul Kelton cautions, focusing too much on the *blankets* risks obscuring other aspects of colonial warfare with far greater epidemiological consequences. As he documents in *Cherokee Medicine, Colonial Germs*, the British forces "chopped down fruit trees, pulled young corn up by the roots, burned a total of 15 towns," and destroyed "an estimated 1,400 acres of crops" in a single campaign.[15] This scorched earth policy produced masses of refugees and upended the quarantine measures the Cherokees had been implementing, allowing the smallpox virus to circulate unimpeded from one community to another across Virginia, Kentucky, Tennessee, Georgia, the Carolinas, and Alabama. Peter Wood estimates that, between starvation and disease, the Cherokees might have lost three-quarters of their population, plummeting to a mere seventy-two hundred in the 1760s from thirty-two thousand in 1685.[16]

But the tribe never gave up, and a century and a half later, when the new smallpox vaccine became available, they would seize upon it and craft a whole new public health strategy. Edward Jenner, who derived the vaccine from cowpox, marveled in 1802, "I am much gratified at the good sense manifested by the Cherokee Indians. Who would have thought that vaccination would already have found its way into the wilds of America?"[17] The London news media was also enchanted. The Cherokees had heard that "the Great Spirit had gifted a white man, over the great water, with a power to prevent the smallpox," reported the May 1803 edition of London's *Gentleman's Magazine*. "It is a pleasing reflection that these untutored savages have spread it throughout their country, and that they are eminently expert in the practice of the new inoculation."[18]

And yet, as Kelton again cautions, what actually happened was a bit more complicated. The Cherokees were not in fact the first to adopt the vaccine; tribes from the Ohio Valley and Great Lakes were ahead of them. And when large-scale distribution did take place in the 1820s, the Cherokees were careful to stick to a "pluralistic approach," retaining many Native beliefs and rituals and grafting them onto Western science.[19] Here as elsewhere, a holistic pandemic narrative is unlikely to feature a single protagonist or a single line of development. It is worth remembering this earlier history of Indigenous public health as we turn to its most recent iterations in the twenty-first century.

When the Cherokee Nation got its first shipment of the Pfizer vaccine in December 2020, there was no question where it would go. "We put Cherokee-fluent speakers at the front of the line," said Principal Chief Chuck Hoskin. "Saving the language" is a top priority at all times, and never more so than during a pandemic.[20]

Cherokee, like many other Indigenous languages around the world, is endangered, with just two thousand fluent speakers, most of them elders. Forty-five of these were lost to Covid-19. The deaths of these keepers of language meant lost libraries of "lifeways, culture, stories." Stung by these losses, the tribe pulled together to get the vaccine out as soon as it arrived. "Our doses have been administered without any lag time," Hoskin said.[21]

The Cherokee Nation, forced at gunpoint to relocate from the Southeast in 1838, now has 141,000 citizens on its reservation in Oklahoma. By February 8, 2021, more than seventeen thousand had gotten both shots, a 12 percent vaccination rate, significantly higher than that of most states. Cherokee speakers, elders, and health care workers had all been vaccinated, and the tribe was able to open up the distribution to those aged fifty-five and older, as well as to teachers and tribal government employees. On February 25, the Cherokee Nation announced that those aged sixteen and older had become eligible.[22] By March 11, the tribe began offering the vaccine to the general public, non-Native as well as Native.[23]

Hoskin attributed this phenomenal success to the decision to put the Cherokee speakers at the head of the line. Given the widespread mistrust among Native communities—especially acute after the federal government sterilized more than a quarter of Native women of childbearing age in 1970[24]—this was the "biggest confidence builder" anyone could have come up with. By inoculating its most revered citizens, the tribe was sending a signal no one could fail to notice. Public health worked best when language preservation was part of a holistic delivery system, creating a sense of purpose as well as a "sense of optimism among our people," Hoskin told CNN.[25]

It also helped that the infrastructure was already in place for the vaccine rollout. The Cherokee Nation is clear-eyed about the nation's health care system and has acted accordingly. "We're a country that doesn't make access to health care part of being a citizen," Hoskin said. "That's a problem during good times, and it's certainly a problem during the pandemic." Not leaving everything to Oklahoma, or the federal government, the Cherokee Nation has been investing for years in its state-of-the-art hospital and clinics, now the largest tribally operated health system in the United States. It has made headline news before. Back in November, *PBS NewsHour* had a story, "How the Cherokee Nation Has Curtailed the Pandemic," featuring the tribe's cutting-edge contact tracing.[26]

The Cherokee Nation is less of an outlier than we might think. Other tribes, without such medical infrastructure, are doing fine as well with the vaccine rollout, thanks in part to the clearly stated goal of protecting endangered speakers. According to an analysis by NPR, Native communities as a rule have been faster and more efficient than the rest of the country in getting shots into people's arms.[27] Given how dire things were at the beginning of the pandemic, this is an unexpected turn of events, to say the least.

Handwashing is difficult on reservations because Native households are nineteen times more likely than white households to lack access to indoor plumbing. "Running water, it would be such a luxury," said Legena Wagner, a member of the Navajo Nation.[28] Other preexisting conditions are just as crushing. Native Americans are 8 times more likely to die of tuberculosis and 2.3 times more likely to die of diabetes.[29] During the early months of the pandemic, they were dying at twice the rate as white Americans.[30] And yet, as Kyle Powys Whyte reminds us, existential threats are nothing new for Native communities; they have always found a way to come out at the other end.[31] "Our genetic memory of past epidemics is very strong," said Chuck Sams, Covid-19 incident commander on the Umatilla Reservation. "Epidemics that came through between 1780 to 1860 wiped out nearly 95 percent of our population. We're the descendants of the 5 percent that survived."[32]

The Rosebud Sioux and Oglala Sioux tribes in South Dakota, with the lowest life expectancy in the United States, represent that 5 percent. Among the hardest hit in the pandemic, they have nonetheless been highly efficient in making language preservation a driving force in public health. Lakota is also an endangered language, again with just two thousand speakers. Elders fluent in that language offer vaccine information on the radio. Call center staffs likewise make appointments and schedule transportation in Lakota. "That's one of the defining features of our response. Our community figures things out fairly well with limited resources," said Alicia Mousseau, vice president of the Oglala Sioux Tribe. Out of a population of about thirty thousand on its reservation, the tribe had vaccinated more than four thousand people by February 1.[33] The Rosebud Sioux Tribe, meanwhile, was vaccinating at double the rate of South Dakota. "We've even had non-Indian people from Sioux Falls and Omaha trying to get in here to get vaccinated because they can't get it over there," said Rodney Bordeaux, president of the tribe.[34]

There is no better example of this sea change than the Navajo Nation. The largest reservation in the United States, it has long been home to nightmarish health crises. The 1918 flu epidemic killed between 10 and 18 percent of the Navajo population.[35] This time around, Covid-19 (Dikos Nitsaa'igii-19, "the big cough" in Navajo) also unfolded swiftly and relentlessly. By April 4, 321 tribal members had already been infected, an increase of fifty-one cases in a single day, with thirteen deaths.[36] By May 18, the Navajo Nation surpassed New York State with the highest infection rate in the country.[37] That infection rate soared to 37.8 percent on November 20.[38]

But other trends were also beginning to emerge. While the Navajo (Diné) language, with 170,000 speakers, is not under immediate threat of extinction, like Cherokee and Lakota, reservation health workers have nonetheless been able to use it as a hook for the vaccine rollout. Daily radio call-in shows and biweekly town hall meetings in Navajo were organized to educate the public. "Utilizing our way of life and teaching helps our people feel it's okay to take the shots," said Jonathan Nez, president of the Navajo Nation. When the first shipment of vaccines arrived in December, three out of four of the residents welcomed them with open arms. By February 8, 33 percent had received the first dose, and 4.3 percent had been fully vaccinated.[39] "The Navajo Nation is beating out every state's coronavirus vaccine rollout," *Forbes* reported on April 4, 2021.[40]

As with the Cherokees in the nineteenth century, Navajo physicians have made a point of grafting Indigenous medicine onto the contemporary drug-based treatment. Michael Tutt, chief medical officer of the Tséhootsooí Medical Center in Fort Defiance, Arizona, cares for a population of thirty thousand by sticking to the art of listening. "My grandmother told me listening is medicine. And what you say, what comes out of your mouth, is medicine. Probably stronger than what you give as medication. When you only treat patients physically, you just throw medications at them. But the Navajo way, we treat them physically, mentally, spiritually."[41]

There is a difference between medicine and medication. The former is much broader, more democratic, an art as well as a science. The Navajo word for this holistic medicine is *hózhó*, a balanced way of walking the earth. It means that the patient has as much input into the healing process as the physician, not just being treated with pills but also being listened to and prayed for. To put *hózhó* into practice, Tutt brings a traditional healer to his mobile rheumatology clinic:

> Sometimes my patients are looking forward more to the traditional healer than to me. That's what I want. Because they feel good when they get a prayer, that things will be all right. To me it's a pure way of praying for somebody. It's Navajo, it's tied to the ground, tied to our surroundings, non-denominational, non-judging. Our way of praying has been going on for 500 years. And it will still be here 500 years from now.[42]

To make sure that the Navajo prayer would last five hundred years, Tutt looks to the next generation for evolutionary continuity. The Tséhootsooí Medical Center has an adolescent care unit, Arizona's first inpatient psychiatric clinic for young Native Americans. "A lot of these kids—I call them scrappers because somehow they've survived this long—have lost their parents to drugs and alcohol," Tutt said. "We take care of them with their addiction; we give them tools to survive their daily life. But one of the things that I think makes a big difference is we instill within the program traditional teaching."[43]

The Navajo Nation can have a future only if there are youngsters to take its way of life forward. Existential threats can be put to rest only if this next generation is equipped for the rocky road ahead, given tools that maximize their chances of survival beyond the long 2020. There is no guarantee, but there is a long history. The Navajos, like other Indigenous communities, have been here before and know what it takes to move on, to make the future thinkable, actionable, and meaningful. Evolution has taught them nothing less.

NOTES

1. "WHO-Convened Global Study of the Origin of SARS-CoV-2, China Part," pp. 6, 58, 155, 8, https://www.who.int/docs/default-source/coronaviruse/who-con vened-global-study-of-origins-of-sars-cov-2-china-part-annexes.pdf.

2. Michael Standaert, "Coronavirus Closures Reveal Vast Scale of China's Secretive Wildlife Farm Industry," *Guardian*, February 25, 2020, https://www.theguardian.com/environment/2020/feb/25/coronavirus-closures-reveal-vast-scale-of-chinas-secretive-wildlife-farm-industry.

3. Emily Feng, "Pandemic Causes China to Ban Breeding of Bamboo Rats and Other Wild Animals," NPR, June 28, 2020, https://www.npr.org/sections/goatsand soda/2020/06/28/883900042/pandemic-causes-china-to-ban-breeding-of-bamboo-rats-and-other-wild-animals.

4. David Quammen, *Spillover: Animal Infections and the Next Human Pandemic* (New York: W. W. Norton, 2012), 366.

5. Smriti Mallapty, "Closest Known Relatives of Virus behind COVID-19 Found in Laos," *Nature*, September 24, 2021, https://www.nature.com/articles/d41586-021-02596-2.

6. Emily Rauhala, "WHO Chief, U.S. and Other World Leaders Criticize China for Limiting Access of Team Researching Coronavirus Origins," *Washington Post*, March 30, 2021, https://www.washingtonpost.com/world/who-wuhan-tedros-lab/2021/03/30/896fe3f6-90d1-11eb-aadc-af78701a30ca_story.html.

7. Steven Quay and Richard Muller, "The Science Suggests a Wuhan Lab Leak," *Wall Street Journal*, June 6, 2021, https://www.wsj.com/articles/the-science-sug gests-a-wuhan-lab-leak-11622995184; Carolyn Kormann, "The Mysterious Case of the COVID-19 Lab-Leak Theory," *New Yorker*, October 12, 2021, https://www.newyorker.com/science/elements/the-mysterious-case-of-the-covid-19-lab-leak-theory.

8. Alina Chan and Matt Ripley, *Viral: The Search for the Origin of COVID-19* (New York: Harper, 2021). Chan is a postdoctoral fellow at Harvard's and MIT's Broad Institute.

9. Amherst to Montgomery, February 24, 1760; quoted in Paul Kelton, *Cherokee Medicine, Colonial Germs: An Indigenous Nation's Fight against Smallpox, 1518–1824* (Norman: University of Oklahoma Press, 2015), 102–3.

10. Amherst to Bouquet, July 7, 1763; quoted in Elizabeth Fenn, "Biological Warfare in Eighteenth-Century North America: Beyond Jeffrey Amherst," *Journal of American History* 86 (March 2000): 1555.

11. Bouquet to Amherst, July 13, 1763; quoted in Fenn, 1556.

12. William Trent, journal entry, June 24, 1763; quoted in Fenn, 1554.

13. "Montreal's Amherst Street Is Officially No More," CBC News, October 21, 2019, https://www.cbc.ca/news/canada/montreal/montreal-amherst-atateken-1.53 28561.

14. Jess Bidgood, "At Amherst College, Some Say It's the Mascot's Turn to Embrace Diversity," *New York Times,* October 31, 2015, https://www.nytimes.com/2015/11/01/us/at-amherst-some-say-its-the-mascots-turn-to-embrace-diversity.html.

15. Kelton, *Cherokee Medicine,* 132.

16. Peter H. Wood, "The Changing Population of the Colonial South, an Overview by Race and Region, 1685–1790," in *Powhatan's Mantle: Indians in the Colonial Southeast,* ed. Gregory A. Waselkov, Peter H. Wood, and Tom Hadley (Lincoln: University of Nebraska Press, 2006), 60.

17. Jenner to Dunning, May 17, 1802, quoted in Kelton, *Cherokee Medicine,* 174.

18. Kelton, 174.

19. Kelton, 174–210, quotation from 177.

20. Harmeet Kaur, "Tribal Health Providers Have Figured Out Key to COVID-19 Success," CNN, February 26, 2021, https://www.cnn.com/2021/02/09/us/tribal-health-providers-covid-vaccine-trnd/index.html.

21. Alex Brown, "In Hard-Hit Indian Country, Tribes Rapidly Roll Out Vaccines," Pew Trusts, February 9, 2021, https://www.pewtrusts.org/en/research-and-analysis/blogs/stateline/2021/02/09/in-hard-hit-indian-country-tribes-rapidly-roll-out-vaccines.

22. Cassidy Mudd, "Cherokee Nation in Phase 3 of Vaccine Distribution," KTUL, February 26, 2021, https://ktul.com/news/local/cherokee-nation-in-phase-three-of-vaccine-distribution-plan.

23. James King, "Cherokee Nation Opens Vaccine to Everyone in 14-County Reservation Area," KTUL, March 11, 2021, https://ktul.com/news/local/cherokee-nation-opens-vaccine-to-everyone-in-14-county-reservation-area.

24. Brianna Theobald, "A 1970 Law Led to the Mass Sterilization of Native American Women," *Time,* November 28, 2019, https://time.com/5737080/native-american-sterilization-history/.

25. Kaur, "Tribal Health Providers."

26. Usha Lee McFarling, "How the Cherokee Nation Has Curtailed the Pandemic," *PBS NewsHour,* November 14, 2020, https://www.pbs.org/newshour/health/how-the-cherokee-nation-has-curtailed-the-pandemic.

27. Kurt Siegler, "Why Native Americans Are Getting the COVID-19 Vaccines Faster," NPR, February 19, 2021, https://www.npr.org/2021/02/19/969046248/why-native-americans-are-getting-the-covid-19-vaccines-faster.

28. Frances Stead Sellers, "It's Almost 2020 and 2 Million Americans Still Don't Have Running Water," *Washington Post,* December 11 2019, https://www.washingtonpost.com/national/its-almost-2020-and-2-million-americans-still-dont-have-running-water-new-report-says/2019/12/10/a0720e8a-14b3-11ea-a659-7d69641c6ff7_story.html.

29. Dana Hedgpeth, Darryl Fears, and Gregory Scruggs, "Indian Country, Where Residents Suffer Disproportionately from Disease, Is Bracing for Coronavirus," *Washington Post,* April 4, 2020, https://www.washingtonpost.com/climate-environment/2020/04/04/native-american-coronavirus/.

30. Chelsea Currizzo, "COVID Mortality Twice as High among Native Americans than Whites," *US News,* December 10, 2020, https://www.usnews.com/news/health-news/articles/2020-12-10/covid-mortality-twice-as-high-among-native-americans-than-whites.

31. Kyle Powys Whyte, "Indigenous Climate Change Studies: Indigenizing Futures, Decoloniziing the Anthropocene," *English Language Notes* 55 (Fall 2017): 153–62; Whyte, "Critical Investigations of Resilience: A Brief Introduction to Indigenous Environmental Studies and Science," *Daedalus* 147 (2018): 136–47.

32. Brown, "Tribes Rapidly Roll Out Vaccines."

33. Kaur, "Tribal Health Providers."

34. Siegler, "Why Native Americans Are Getting COVID-19 Vaccines Faster."

35. Erin Blakemore, "How Influenza Devastated the Navajo Community in 1918," *JSTOR Daily,* July 13, 2020, https://daily.jstor.org/how-influenza-devastated-the-navajo-community-in-1918/.

36. Hedgpeth et al., "Indian Country."

37. Holly Silverman, Konstantin Toropin, Sara Sidner, and Leslie Perrot, "Navajo Nation Surpasses New York State in the Highest COVID-19 Infection Rate in the US," CNN, May 18, 2020, https://www.cnn.com/2020/05/18/us/navajo-nation-infection-rate-trnd/index.html.

38. Jade Begay, "How Navajo Physicians Are Battling the COVID-19 Pandemic," *Smithsonian,* March 2021, https://www.smithsonianmag.com/science-nature/healers-navajo-nation-pandemic-covid-19-180976994/.

39. Kaur, "Tribal Health Providers."

40. Carlie Porterfield, "Here's Why the Navajo Nation Is Beating Out Every State in Coronavirus Vaccine Rollout," *Forbes,* April 4, 2021, https://www.forbes.com/sites/carlieporterfield/2021/04/04/heres-why-the-navajo-nation-is-beating-out-every-states-coronavirus-vaccine-rollout/.

41. Julia Flaherty, "For This Navajo Doctor, Listening Is Medicine," *Tufts Now,* April 15, 2019, https://now.tufts.edu/articles/navajo-doctor-listening-medicine.

42. Flaherty.

43. Flaherty.

5 Environmental Warnings Unheard, from 1962 to 2020

The emergence of SARS-CoV-2 in 2019 in China has confirmed scenarios built by microbiologists in the 1980s on the emergence of infectious diseases. Joshua Lederberg and Stephen Morse warned us that "we have never been so vulnerable" because of the growing interdependencies between human societies at the scale of the planet and their growing impact on the nonhuman world.[1] Consequently, they argued, we had to prepare for new diseases by monitoring the animal reservoirs where pathogens silently mutate before spilling over to humans. Techniques of preparedness, such as sentinel devices, exercises of simulation, or stockpiling of vaccines and drugs, were transferred from the world of civil defense to all kinds of hazards at the end of the Cold War, as part of a biosecurity apparatus reinforced by 9/11.[2] We have thus come to conceive of emerging pathogens as enemies whose invisible paths must be followed before they trigger catastrophic events through infectious outbreaks. SARS-CoV-2 has often been conceived as a revenge of bats and pangolins against the illegal trade that transformed them into commodities, as if viruses could be considered weapons of the weak against a tantalizing humanity.[3]

I want to trace the meaning of SARS-CoV-2 as a warning of environmental changes to a longer genealogy. Rather than as enemies enacting revenge against us, we should conceive of bats as a parallel order of mammals who occupied the planet long before humans and adapted to a diversity of microbes that strengthened their immune systems that allowed them to fly. The emergence of SARS-CoV-2, in this perspective, is a sign of disruption of this equilibrium between two parallel orders of flying mammals: those that developed long ago a light metabolism and those that have developed recently a costly and probably unsustainable metabolism. Rather than as a reservoir for pathogens silently mutating before jumping to humans, we should see bats as a reserve of possibilities to live in interspecies colonies through different environments.[4]

To think about SARS-CoV-2 ecologically, I want to return to the year 1962, when this coexistence between orders of living beings was described and when warning signals of its disruption were sent. As the world was then at the peak of decolonization and of the Cold War, with the end of the Algerian War and the Cuban Missile Crisis, new images were produced of worlds entering a process of extinction. Information about invisible entities, such as toxic chemicals or emerging microbes, was available at the same time as new representations of societies who entered in relation with their environments through narratives about the plants and animals. I want to come back to what was known in ecology, microbiology, and anthropology in three important works published in 1962.

The year 1962 is when Rachel Carson's classic book *Silent Spring* was published, considered foundational for environmental protection in the United States, as it raised awareness of the effects of DDT so compellingly that public outcry led to the chemical's withdrawal. Carson was concerned by the fate of birds because, owing to their place in the food chain, they were exposed to the massive doses of pesticides consumed by insects and fish. While chemical companies observed the effects of pesticides like DDT in laboratories on different animal species, she realized that when a bird eats a fish that ingested insects with DDT, the dose in the bird's body is one hundred times what it would have ingested by itself. Carson introduced an ecological approach in toxicology because she looked at the combination of toxic molecules in trophic chains. As a marine biologist, Carson had learned to take the perspective of fish on their dangerous environments. "I have spoken of a fish fearing his enemies not because I suppose a fish experiences in the same way that we do, but because I think he behaves as though he were frightened."[5] Carson initially thought of giving her book the title "Man against the Earth" or "A War on Nature" to describe the threat of pesticides on fish and birds, but she chose *Silent Spring* to convey the experience of a nature lover who feels that natural species are missing. "To the birdwatcher, the suburbanite who derives joy from birds in his garden, the hunter, the fisherman or the explorer of wild regions, anything that destroys the wildlife of an area for even a single year has deprived him of a pleasure to which he has a legitimate right." Carson's book was an attempt to go beyond that human point of view and describe what could be a "poisoned environment."[6]

Carson argued for a democratization of knowledge about pesticides, which remained in the hands of toxicologists and governments. She noted that the fear of poison that concerned only aristocratic families in castle plots—such as the famous Borgias—now concerned every citizen living in a quiet environment: "every human being is now subjected to contact with dangerous chemicals from the moment of conception until death."[7] Her book mixes poetic nature writing with technical knowledge on the composition of chemicals and the statistics of cancer in locations where these pesticides are spread, as the number of deaths from cancer in the United States had increased from 4 percent in 1900 to 15 percent in 1958. The strength of Carson's work is to frame pesticides as one entry in the web of solidarities that constitute the natural environment: not only insects, fish, and birds but also water, soil, and plants. She refuses the argument of a tragic choice between protecting trees and protecting birds. "By one of the ironies that abound throughout the field of chemical control, we may very well have neither if we continue on our present, well-traveled road. Spraying is killing the birds but it is not saving the elms."[8] It is impossible to predict which species will be destroyed by a pesticide and which will be protected because all species live in interdependency, but it is possible to observe the number of dead animals after the spraying of pesticides. Carson's general argument is that humans are too entangled with their environment to stand apart, as if they could control it. Their action is too direct. "We are walking in nature like an elephant in the china cabinet."[9]

Carson often compared pesticides to two other invisible entities in the modern environment: radiation and microbes. Carson herself had to submit her body to radiation to decrease her cancerous tumors. The nuclear bombs in Hiroshima and Nagasaki allowed physicians to study the effects of radiation and to give a positive image of its use in medicine. In the context of widespread fears of nuclear war, this strategy was aimed at raising awareness of the threat of pesticides by reference to a more dreaded threat. On the other side, Carson compared pesticides to vaccines, which, rather than the "magic bullet" of antibiotics that eliminated bacteria, used attenuated microbes to produce immunity. Carson requested a rational use of pesticides and looked for alternative ways to kill invasive insects, such as sterilization. For her, the twentieth-century rediscovered for radiation and pesticides what the nineteenth century had learned of microbes:

the necessity to understand relations between beings composing an environment before trying to eradicate one kind of them.

Carson assumed that microbes came from nature and pesticides from humans. "The outlook is more encouraging than the situation regarding infectious disease at the turn of the century. The world was then full of disease germs as today it is full of carcinogens. But man did not put the germs in the environment and his role in spreading them was involuntary. In contrast man has put the vast majority of carcinogens into the environment, and he can, if he wishes, eliminate many of them."[10]

However, the idea that humans had no impact on the microbes composing their environment was questioned in another field of knowledge, the ecology of infectious diseases.[11] One of the landmarks of this medical thinking, Frank Macfarlane Burnet's *Natural History of Infectious Diseases*, first published in 1953, came out in a second version in 1962. The echoes between this book and Carson's, though unheard at that time, are worth mentioning to think through the challenges of our own time.

Burnet is considered the founder of Australian microbiology. After receiving a PhD in medicine at the University of London in 1928, he returned to his native Australia, where he studied the pandemic of psittacosis, a disease transmitted from parrots to humans, infecting 800 people worldwide, 112 of which died. Burnet found the bacterium that causes the disease, cultivated it in a chicken embryo, and showed that a wide range of species of Australian birds carried this bacterium, although their strains were not pathogenic. He concluded that the transportation of birds from Australia to Europe in stressful conditions had made this bacterium pathogenic. At the same time, Karl Friedrich Mayer showed that parrots transported from South America to North America transmitted the disease during and after their boat trips.[12] Burnet also successfully cultivated the influenza virus on chicken embryos, which made possible the production of vaccines against influenza. He won the Nobel Prize in 1960 for his research on immunology. Two of his students, Robert Webster and Graeme Laver, showed that wild birds had antibodies to influenza even if they didn't have symptoms of the disease and collected influenza viral strains among wild birds to follow the mutations of the virus that could cause a pandemic.[13] The conclusions of Burnet's psittacosis research in the 1930s was applied to avian influenza in the 1960s: even if wild birds carry influenza viruses without symptoms, their concentration in dense bird populations by human intervention, such as poultry farms in China, could lead to the emergence of a pathogenic strain.

Burnet's *Natural History of Infectious Diseases* thus adds to the eighteenth-century observations of nature made by microbiologists who trace the mutations of microbes in the different animal species composing an environment:

> Since the eighteenth century, there have always been educated men of some leisure with a natural interest in the activities of animals and plants. Many of these amateur naturalists, from Izrael Walton and Gilbert White onward, have written about the way animals make a living. The habits of birds in feeding, courting and nesting have attracted the interest of many. Others have spent years unraveling the life history of insects. In more recent years, the essentially amateur type of observer has been supplemented by the professional biologist, whose more systematic investigations in the field once known as nature study have raised its dignity to the science of ecology.[14]

For Burnet, who had been a passionate beetle collector in his youth, the microbiologists had to think at the level of the ecosystem to understand the coevolution between animals, plants, and microbes. If microbes live as parasites in animals and plants, who host them for mutual benefit, a disease appeared a sign that the balance between species had been altered, as if nature were using microbes against invasive species to return to equilibrium. "Nature has always seemed to be working for a climax state, a provisionally stable ecosystem, reached by natural forces, and when we attempt to remould any such ecosystem, we must remember that Nature is working against us."[15] Burnet was particularly worried about the effects of war and migration on the emergence of new infectious diseases and trusted that immunology could develop good distances between living species following the laws of evolution.

The idea that nature sends humans warning signals of the disruption of stable ecosystems seems to resonate with our time, even if the recent transformations of ecology have questioned the model of a stable ecosystem. It also resonates with the knowledge of non-Western societies who perceive signs in their environment, even if they don't integrate these signs in general laws of nature. Claude Lévi-Strauss's *La pensée sauvage*, also published in 1962, is all the more interesting to read in that perspective, because

he questions Western modes of integration of "nature."[16] Translated in
1964 with the title *Savage Mind*, it has recently been translated in a new edition under the title *Wild Thoughts*. Indeed, Lévi-Strauss conceives of thinking
as a means to attenuate tensions in the perceived environment by connecting empirical qualities. For instance, when Hidatsa hunters dig a hole in
which they hide to attract eagles, they invoke the spirit of the wolverine
because the wolverine is the only animal in their environment that never
falls into traps. Hunting societies, following Lévi-Strauss, have developed
modes of classification of animals and plants that stabilize the effects of
contingent events, such as demographic changes, arrivals of newborns, or
emergences of new diseases.

This demonstration allowed him to criticize the hypothesis of totemism,
which assumed that society projected its categories onto natural entities,
considering them as ancestors or allies. The totemic hypothesis didn't give
enough credit to the attention paid by hunting societies to the diversity of
their environment, where they could find names and remedies for new
diseases. "So little is the species 'grid' confined to sociological categories
that (notably in America) it serves to order a domain as restricted as that
of diseases and remedies. The Indians of the South-East United States
attribute pathological phenomena to a conflict between men, animals and
plants. Vexed with men, animals sent them diseases."[17] For Lévi-Strauss,
this narrative showed that hunting societies could extend their classifica-
tions to include diseases, because to name a disease is to begin an inquiry
into its remedy.

Lévi-Strauss assumed that this knowledge of hunting societies had
become marginal with the Neolithic revolution, which led to privileg-
ing stable entities in the resolution of practical problems. The invention
of pottery and the domestication of animals and plants have led to the
division between two modes of thinking, which he called *tinkering* and
engineering. They are "two strategic levels at which nature is accessible to
scientific inquiry: one roughly adapted to that of perception and the imagination, the other at a remove from it."[18] While the birth of mathematics
strengthened this distinction between two modes of knowledge, the invention of microbiology and the theory of biological information filled the
gap between them. They showed that there is a "heuristic value . . . in
treating the sensible properties of the animal and plant kingdoms as if they
were the elements of a message and in discovering 'signatures'—and so
signs—in them."[19]

Indeed, virus hunters who followed the mutations of influenza in Australia and North America, at the moment when Lévi-Strauss writes this sentence, perceived the signs of ecological disruption in the discontinuities of genetic sequences, and they imagined pandemic events to mitigate their catastrophic consequences. They built alliances with birdwatchers to closely monitor the environments in which viruses can be collected and store them in biological archives.[20] The alliance of the microbiological knowledge developed by Burnet and the ecological sensibility developed by Carson leads to a reinvigoration of the techniques of anticipation described by Lévi-Strauss as "savage mind" or "wild thoughts." At a moment like the long 2020, when societies on the verge of extinction meet with animal species threatened by the impact of domestication—what we now call the Anthropocene—possibilities of knowledge appear at the level of perception, allowing humans to imagine a future with animals: a future in which animals live at a good distance from humans and in which disease signals that these distances have been breached; a future in which animals carrying signs of diseases are not eradicated as scapegoats but are attentively followed as sentinels of vulnerabilities they share with humans.

NOTES

1. Stephen S. Morse, ed., *Emerging Viruses*, 1st ed. (Oxford: Oxford University Press, 1993).

2. Andrew Lakoff, *Unprepared: Global Health in a Time of Emergency* (Oakland: University of California Press, 2017).

3. Andreas Malm, *Corona, Climate, Chronic Emergency: War Communism in the Twenty-First Century* (London: Verso, 2020).

4. Lin-fa Wang and Christopher Cowled, *Bats and Viruses: A New Frontier of Emerging Infectious Diseases* (New York: John Wiley, 2015).

5. Rachel Carson, *The Sea around Us* (1951), quoted in Linda Lear, *Rachel Carson: Witness for Nature* (New York: Henry Holt, 1997), 91.

6. Rachel Carson, *Silent Spring* (Boston: Houghton Mifflin Harcourt, 1962), 86–87.

7. Carson, 15.

8. Carson, 114.

9. Carson, 78.

10. Carson, 242.

11. Warwick Anderson, "Natural Histories of Infectious Diseases: Ecological Vision in Twentieth-Century Biomedical Science," *Osiris*, 2nd Series 19 (2004): 39–61.

12. Frank Macfarlane Burnet, "Enzootic Psittacosis among Wild Australian Parrots," *Journal of Hygiene* (1935): 412–20; Mark Honigsbaum, "'Tipping the Balance': Karl Friedrich Meyer, Latent Infections, and the Birth of Modern Ideas of Disease Ecology," *Journal of the History of Biology* 49, no. 2 (2016): 261–309.

13. Robert Webster, *Flu Hunter: Unlocking the Secrets of a Virus* (Dunedin, New Zealand: Otago University Press, 2018).

14. Frank Macfarlane Burnet, *Natural History of Infectious Diseases* (Cambridge: Cambridge University Press, 1962), 5.

15. Burnet, 15.

16. On the difficulties of using the notion of nature for non-Western societies, see Philippe Descola, *Beyond Nature and Culture* (Chicago: University of Chicago Press, 2013).

17. Claude Lévi-Strauss, *The Savage Mind* (London: Weidenfeld and Nicolson, 1966), 164.

18. Lévi-Strauss, 15.

19. Lévi-Strauss, 268.

20. Frédéric Keck, *Avian Reservoirs: Virus Hunters and Birdwatchers in Chinese Sentinel Posts* (Durham, N.C.: Duke University Press, 2020).

6 The Backdrop of the Post-Truth

RODERICK A. FERGUSON

This chapter analyzes the long 2020 by focusing on post-truth discourses or the practices by which objective facts are demoted as elements to shape policy and public opinion and personal beliefs and feelings are exalted as determinants of public and political sensibilities. In the U.S. context, most of the commentary on the post-truth moment revolves around Donald Trump. During the 2020 election year, Trump claimed that if he lost to Joe Biden, it would be because of voter fraud. When he did lose the presidency, he engaged a systematic campaign to discredit the election process and foment political unrest. As the editors of this volume note, "[Trump's] incessant months-long Twitter and media campaign to invalidate the election had its desired effect, sowing chaos and fueling his cult of personality, leading thousands of Trump loyalists to stage an attempted coup at the nation's Capitol on January 6, 2021."

While Trump is the most spectacular U.S. president in modern history to promote and manipulate post-truth politics, we focus unduly on him at great historical costs. By fixing our analysis on Trump, the post-truth moment is understood to emanate from the idiosyncrasies of a particular individual figure. As the moment in which the authority of facts is degraded, the post-truth is, hence, framed as something that can be explained through the discrete occurrences of a particular campaign and a particular presidency.

Other accounts of the post-truth horizon engage it as a breakdown of norms of accountability concerning evidence and rational argumentation. Moreover, most of the coverage about the post-truth frames it as an ideological matter whose outcomes might be racist or sexist here and there but

53

whose origins can be simply understood as irrationalities that have little to do with social hierarchies or exclusions. For instance, charges that Barack Obama was not born in the United States or that Hillary Clinton was the originator of "birther" claims may be racist and sexist expressions of the post-truth, but post-truth discourse is not in itself seen as emanating from social exclusions.

Those framings of the post-truth are in many ways symptomatic of what this chapter attempts to diagnose—that is, the long-cultivated resistance to truth and history that has come to characterize the political and social ethos within this country. Moreover, that ethos cannot be explained simply through Trump. Indeed, it precedes him. It also cannot be explained as an idiosyncratic occurrence. In fact, it is part of a deliberate and well-planned historical formation. It is a historical formation that is also not disconnected from social ideologies of race, class, gender, and sexuality but firmly rooted in them.

The ideological origins of the post-truth moment are evident especially in its development in the 1980s onward. In that moment, the ideological connotations of the post-truth discourse were most evident during the Reagan and Bush years. In fact, the current post-truth moment inherits these earlier iterations from the 1980s. Those earlier moments were responding to the various critiques of forms of power coming from art, activism, and scholarship. One way of thinking about the origins of the post-truth is to read them as efforts to resist the critical and affective inroads attempted by antiracist, feminist, anticapitalist, and queer formations. This talk, therefore, investigates the post-truth ethos in the United States as a backlash not simply to the status typically enjoyed by the factual and the empirical but to the affective inroads made by antiracist, queer, and feminist intellectual production. As such, the post-truth moment represents not only the demotion of empirical knowledge but the unseating of historical and cultural knowledge about racial, gender, and sexual minorities and its potential to disrupt the coherence of subjects privileged by race, gender, and sexuality and the innocence of the U.S. nation-state. As such, I would like to offer the post-truth moment as a mode of resistance to the critical knowledges produced in activist, academic, and artistic contexts and to the affective agendas that those knowledges presumed—that is, the ways in which those critical knowledges were attempting to effect change at the level, not only of the social, but of the subjective as well. As a culmination of post-truth practices from bygone eras, the long 2020 was seeded in decades past.

POST-TRUTH IN THE 1980S

The category "post-truth" was first used in a 1992 article written by the late Serbian American writer Steve Tesich. In "The Watergate Scandal: A Government of Lies," Tesich draws attention to the deliberate subterfuge and misleading of the American public during the Reagan and Bush years. After truth prevailed because of pressures from social protest, media, and legislation responding to Vietnam and Watergate, Tesich identified a shift. As he states, "In the wake of that triumph something totally unforeseen occurred. Either because the Watergate revelations were so wrenching and followed on the heels of the war in Vietnam, which was replete with crimes and revelations of its own, or because Nixon was so quickly pardoned, we began to shy away from the truth."[1] Those moments occasioned not only a shift away from truth but U.S. society's capacity to stomach the truth as well. As he argues, "We came to equate the truth with bad news and we didn't want bad news anymore, no matter how true or vital to our health as a nation. We looked to our government to protect us from the truth."[2]

The social turn away from truth, Tesich goes on to argue, provided a kind of cover for the Iran–Contra scandal, which he describes as "far more serious and un-American than the crimes for which Nixon was kicked out of office." As he says, "These latest crimes attacked the very heart and soul of our Republic. A private little government was created to pursue a private foreign policy agenda and thereby circumvent the law of the land, the Congress, the Constitution itself." Known as the Iran–Contra Affair, senior administrative officials within the U.S. government sold arms to Iran in the hope that those arms would then be sold to the right-wing rebel group in Nicaragua known as the Contras. Iran was the subject of an arms embargo at the time, and the Boland Act Amendment of 1982 had prohibited the further sale of U.S. arms to the Contras. Relating this breach within American government to authoritarian regimes, Tesich goes on to say, "The hidden layer of government, which diminishes democratic institutions to a series of front organizations, is a well-known feature of 'totalitarian' regimes." There is a "government line" presented to the public and a "party line" that functions in the backrooms. As he says, "The line in this case was the Republican Party line, but it was no different in its implementation and its implications from the Communist Party line to the pre-Gorbachev Soviet Union."[3]

As Vietnam and Watergate provided openings for Iran–Contra, they all produced the conditions for the deceptions of the Gulf War, according to Tesich. Discussing the Gulf War, he points to the State Department's own declassification of the diplomatic cables of U.S. ambassador April Glaspie, who—contrary to the cables—told the Senate that Saddam Hussein was warned not to violate the territorial integrity of Kuwait. Commenting on this, Tesich argues, "It now turns out that it was all a lie. But the fact that the Bush Administration felt safe in declassifying those cables shows it was no longer afraid of the truth because it knows the truth will have little impact on us."[4]

The post-truth for Tesich had implications broader than any one particular administration. As an ideology that stretched across various presidential administrations, it cannot then be understood under its present-day logic as a matter of the idiosyncrasy of the Trump presidency. It is and has been—as Tesich argues—a matter of American statecraft for more than thirty years. Indeed, the post-truth, for Tesich, denoted the moment in which the government fundamentally abrogated ethical responsibility to ideals of truth and equity. Tesich writes, for instance, "The Gulf War is over but the war at home goes on. The gulf between rich and destitute widens—between those of us who live in a modern postindustrial nation and those of us who live in the Third World countries of our inner cities." As he suggests, the post-truth is simultaneously a racial and class project, one in which the authority of truth and fact is downgraded by entities that are in theory supposed to uphold that authority, downgraded for the good of racial, class, and, in the case of Nicaragua, imperial subjugation.

Tesich asserts that the post-truth produced a devastating intellectual and moral crisis, one that can be seen in the state's rejection of critical education and the people's acceptance of that rejection:

> We keep asking why the level of our children's intelligence and competence, as measured by all the tests, keeps dropping. The reason is very simple: We don't want them to be well-educated. The last thing we want now is for an intellectually and spiritually vigorous generation to confront us with the question of what we have done to this country.[5]

The post-truth was part of an elaborate system that educates and convinces people away from truth as an instrument of critical engagement between the people and apparatuses of power. This system, for Tesich, is what causes a democracy to teeter toward totalitarianism: "All the dictators up to now," he says, "have had to work hard at suppressing the truth. We, by our actions, are saying that this is no longer necessary, that we have acquired a spiritual mechanism that can denude truth of any significance. In a very fundamental way, we, as a free people, have freely decided that we want to live in a post-truth world." Hence the post-truth is not the diagnosis of a benighted head of state; it is the diagnosis of a social formation in which the state and its people are implicated.

THE INTERSECTIONAL STRUGGLES AGAINST THE RESISTIVE POWERS OF THE POST-TRUTH

The cultural turn away from the authority of truth was part of a hegemonic struggle between elite efforts to subjugate knowledge and critical efforts to disinter that knowledge. Indeed, the moments that Tesich uses to periodize the post-truth—the Vietnam War, the Watergate scandal, the Iran–Contra Affair, and the Gulf War—were also periods characterized by vigorous responses in terms of social movements, art, and criticism. The artists, activists, and scholars who produced those responses would ask the nation and its people to confront the truth in all its historical and social unpleasantness, an unpleasantness that has racial, gender, sexual, and class contours. This would not only involve an intellectual encounter with the truth of state and social violence; it would also entail an affective and psychic confrontation with ongoing histories of violence. Those critiques had an explicitly affective and psychic agenda, one designed to tear down the American self's strategies of resistance where critiques of authority were concerned. These critiques and their related affective and psychic agendas were prominently seen in intersectional engagements with race, gender, class, and sexuality, engagements designed to tear down a national armory of ideological and psychic resistances designed to bolster state nationalism and systemic exploitations within and outside the United States. Put plainly, the 1980s were a moment in which the post-truth and critiques of it revealed themselves to have simultaneously ideological and psychic agendas.

A long list of work coming out of the 1970s and 1980s attempted to address the importance of a psychic confrontation with and working through of racial, gender, class, and sexual exploitations that characterize both the U.S. nation-state and Western civilization. Think, for instance, of Toni Morrison's 1970 novel *The Bluest Eye* about a little Black girl who longs for the one thing that would make her life complete—a blue eye. Morrison used the novel to address the psychic life of racism and the ways in which that life was promoted by media and by standards of beauty. Consider as well the Combahee River Collective's linking of psychological dispossession with structural exclusions in their 1977 "A Black Feminist Statement." Addressing the dual structural and psychic assault of racial, gender, and sexual power, they wrote, "We are dispossessed psychologically and on every other level, and yet we feel the necessity to struggle to change the condition of all black women." In "Poetry Is Not a Luxury," first written for the journal *Chrysalis* in 1977, Audre Lorde said this about the psychic agendas of gender and sexual domination as it pertains to women: "For within the living structures defined by profit, by linear power, by institutional dehumanization, our feelings were not meant to survive. Kept around as unavoidable adjuncts or pleasant pastimes, feelings were expected to kneel to thought as women were expected to kneel to men."[6] Reading power as partly the distortion and domination of the affective and understanding dreams to be the landscapes where freedom might be imagined, she went on to write, "Those dreams are made realizable through our poems that give us the strength and courage to see, to feel, to speak, and to dare."

In another context, Lorde continued her interest in the psychic life of power and freedom. For instance, in February 1982, Lorde delivered a lecture for Malcolm X Weekend at Harvard University. In that lecture, titled "Learning from the Sixties," Lorde addressed the political and affective dimensions of Black radical struggles, writing, "One of the most basic survival skills is the ability to change, to metabolize experience, good or ill, into something that is useful, lasting, effective. Four hundred years of survival as an endangered species has taught most of us that if we intend to live, we had better become fast learners. Malcolm knew this."[7] We might think of Lorde's use of the metabolic metaphor as a model for confronting historical exigencies and traumas. As such, the metabolic metaphor implies processes by which those traumas and exigencies are synthesized and broken down to produce new forms of social and subjective mobilizations.

In this instance, historical violence is metabolized as the antithesis of the post-truth's evasion of historical confrontation. As a metabolic gesture, to confront history is to synthesize and break down the contradictions, traumas, and violences of nation-states. Discussing the developing role of U.S. empire in Latin America in the early 1980s, soon after the Iran–Contra Affair was developing but before its exposure, Lorde wrote, "We are functioning under a government ready to repeat in El Salvador and Nicaragua the tragedy of Vietnam, a government which stands on the wrong side of every single battle for liberation taking place upon this globe."[8] Here Lorde was using her speech to underline the necessity of producing oneself as a subject who can point toward the ugliness that is concealed by the state. Like many other writers and artists during the period, Lorde would help establish the confrontation with the unpleasant truths of history as the horizon of intellectual production and psychic possibility.

In Pratibha Parmar's 1991 film about Angela Davis, June Jordan, and Alice Walker—*A Place of Rage*—the theorist and filmmaker Trinh T. Minh-Ha discusses the ways in which African American women's literature set that standard for her when she migrated to the United States in the 1970s:

> What I remember during my first years in the States, I remember being very impressed, particularly impressed by the work of African American playwrights and poets. And of course I remember the poetry of June Jordan, being the first few works by Black women that I read at the time. The poems have an ability to walk right into the heart and awaken a deep, plural anger for brutal violence and injustice.[9]

For Trinh, African American women's cultural production was key to producing a psychic confrontation with the hard truths of violence and injustice. More pointedly, she points to African American women's literature as a technology that set into motion a run-in between the subject and history, between the reader and the social world, a run-in that is unpleasant and necessary, one involving lessons in—to use the words of Columbian artist Doris Salcedo—"how human life is manipulated by calculations of power."

The 1970s and 1980s represent moments in which dominant forces attempted to erect psychic armories against the critique of the state and forms of inequality. In addition, they were moments in which counterhegemonic forces attempted to produce critiques of the state and the inequalities that it generated and encouraged. In addition, those decades signify periods in which those counterhegemonic forces worked to produce psychic and subjective dispositions that could hold those critiques in awareness. In doing so, they were struggling against a developing post-truth milieu that insisted on the right of American citizens, in particular, to be unencumbered by the other and the historical exigencies that surrounded the other.

RESISTANCE AND THE RIGHT TO BE UNENCUMBERED

So far, I have argued that post-truth discourse does not originate simply with the Trump administration, that its history stretches back—as Steve Tesich argued—to at least the 1980s during the Reagan and Bush years. Moreover, I have asserted that post-truth ideology has for decades attempted to resist the critical *and* affective inroads of cultural and academic production around race, gender, sexuality, and class and that the post-truth ideology is a system of resistance to the persuasive powers of that production. If post-truth discourse, as Tesich suggests, addresses itself not only to the government's operations but to the people's beliefs and dispositions, then post-truth discourses identify psychic life as a main target of their activities, indeed, as the basis for a resistance to historical confrontation and as the seedbed of the right to be unencumbered.

In terms of fields, psychoanalysis has the longest engagement with psychic resistance as an analytical object and practice of the mind. The psychoanalytic and education theorist Deborah Britzman contextualizes Freud's invention by writing,

> He turned his attention away from enlightenment to ordinary experiences of fear, anxiety, and desire in human relationships and wondered about resistance to change, the defense of perfection, and the ego's compromises. Freud was also writing in a world at war and saw for himself the violence, destruction, and hatred between and within nations. His big question then was not so much why we need knowledge but *why we don't want it.*[10]

As Britzman suggests, national strife and social animosities provided the social contexts in which Freud would deliberate upon resistance as a psychic operation involving memory, repetition, and resistance. This context would, in a sense, point to historical confrontation as the backdrop for Freud's reflections on why we don't want knowledge.

In his 1914 paper "Remembering, Repeating, and Working Through," for instance, Freud posits resistance as the process by which the subject represses memories only to have them resurrected in action. As he states, "the patient does not *remember* anything of what he has forgotten and repressed, but *acts* it out. He reproduces it not as a memory but as an action; he *repeats* it, without, of course, knowing that he is repeating it." What the subject will not confront through consciousness is then exiled to the unconsciousness of the body's actions. Freud designed psychoanalysis as a method by which subjects would confront the insistent material that they resisted and repressed. Discussing this operation, he argued, "First and foremost, the initiation of the treatment in itself brings about a change in the patient's conscious attitude toward his illness. . . . The way is thus paved from the beginning for a reconciliation with the repressed material which is coming to expression in his symptoms, while at the same time place is found for a certain tolerance of the state of being ill."[11] As a science, psychoanalysis aspired to produce a new relationship between the subject, the material that the subject repressed, and the subject's illness. As Freud's passage suggests, psychoanalysis was attempting to promote subjects who could do the hard and agonizing work of confrontation and accept that work as the condition for emotional and social life.

Psychoanalysis's task would set it apart from its peers in the social sciences and humanities. In *The Order of Things,* Foucault noted the ways in which psychoanalysis was distinct from the other human sciences because of this aspiration:

Whereas all the human sciences advance towards the unconscious only with their back to it, waiting for it to unveil itself as fast as consciousness is analysed, as it were backwards, psychoanalysis, on the other hand, points directly towards it, with a deliberate purpose—not towards that which must be rendered gradually more explicit by the progressive illumination of the implicit, but towards what is there and yet is hidden, towards what exists with the mute solidity of a thing, of a text closed in upon itself, or of a blank space in a visible text, and uses that quality to defend itself.[12]

Here Foucault points to the psychoanalytic apparatus as one that trains its powers on an economy of the visible and the hidden, the true and the unspeakable. Because of this, we might aptly say that psychoanalysis was the first science to exhibit and demand real courage.

The visible and the hidden take on a different character in settings like the United States. Indeed, in social contexts where those minoritized by differences of race, gender, sexuality, and class become part of the landscape of the unspeakable and the invisible, what is repressed and resisted ceases to be exhausted by the inner workings of the psyche and becomes part of the external dramas of the social. In those contexts, what must be resisted are the various histories and critiques that the other invokes. If psychoanalysis is about addressing the unrepresentable at psychic levels, then the cultural production conducted along feminist, queer, and antiracist lines is about engaging the unrepresentable at the levels of the psyche and of the social.

In contrast to psychoanalysis's call for subjects to refute psychic resistance, we are now in a moment that attempts to normalize that resistance and establish it as a right. Discussing this as the right to be unencumbered, theorist Jodi Melamed argues, "We are experiencing a partial remaking of rights under the combined pressure of the ultracapitalist radical right, a block that leads today for extractive, financial, and corporate global capitalism, and the political resurgence of a libertarian-leaning ethno-nationalism, which we can think of as a highly individualistic (neoliberalized), lightly veiled version of white supremacy."[13] Touching on how the discourse of rights plays into this, Melamed argues, "These forces come together around relatively new articulations of 'rights,' which grow out of relatively old 20th century libertarian notions of economic liberty, and are routed through the First Amendment, anti-discrimination claims, and civil rights redone as libertarian counterrights. They amount to this: *the 'right' to be unencumbered by concern for the wellbeing of others and the planet.*"[14]

As Melamed states, there is a close link between white racial ideologies and the "right to be unencumbered." In fact, in the context of the United States, whiteness has presented itself—thinking here of Freud's paper again—as the resistant subjectivity par excellence. Talking about the resistive properties of white subjectivity in his 1965 essay "White Man's Guilt," James Baldwin argues,

[People] who imagine that history flatters them (as it does, indeed, since they wrote it) are impaled on their history like a butterfly on a pin and become incapable of seeing or changing themselves, or this world.

This is the place in which it seems to me most white Americans find themselves. Impaled. They are dimly, or vividly, aware that the history they have fed themselves is mainly a lie, but they do not know how to release themselves from it, and they suffer enormously from the resulting personal incoherence.[15]

Similar to psychoanalysis, Baldwin offers a "treatment" meant to get the subject in general but the white subject in particular to develop a different relationship with historical confrontation. He writes,

In great pain and terror one begins to assess the history which has placed one where one is and formed one's point of view. In great pain and terror because, therefore, one enters into battle with that historical creation, Oneself, and attempts to recreate oneself according to a principle more humane and more liberating; one begins the attempt to achieve a level of personal maturity and freedom which robs history of its tyrannical power, and also changes history.[16]

If the psychoanalyst, to use Freud's language, must "allow the patient to become more conversant with this resistance with which he has now become acquainted, to work through it, to overcome it, by continuing, in defiance of it, the analytic work according to the fundamental rule of analysis,"[17] then Baldwin calls for a similar working-through and overcoming, not of an abstract resistance, but rather of a historically laden one that is contoured by the irksome truths of racism, empire, heteropatriarchy, homophobia, ableism, and class exploitation. As Baldwin, Lorde, the Combahee River Collective, and Freud imply, confrontation is work, and doing that work is our only possibility for human and social advancement.

THE POST-TRUTH AND THE RIGHT TO BE UNENCUMBERED IN THE HISTORY OF SEXUALITY

If psychoanalysis has had the longest engagement with psychic resistance, then it is social movements and the interdisciplinary and intersectional inquiries that have accompanied them that have had the longest engagement with the acceptance of new knowledge and new transformations as a psychic assignment. In this context, work by folks engaged in sexual liberation has proven to be of great significance. Within this assemblage of artists, activists, and intellectuals, we can find models of people who made the confrontation with history the condition for living. Consider, for example, these words from artist David Wajnarowicz's *Close to the Knives: A Memoir of Disintegration*:

> Dismissal is policy in America. Our elected "representatives" have come up with a fail-safe system of symbols based on a prehistoric moral code built by other humans, years, decades, or even many centuries ago. . . . In this country the elected representative has only to attach one of these symbols from the moral code to any social problem and people who are not immediately affected by that problem feel safe and distanced. If there is homelessness in our streets it is the fault of those who have no homes—they *chose* to live that

way. If there is a disease such as AIDS it is somehow the fault of those who contract that disease—they *chose* to have that disease. If three black men are shot by a white man on a subway train—somehow they *chose* to be shot by that man.[18]

If we take Wajnarowicz's remark as a thesis about the critical possibilities of sexuality, we could say that the critique of sexuality here observes the operations of power within race and poverty as well as sexuality. We might also venture that sexuality is a confrontation with dismissal as a psychic and social technology, as a mode of statecraft and a form of governmentality in advanced liberal and socially heterogeneous societies. Moreover, sexuality denotes the critique of how the state promotes its individuals to understand themselves as distant from the people and the contradictions around them. As such, this critique of sexuality goes to the heart of the moral crisis engendered by the post-truth. Lastly, for Wajnarowicz, we might say that sexuality counteracts the post-truth's "right to be unencumbered" with the necessity of being yoked to history and its others.

To counteract the post-truth and to end the long 2020, we need to turn to the histories of progressive social movements and interdisciplinary formations—not only to learn from their tactics or to take inspiration from their courageous efforts. We need to reacquaint ourselves with them to learn how to encounter and *feel* new knowledge and new experiences as necessary for our collective survival rather than threats to our existence. In doing so, we would be taking as our models formations that have made it their business to run toward the truth rather than away from it.

NOTES

1. Steve Tesich, "A Government of Lies," *The Nation*, January 6–13, 1992, 12.

2. Tesich, 12.

3. Tesich, 12.

4. Tesich, 13.

5. Tesich, 13.

6. Audre Lorde, *Sister Outsider: Essays and Speeches* (New York: Crossing Press, 2007).

7. Lorde.

8. Lorde.

9. Pratibha Parmar, dir., *A Place of Rage* (United States, 1991).

10. Deborah Britzman, *A Psychoanalyst in the Classroom: On the Human Condition in Education* (Albany: SUNY Press, 2015), 41, emphasis added.

11. Sigmund Freud, "Remembering, Repeating, and Working-Through," *Standard Edition* 12 (1914): 147–56.

12. Michel Foucault, *The Order of Things: An Archaeology of the Human Sciences* (New York: Vintage, 1973), 374.

13. Joni Melamed, "The Proliferation of Rights-Based Capitalist Violence and Pedagogies of Collective Action," *American Quarterly* 70, no. 2 (2018): 179.

14. Melamed, 180.

15. James Baldwin, "White Man's Guilt," in *James Baldwin: Collected Essays,* ed. Toni Morrison (New York: Library of America, 1998), 723.

16. Baldwin, 723.

17. Freud, "Remembering, Repeating, and Working-Through."

18. David Wajnarowicz, *Close to the Knives: A Memoir of Disintegration* (New York: Open Road Media, 2014).

7 Crippin' the Long 2020

As If Disability Matters

NIRMALA EREVELLES

THE COVID-19 PANDEMIC, JANUARY 2020

We did not know, then, as we watched the mirrored ball slowly descend in New York's Times Square, that after two short months of "normal" life, we would be haunted by an isolating silence and the dread of the long 2020 stretching before us. For many of us, "normal" was the reassurance that our privileged lives would continue uninterrupted as we made complicated plans for our consumptive desires in a global paradise created for our pleasure. When the proverbial shoe dropped and the World Health Organization (WHO) confirmed that we were indeed in a global pandemic, we panicked. For those of us accustomed to weathering global crises with the comforting assurance that we are safely protected from tragedies bolstered by our exceptionalism, there was disbelief that this was real. Too far away from us, for sure. We have better medical infrastructure than any other nation in the world, of course. We were never afraid before, so why now? But then, people like us began to die. They were not just the huddled masses in far-off lands. Or elderly residents warehoused in segregated nursing home facilities. Or mostly folks with chronic illnesses and comorbidities who were never meant to survive anyway. Instead, they were our neighbors, our friends, our celebrities, our heroes, whom even our most sophisticated respirators and powerful drugs could not aid in their desperate attempts to take a breath. And as our morgues filled up, so that we had to stack bodies in makeshift freezer trucks, and as fatigued doctors and nurses and public service employees pleaded with the nation for basic safety equipment, and as our cafés, schools, theaters, and businesses were shuttered, our airplanes grounded, our streets haunting in their stillness, we fought for toilet paper and scarce food supplies and shook our heads in fearful despair, muttering, "What's going on? . . . What's going on?"

A year later, it is this yearning for the "normal" we once enjoyed that bears critical reflection. It is this "normal" that thrives on embracing a social that has little tolerance for the vulnerabilities that reconfigure time, space, and embodiments. It is this "normal" that urges us on our relentless quest to surge ahead and consume the products of transnational capitalism, no matter its often violent and exploitative commitment to profits rather than people. It is this "normal" that has historically always sorted out what is anointed from what is "matter out of place"[1] and rendered the latter disposable collateral that is essential for fueling the engines of progress. It is this "normal" that has historically treated precarity as the necessary by-product for reimagining techno-fantastical futures. It is this "normal" whose very existence has required abnormality, deviancy, and disability to buttress its own centrality in the everyday, while simultaneously ensuring the forcible segregation of these same "others" from life's daily rhythms to preserve the fiction of an untroubled, predictable future.

For some of us, suddenly "woke" to the startling new reality that disrupted our routine worship of the "normal," this pandemic felt like a eureka moment—where the harsh inequalities of everyday life and its attendant discomforts demanded from us an earnest call to action that nevertheless struggled to materialize. For many others, however, this recognition of everyday adversity was not novel. In fact, their everyday realities of isolation, scarcity, economic desperation, diminished life possibilities, and disposability predated this pandemic. The difference was that the vicissitudes of their daily existence now mirrored the experiences of those who, before the pandemic, had barely given thought to forging solidarity with those whose lives seemed radically different from their own. But although the opportunity for building radical coalitions to disrupt the dehumanizing violence of the "normal" could have metamorphosed into tangible transformative possibility, there is now a numbing recognition that we might have squandered the opportunity in our relentless yearning for the familiar, the routine, the habitual—and, in doing so, inadvertently reproduced the very degradations that can destroy us all.

I began this essay by deconstructing the narrative that we are living in "unprecedented times" and that going back to "life as normal" is what we most earnestly desire. I reject this yearning for the "normal" from a critical transnational materialist feminist disability lens[2] by demonstrating how this "normal" is in fact rooted in acts of brutal violence that preceded this pandemic, shattering our blithe visions of a neoliberal ableist future. I use two historical events to argue that we have lived through other pandemics long before Covid-19 brought the world to an abrupt halt: the ongoing racial violence that gave rise to the Black Lives Matter Movement in 2014 and our racist response to the Ebola outbreak in West Africa that same year. My earnest provocation in this essay is to paint with broad strokes a portrait of the pandemic as a "long" moment of transformative possibility, with the wherewithal to discompose the ableist, heteronormative, white supremacist, and exploitative conventions of normativity in an effort to reimagine what Alison Kafer has described as "crip futurity."[3] Kafer writes,

> I am particularly interested in uncovering the ways the disabled body is put to use in these future visions attending to both metaphorical and "corporeal presence and absence." . . . Rather than assume that a "good" future naturally and obviously depends on the eradication of disability, we must recognize this perspective as colored by histories of ableism and disability oppression [and I might add imperialist and settler colonialist oppressions as well].[4]

I cite Kafer here because the particular terror that we have faced during this pandemic is the terror of the proliferation of disabled bodyminds, seemingly one of the most dreaded outcomes of a pandemic. In fact, we have all been privy to laments about the prospects of "Covid brain," debilitating physiological impairments, chronic pain, depressive mental states, and other disabilities—all conditions that render bodyminds so vulnerable and debilitated that they no longer function at their presumably formerly efficient and profitable capacities. In fact, these ableist constructions of disability as debilitating difference are touted widely as the single most pressing incentive to urge the privileged to mask up, maintain social distancing, and get vaccinated—not so much as efforts to ensure our collective survival but rather to halt the proliferation of disability in a techno-fantastical future that abhors vulnerabilities. Such exhortations protect a neoliberal, exploitative, and accumulative economy that rejects the inefficiencies that such debilities portend.

I am not urging that we abandon safety measures during this pandemic. Rather, my argument is to extend Kafer's challenge to reimagine crip futures that simultaneously disrupt the political economy of transnational capitalism in its subservience to the brutal reach of Empire. By Empire, I am broadly referring to the political-economic structures of transnational capitalism committed to the processes of extraction, accumulation, exploitation, and necropolitics, deployed both within and without the traditional boundaries of the nation-state.[5] In fact, the violent practices of Empire utilize the labor of disability as the rallying cry for the reinstatement of the normal that focuses predominantly on the annihilation of disability rather than organizing around the "care work" that is essential for our collective survival.[6] I call this labor that disability is called to do *exploitative* and *cannibalistic*, because the hypervisibility of disability simultaneously becomes the rallying cry for foregrounding the appalling flaws in public health initiatives directed toward multiply marginalized communities, while at the same time demanding that these initiatives swiftly annihilate disability from community life. As such, disability as a social and political category of difference becomes the centripetal force about which the global response to the pandemic revolves; by doing so, it becomes the victim of its own deployment.

This lethal contradiction becomes apparent when paying attention to the discursive and material fields of intelligibility that have emerged out of this pandemic. When ventilators were in short supply in the United States, medical personnel resurrected formulas that even in prepandemic times were utilized to determine the "value of a statistical life" of multiply marginalized people—a eugenic calculation to determine who should live and die.[7] The scandal within the Cuomo administration (where Covid-19 patients were sent back to nursing homes to convalesce and the number of deaths went undercounted in institutions rife with chronic understaffing, obsolete medical technology, and dire neglect) was typical of the treatment of multiply marginalized communities who are conceived of as disposable.[8] We have come to accept the inevitability that in moments of scarcity—whether of ventilators, vaccines, or access to medical care and safe housing—disabled people living in multiply marginalized communities are at the back of the proverbial bus. Additionally, we have failed to connect the past isolation (both geographic and psychic) of people living in multiply marginalized communities to carceral spaces (like special education classrooms, alternative schools, boarding schools, immigration detention centers [i.e., cages], group homes, nursing homes, and the prison–industrial complex) or to the exacerbation of psychic pain and trauma that comes with recognizing one's disposability.[9] It is interesting to note that this persistent experience of disposability is also of pandemic proportions—a pandemic that we have been unwilling to eradicate. Once reserved only for those who were considered innately expendable and thereby went unnoticed, I argue here that the necropolitics of pandemic proportions is more prevalent than we are willing to admit and thereby proffers us a framework to refuse normality and embrace a transnational vision of crip futurity for our collective survival through interdependent care.

FERGUSON, MISSOURI, 2014

In the hot August sun, a brown body lay facedown on the bloodied blacktop, partially covered by a sheet for four long hours. The yellow police tape separating the slowly gathering crowd on the grassy roadside from the dead body seemed ineffectual in containing the soon-to-be outrage that would spark a movement—Black Lives Matter. By nightfall, the unearthly silences that marked the scene of murder would be replaced by the whine of bullets; the crackle of tear gas; the sirens; the shattering glass; and screams of pain amid fire, smoke, blood, and a mounting, desperate rage. The state police, intent on protecting private property, belligerently faced off against a mass of brown, Black, and white bodies with hands raised up to say "don't shoot!" But the police shootings continue unabated as more bodies fall—almost all of them brown and Black, many of them disabled. Their names include Darien Hunt, Ezell Ford, Omar Abrego, Tamir Rice, Tanesha Anderson, Rumai Brisbon, John Crawford III, Keith Vidal, Kajieme Powell, Akai Gurley, Sandra Bland, Eric Garner, Michelle Cusseaux, Jack Jacquez, Jason Harrison, Yvette Smith, Louis Rodriguez, Rayshard Brooks, Daniel Prude, Dontre Hamilton, David Latham, Maria Godinez, Korryn Gaines, Dante Wright, Breonna Taylor, and George Floyd—to name only a few.

This incomplete roll call of unarmed, murdered brown/Black/disabled/trans bodies has inspired another slogan in the face of this epidemic of violence: "I Can't Breathe," a phrase that George Floyd also used before his last breath.[10] I use the term *epidemic* tentatively, fearful in drawing on a medical term to talk about a social, political, and economic phenomenon. Almost every dictionary I consulted describes an epidemic as the rapid spread of an infectious disease to a large number of people in a context where the disease is not normally prevalent.[11] What apparently prompts an epidemic is its increased virulence when introduced in a novel setting, often triggered by changes in host susceptibility to the infectious agent. As such, an epidemic does not necessarily have to be contagious, only prolific, encroaching beyond the body also to be implicated in the destruction of human relations and disruption of social life. The terms *epidemic* and *endemic* are also used interchangeably, even though they are not synonymous. While an epidemic is described as rapidly spreading between bodies in a short period of time, the term *endemic* refers to disease that is chronically prevalent in a specific context and region and is sometimes assumed to be native to the region.[12] Following this logic, whereas an *epidemic* can be halted in its tracks through concerted efforts to eradicate it, a disease that is *endemic* is assumed to be stubbornly resistant to any and all interventions.

So, are the almost daily murders of brown/Black/disabled bodies a recent epidemic, or are such murders endemic to U.S. society, given its brutal history of settler colonialism, slavery, imperialism, and transnational capitalism? What are the implications of reading these murders through these two radically different lenses? Furthermore, how does the deployment of a medical model to address an epidemic of violence shape the way we read the social? Where does the locus of pathology lie: in the bodies of the fallen citizens or in the police who serve the militarized state? Will our efforts at transformation appear inadequate given that the roots of endemic violence arise from a violent pathology that is assumed to be "natural" to U.S. society? Also, what kinds of interventions does a medical model inspire when violence is viewed as a disease that needs urgently to be eradicated? And will that foreclose alternative interventions that could foreground an ethics of care for others in our simultaneously well-connected and yet hopelessly divided world?

Unfortunately, this epidemic of violence has not been limited to our national borders but is also evident on a transnational scale. Since 2014, we have borne witness to an increasing threat of the state using militarized violence against its own racialized/disabled/poor citizens: the ruthless bombing of the Gaza Strip by the state of Israel; the use of U.S. military drones to drop bombs on civilians and terror suspects alike in Afghanistan, Iraq, and Syria; the occupation of the state of Kashmir by the Indian Army; the reports of torture by the U.S. military of Iraqi and Afghan prisoners; the slaughter of innocent victims by the Boko Haram in Nigeria; the civil wars in Syria; the murders at the Charlie Hebdo offices; ISIS and its ruthless, televised beheadings of journalists and international aid workers; and a resurgence of Islamophobia with deadly consequences for Muslim citizens in Europe, the United States, and South Asia. The steady stream of brown and Black bodies leaving war-torn homelands and crowding onto tiny shipping vessels that capsize in emerald waters, washing death onto shorelines, is reduced to barely a news headline, while other refugee bodies tiredly trudge across barbed wire borders, playing a modern version of the Middle Passage, then to be kicked and spat upon and herded in refugee camps. Where is the love?

The vast majority of the victims of these epidemics continue to be brown/Black/disabled bodies, prompting the question whether these deaths should be understood within the context of a pandemic that raises the stakes because its infectious and diseased effects (violence) have now spread through human populations across a large region, for instance, multiple continents or even worldwide.[13] What kind of response does a pandemic require as per a medical model? Or is such pandemic violence endemic to the human condition, where it is argued that there will always be some bodies that will be "naturally" cast as victims of some other bodies' violence and hence require no intervention, because how can one interrupt the transitory and random hands of fate?

EBOLA, WEST AFRICA, 2014

Early spring 2014 ushered in its own violent medical epidemic—the spread of the Ebola virus, a severe hemorrhagic fever with a fatality rate ranging from 25 to 90 percent in humans. According to a WHO report, the virus was transmitted to people through contact with the blood, secretions, organs, or other bodily fluids of infected animals, such as chimpanzees, gorillas, fruit bats, monkeys, forest antelope, and porcupines found ill or dead in the rainforest. A similar argument was made regarding Covid-19.[14] The virus then rapidly spread in the human population through human-to-human transmission, beginning in Guinea, then spreading to neighboring Sierra Leone and Liberia, by air to Nigeria, and by land to Senegal. Because these small nation-states already wracked by civil wars had weak health systems, lacking human and infrastructural resources, stemming the deadly march of the epidemic through impoverished populations was difficult.

The Centers for Disease Control and Prevention (CDC) has reported 28,616 (suspected, probable, confirmed) cases in Guinea, Sierra Leone, and Liberia and 11,310 deaths.[15] Other nations that reported cases were Nigeria (20), Mali (8), the United States (4), the United Kingdom (1), Spain (1), and Senegal (1). While early supportive care with rehydration and symptomatic treatment improved survival, there initially were no licensed therapies until one was identified and used for some U.S. citizens who survived the deadly illness. More often than not, African citizens were subjected to problematic modes of surveillance, incarceration, and discrimination if suspected of being carriers of the virus. Again, similar treatment was meted to Asian Americans during the current pandemic. Note the similarities and differences with how we have dealt with Covid-19.

In both contexts—the transnational pandemic of violence (state violence) and the violent medical epidemic (Ebola and Covid-19)—the immediate response has been to pathologize those who have been the victims of these pandemic/epidemic outbreaks. Here race and disability are implicated simultaneously as both the cause and outcome of epidemic violence. For example, the murder of Eric Garner, the Staten Island African American man who died when the police placed him in a chokehold, was blamed on his obesity, asthma, and heart disease rather than the excessive force used by the police.[16] Interestingly enough, regarding death by chokeholds, Robert McRuer, in his book *Crip Theory*, mentions in passing that the Los Angeles Police Department justified the deaths of gang members of the Crips and Bloods at the hands of the police by claiming that the carotid chokehold, when placed on African Americans, did not open up as fast as it does on "normal" people.[17] Similarly, instead of garnering medical and other resources that are desperately needed in the African countries battling Ebola, Africans exposed to the Ebola virus were simultaneously blamed for inadequate health knowledge and backward social practices (i.e., perceived natural impairments) in contracting the virus. Moreover, if the victims of any of these epidemics survived the violence, they were bound to acquire disabilities as a result of inadequate care and other untreated side effects.

Scholars of both critical race theory and disability studies know well the dangers of pathologizing bodies. Since pathology is closely associated with the medical model, the emphasis is on cure rather than care. Here the intent of a pathological intervention is the single-minded decision to destroy the isolated contravening agent assumed to have been the cause of the epidemic in the first place. As a result, because the victims of these pandemics are perceived as the very embodiment of pathological difference, they become the objects of destruction rather than the subjects of care. Claiming that their pathologized bodies locate them outside the boundaries of humanness, the violence that is done to them is justified because they are seen as the state of exception existing within the zone of bare life.[18] Thus the pathologization of Michael Brown as dangerous thug

not only contributed to his brutal murder in front of witnesses in broad
daylight but also allowed his broken body to lie carelessly on the hot tar-
mac untended for more than four hours. Similarly, the disinterested global
response to the Ebola epidemic in countries in sub-Saharan Africa until it
threatened the countries in the Global North was also justified based on the
pathologization of African people via the deployment of a necropolitics
that casually consigned their pathologized bodies to what Achille Mbembe
has described as "death worlds."[19]

In this essay, I foreground the dangers of pathologization in the context
of epidemics of violence and violent epidemics at the simultaneous intersection of race, disability, and class. Most of the discussion of the epidemics that I have described here has been located within the critical discourses
of race. But, I argue, so much of the violence does not stem solely from
structural racism but in the complex ways that it intersects with ableism
in the creation of "bodies that do not matter" in the same ways as bodies
that are deemed normative. In a blog post sponsored by the Hampton
Institute, Sonasha Braxton argues that in a historical context where "there
exists an increasingly visible disproportionate response to the 'inconvenient'
and 'deadly' presence of Black bodies and what they embody both literally
and metaphorically . . . an exploration into how Ebola became a racially
constructed politically pliable discourse must necessarily ensue."[20] While I
cannot include a more in-depth discussion that Braxton suggests is necessary in this essay, I will briefly mention the transnational context in which
there has been a continuous history of medical violence directed toward
people of color living in the Global South. There are continuities between
the "Mississippi appendectomies" conducted in the southern United States
as late as 1963 and the more recent allegations (that are being investigated)
of forced hysterectomies of undocumented women in ICE custody in the
United States.[21] Settler-colonial states like the United States and Canada
have historically propagated such eugenic policies and continue to do so
even today against Indigenous communities. Here the very logic of intersectional difference along the axes of race, class, disability, and gendered
identity is so imbricated in eugenic practices that it could be considered a
pandemic—one that has survived for almost a century.

ENVISIONING CRIP FUTURES VIA THE POLITICS OF CARE

Even as I map out the constitutive relationship between racist and ableist
pathologies that have continued to justify pandemics of violence and violent

pandemics directed against brown/Black/disabled people, I want to be very clear that I do not intend to reproduce ableist pathologies that frame disability as a precarious condition settling into a "slow death."[22] Following Tanya Titchkosky, there is an urgency to read and write disability differently for a more radical counternarrative.[23] In *Feminist, Queer, Crip,* Kafer calls feminist, queer, and environmental theorists and activists to account for the ableism that is intertwined in their transgressive/oppositional visions for a future, one that explicitly (or implicitly) excludes the possibility of disability and comes at a huge cost to the disability community.[24] She therefore asks, What does it mean to choose futures for disability?

Kafer's question has been answered by legions of disability activists and scholars in disability pride parades, in vibrant disability justice movements, in the transgressive aesthetics of disability art, in the angry protests against the medical–industrial complex, against incarceration in both prisons and institutions, against sterilization, against segregation in education, against nursing homes, and, more recently, in the newly expanding scholarship and protests against neoliberal doctrines that are anathema to crip futurity.[25] But these protests should also give us pause, given Rachel Gorman's blunt and thoughtful assertion that disability studies/crip theory, like other social theories, has inadvertently reconstituted the disabled subject as white, creating a disability rights consciousness that she describes as a kind of disability nationalism akin to Jasbir Puar's critique of homonationalism in the context of the problematic racialization of queer politics.[26] What allegiances do disabled people located at the crossroads of shifting identities have with a largely white, middle-class disability rights movement in the Global North? And how would our contradictions in the face of these real struggles enable us to imagine futures that do not rely on the exploitation and colonization of others? In short, I am asking, how do we care?

Mary-Jean Hande and Christine Kelly argue that in contemporary disability politics, issues of care are taken up via discourses of "inclusion," "accessibility," and "daily living supports" in ways that erase the material effects of living with disabilities.[27] Issues of care have become a multimillion-dollar business such that, according to McRuer, disability has become "corporealized, destigmatized, identified, and integrated . . . (out and proud) into the circuits of global capital," while disabled bodies are simultaneously being incarcerated in nursing homes and/or state institutions and medicalized against their will in what he calls the "state securitization and incarceration" of disabled bodies.[28] In critical opposition, some of the most thoughtful critiques of care have come from disability studies scholars like Hande and Kelly, who have focused on how the "legacies of care" have also historically been structured by exploitive and oppressive relations, "from subtle coercions played out on the microscale between disabled people and those who support them, to mass institutionalization of disabled bodies undertaken in the name of 'caring for' people with disabilities [as well as] the exploitive structures that coerce women, especially women of color, into what Nakano-Glenn terms 'racialized gendered servitude.'"[29]

Adding to this rich body of work on care and its critique, I want to add another dimension to the discussion on care: the material conditions within which "care" is constructed as an urgent need and the conditions under which it is meted out. In our blatantly unequal context, "care" is valorized within a context of consumption where disabled tourists are involuntarily conscripted as profitable neoliberal subjects for transnational capitalism. I use the term *involuntarily* here to foreground the probing reach neoliberal practices have in all aspects of the relations of consumptions. I argue, then, that the neoliberal relations of consumption are enabled by the most violent and exploitative relations of production—a discussion that is rarely (if at all) engaged by radical theorists and activists. Examining care via transnational capitalism's production relations takes on a distinctly imperialist/neocolonial turn within the broader context of Empire if (or rather when) critical disability studies/crip theory and other radical theories begin to engage the historical contexts where sites of "care" become "normalized" sites of violence.

For example, I call upon all of us to witness the brutality that barricades citizens behind the rubble in the West Bank and the Gaza Strip mediated by the tense relationships between Palestinian territories and Israeli settlements. Moreover, these normalized sites of violence—known formally as "national borders"—become unremarked sites where the conditions for care as an urgent need proliferate with disability as a routine outcome of such violent exclusion and differential access. A similar argument could be made about the U.S.–Mexican border, where unaccompanied immigrant children are being herded out of deplorable immigration detention centers where they had been earlier warehoused for deportation, even while being subject to unimaginable physical and emotional stresses—another example of disability proliferation at the intersection of race, nation, imperialism, exploitative labor, antagonistic class relations, and profit. Here, once again, the discourse of care is bandied about as an argument against involuntary incarceration that is not limited to the locale of prisons, asylums, nursing homes, and institutions but should also include immigration detention centers and border control policies,[30] connected to the violent political economy of globalization that enables capital, but not racialized labor, to cross borders with impunity. Discussions of access, therefore, have also to engage the transnational political and economic conditions that require laboring bodies to cram themselves into overheated, closed spaces; stagger across the burning sands; or cling desperately to inner tubes across stormy oceans. In these contexts, lack of care is not just a gross denial of one's human rights as global citizens; it is also an instrument of physical harm, disappearance, and even death.

I now return to an argument made early on in this essay regarding the labor that disability is called upon to do. These invocations of disability as pathological difference are central to the production and enablement of "empire" vividly described by Jasbir Puar in *The Right to Maim,* where she describes how "the Israeli state manifests an implicit claim to the 'right to maim' and debilitate Palestinian bodies as a form of biopolitical control and as central to the scientifically authorized humanitarian economy."[31] Puar calls this a "speculative rehabilitative economy" of debilitation (making of disability)—marking the shift "from the production of populations available for injury to the targeting of populations to be injured . . . where the idea is to shoot in order to cripple."[32] Here maiming results in the dual production of permanent disability via the infliction of harm and "the attrition of life support systems that might allow populations to heal from harm."[33] Whereas Puar invokes the Foucauldian concept of biopolitics and the Deluezian construct of assemblage to support her conceptual shift from disability to debility, my argument conceives of disability as a historical materialist construct whose labor is appropriated for the social production of difference. In other words, I make the production of disability central to the maintenance of Empire and its violent ideologies; its material practices of anti-Blackness; its imperialist practices of extraction, exploitation, and appropriation; and the brutal necropolitics that include the "right to maim." Yet, even though disability is central to the production of Empire, disability is, nevertheless, invoked as an inevitable pathology—the outcome of such unspeakable violence.

I conclude by taking up the argument that Jina Kim makes regarding infrastructure in her exploration of the "Anatomy of the City," where infrastructure refers not only to the "equipment, facilities, services, and supporting structures needed for a city's or region's functioning . . . but also [to] organizational systems like health care, emergency services, education, and law enforcement"—the services "indelibly tied to a city's well-being."[34] Kim argues that state infrastructure creates a discourse of dependency that utilizes the labor of disability to shift its own failures onto the bodies most harmed by this violence. Similar discourses abound in response to Covid-19. But disability justice activists have refused these shaming monikers of dependency, opting instead for care work and disability justice in terms of interdependency that enables the survival of vulnerable life.[35] Here I turn to Alison Kafer's more inclusive notion of "crip kin":[36]

> Whether thinking through the necessity of imagining kin differently in the age of climate change . . . or reckoning with the ways in which kinship networks have been pathologized, decimated, and destroyed through slavery, mass incarceration, settler colonialism, and eugenics . . . kin is a site of power, friction, and potentiality.[37] . . . Kin do not inhere in particular categories or relations but emerge *as an effect of social struggle.* . . . Thus, we can best find and make crip kin in becoming more aware of the deployment of disability in narratives of war violence and rehabilitation . . . the uneven distributions of technology . . . the possibility that new kinship imaginaries can be conscripted into neoliberalism, . . . and the assemblage of racist, ableist, sexist, and imperialist logics in the assumption that "human" is the only animacy that matters.[38]

If we can recognize how the normative discourses of the long 2020 pandemic are shaped by interrelated violences, then we can challenge the infrastructures that fail us through interdependent practices of care and build a solidarity movement that is truly transformative.

NOTES

1. Mary Douglas, *Purity and Danger: An Analysis of Concepts of Pollution and Taboo* (New York: Routledge, 2003).

2. Nirmala Erevelles, *Disability and Difference in Global Contexts: Enabling a Transformative Body Politic* (New York: Springer, 2011).

3. Alison Kafer, *Feminist, Queer, Crip* (Bloomington: Indiana University Press, 2013).

4. Kafer, 3.

5. Achille Mbembe, *Necropolitics* (Durham, N.C.: Duke University Press, 2019).

6. Leah Lakshmi Piepzna-Samarasinha, *Care Work: Dreaming Disability Justice* (Vancouver, B.C.: Arsenal Pulp Press, 2018).

7. Chris Conover, "How Economists Calculate the Costs and Benefits of COVID-19 Lockdowns," *Forbes,* March 27, 2020, https://www.forbes.com/sites/the apothecary/2020/03/27/how-economists-calculate-the-costs-and-benefits-of-covid -19-lockdowns/.

8. Michael Gold and Ed Shanahan, "What We Know about Cuomo's Nursing Home Scandal," *New York Times,* April 28, 2021, https://www.nytimes.com/article/.

9. Liat Ben-Moshe, Chris Chapman, and Allison C. Carey, eds., *Disability Incarcerated: Imprisonment and Disability in the United States and Canada* (New York: Palgrave Macmillan, 2014).

10. Maanvi Singh, "George Floyd Told Officers 'I Can't Breathe' More than 20 Times, Transcripts Show," *The Guardian,* July 9, 2020, https://www.theguardian.com /us-news/2020/jul/08/george-floyd-police-killing-transcript-i-cant-breathe.

11. *Merriam-Webster Dictionary,* s.v. "epidemic," https://www.merriam-webster .com/.

12. W. Ian Lipkin, "Epidemic, Endemic, Pandemic: What Are the Differences?," *Public Health, Global Health, Infectious Disease,* https://www.publichealth.columbia .edu/public-health-now/news/epidemic-endemic-pandemic-what-are-differences.

13. Lipkin.

14. World Health Organization, "Ebola Virus Disease," https://www.who.int/ health-topics/.

15. Centers for Disease Control and Prevention, "2014–2016 Ebola Outbreak in West Africa," https://www.cdc.gov/vhf/ebola/history/.

16. Nia-Malika Henderson, "Peter King Blames Asthma and Obesity for Eric Garner's Death. That's a Problem for the GOP," *Washington Post,* December 4, 2014.

17. Robert McRuer, *Crip Theory: Cultural Signs of Queerness and Disability* (New York: New York University Press, 2006).

18. Giorgio Agamben, *Homo Sacer: Sovereign Power and Bare Life* (Palo Alto, Calif.: Stanford University Press, 2020).

19. Mbembe, *Necropolitics,* 92.

20. Sonasha Braxton, "Kind of Blue, Part II: The Racialization of Ebola, Media Misrepresentations, and What We Can Learn from Chris Brown—#DoAllBlacklives matter?," *Hampton Institute Blog,* February 4, 2015, https://thehamptoninstitute.word press.com/.

21. Tina K. Sacks, "The Mississippi Appendectomy: Race and Reproductive Healthcare," in *Invisible Visits: Black Middle-Class Women in the American Healthcare System,* 93–112 (Oxford: Oxford University Press, 2019); Catherine E. Shoichet, "In a Horrifying History of Forced Sterilizations, Some Fear the US Is Beginning a New Chapter," CNN, September 16, 2020, https://edition.cnn.com/2020/09/16/us/ice-hysterectomy -forced-sterilization-history/index.html.

22. Lauren Berlant, "Slow Death (Sovereignty, Obesity, Lateral Agency)," *Critical Inquiry* 33, no. 4 (2007): 754–80.

23. Tanya Titchkosky, *Reading and Writing Disability Differently* (Toronto, Ont.: University of Toronto Press, 2020).

24. Kafer, *Feminist, Queer, Crip,* 44.

25. See the websites of Sins Invalid, "Sins Invalid: An Unshamed Claim to Beauty in the Face of Invisibility," https://www.sinsinvalid.org/; Mia Mingus, "Leaving Evidence," https://leavingevidence.wordpress.com/about-2/; and Leroy Moore and Lisa (Tiny) Gay Garcia, interviewed by Amy Goodman, "Disability Rights Activists Take on Twin Pandemics of Racist Police Brutality and COVID-19," *Democracy Now,* July 13, 2020, https://www.democracynow.org/2020/7/13/disability_rights_activists_take_on_twin.

26. Rachel Gorman, "Disablement in and for Itself: Toward a 'Global' Idea of Disability," *Somatechnics* 6, no. 2 (2016): 249–61; Jasbir K. Puar, *Terrorist Assemblages: Homonationalism in Queer Times* (Durham, N.C.: Duke University Press, 2018).

27. Mary-Jean Hande and Christine Kelly, "Organizing Survival and Resistance in Austere Times: Shifting Disability Activism and Care Politics in Ontario, Canada," *Disability and Society* 30, no. 7 (2015): 961–75.

28. Robert McRuer, "Epilogue: Disability, Inc.," in *Disability Incarcerated,* ed. Liat Ben-Moshe, Chris Chapman, and Allison C. Carey (New York: Palgrave Macmillan, 2014), 274.

29. Hande and Kelly, "Organizing Survival," 963.

30. Mansha Mirza, "Occupational Upheaval during Resettlement and Migration: Findings of Global Ethnography with Refugees with Disabilities," *OTJR: Occupation, Participation, and Health* 32, no. 1_suppl (2012): S6–S14.

31. Jasbir K. Puar, *The Right to Maim* (Durham, N.C.: Duke University Press, 2017), 128.

32. Puar, 129.

33. Puar, 143.

34. Jina B. Kim, "Anatomy of the City: Race, Infrastructure, and US Fictions of Dependency," PhD diss. (University of Michigan, 2016), 28.

35. Sins Invalid, "Social Distancing and Crip Survival: A Disability Centered Response to COVID-19," March 19, 2020, https://www.sinsinvalid.org/news-1/2020/3/19/social-distancing-and-crip-survival-a-disability-centered-response-to-covid-19.

36. Alison Kafer, "Crip Kin, Manifesting," *Catalyst: Feminism, Theory, Technoscience* 5, no. 1 (2019).

37. Kafer, 6.

38. Kafer, 28–29, emphasis added.

8 The Last Season

The Cruel Optimism of Generic Futurity

REBECCA WANZO

African American comedian Frank White posted a short video, "How Angels Watching Earth 2020," in July 2020.[1] He often does religious-themed comedy, and in this piece, White wears faded jeans, a white shirt, and a feathered halo on his head, cheap wings askew and bunched up behind his back in an armchair. We see the light of the television reflected on his face. Joe's "Big Rich Town," the theme song that opens the Black crime prime-time soap opera *Power,* can be heard. A woman off-camera asks him what he's watching. He is engrossed in the new season of *Earth 2020* and catches her up on new plot developments. Last season, "your boy the orange dude, with the red hat," started "wildin' out from episode one." Then a pandemic happens, everybody's sick, people are on "lockdown," and "you can't even go see your side chick." After that, he recounts, the cops start killing Black people, and the woman off-camera interjects: "Didn't that happen last season?" He replies, "That happen every season" but that this season is different because "white people mad." He goes on to say that in episode 7, "they just cut unemployment," and he doesn't know what will happen now. "They're talking about how this the last season."

The opening site gag deploys incongruity to produce humor, which may remind some viewers of the 1936 film *The Green Pastures* but will definitely be a point of affective cathexis for those familiar with the comical rendition of a Black colloquial heaven evoked in Black church storytelling. But the inspiration for the piece is clear to a broad audience outside the culturally specific humor. Many of us will recognize the new communal practice of framing calendar years as either malevolent actors or a sequence of events that can be tidily contained in a singular plot that comes to an end on December 31, a tidiness that concepts like the "long 2020" disrupt. Calling attention to 2020 as a "situation" is the most recent example of imparting years with agency and describing them as "the worst."[2]

The fact that calendar years have become antagonists in arbitrary constructions of time limits to suffering is illustrative of what Lauren Berlant terms "cruel optimism."[3] This optimism has taken the form of a genre of narrative and narration—"the worst" as genre mash-up that will end with a better future. Google Trends suggests that the idea of the "worst year" began appearing regularly in 2010 in Google searches. New sources had previously reported when corporations had their worst years ever. Tragedy-struck individuals had the worst years of their lives. There were, undoubtedly, moments that people identified as cursed, unparalleled, and devastating. Many more lives had been lost in various years. But it took social media storytelling to create the conditions under which people would construct a collective narrative of years as nadirs.

In 2016, *New Yorker* staff writer Jia Tolentina was one of a number of commentators who began condemning the tendency toward the "worst year" designation.[4] The year 2016 began with people declaring that the deaths of Prince and David Bowie marked the year as the worst and ended with Donald Trump's election. The months in between were filled by the perennial celebrity deaths, mass shootings, and natural disasters. The atemporality of the events that are nonetheless marked as the "worst" makes the hyperbole of the affective condemnation of an arbitrary time interval transparent. I experienced Prince's death as a tragedy and collectively mourned with other fans, but the unnuanced excesses of the internet highlight its struggle with proportionality and scale.

I hope that the rhetorical habit of characterizing years as the "worst" will be put to rest in 2020. The year may very well mark a break with this practice, as the people who predominately have been positioned to be cavalier about such pronouncements may have actually experienced the Covid-19 rupture as a nadir. In other words, while we know many people have been living in precarity and will continue to do so, part of the experience of 2020 was introducing precarity into a larger number of lives. Even that demonstrates deep divergence—people lived very different pandemics.

It is the fact that people inhabit different space-times that should push us to end such framing. For the worst is always yet to come. If it is not your worst, it is someone's. There are eighty million refugees and displaced people around the world.[5] Poverty and violence are perpetual threats, and various identity factors increase vulnerability. Living in and with the Anthropocene guarantees that the worst is yet to come—the planet is warming, fires are raging, ice caps are melting, and species are dying. Categorization of the worst as relative might seem simply to be trivially true, but I do think it speaks to the atemporal, ahistorical, and fragmented storytelling in social media. Social media is paradoxically a place where nothing is forgotten and everything is. Past affect and injury are a search away but buried under the deluge of the present unless they serve the present. If the present is always our worst, it promises the idea of a better future even if the arbitrariness of the calendar year inevitably leads us to be stuck in another nadir when the "worst" affectively seems to strike again.

However, scholars who explore the question of the "worst" year through data sets and archaeological evidence argue that various "presents"—the twenty-first century, the twentieth century, or any period that is not prehistoric—are demonstrably less violent. Steven Pinker's *The Better Angels of Our Nature* offers the most prominent version of this argument, but other scholars, such as a group of mathematicians who looked at the history of battle deaths in an essay published in 2020, also argue that this time is not "the worst."[6] In contrast, scholars like philosopher John Gray question the utility of data sets in the "Long Peace" thesis. He argues that Pinker's framing of the Enlightenment as producing less cruelty willfully ignores how it was the foundation for scientific racism, colonialism, genocide, and other illiberal espousals of violence.[7] Battlefield deaths, in the counterargument to the "Long Peace," are a poor proxy for measuring progress when the nuclear threat of mass destruction has served as a deterrent and thus encouraged, instead, necropolitics and slow violence. For Gray, this is big data as divination, another misguided attempt to use science to "bolster faith in the future."[8]

Social media narrative framing of the year as "the worst" also works to provide hope for the future. Twitter, news articles, blogs, Facebook, memes, gifs, and Instagram construct a narrative about a year. It is repetitive and not organized but curated through repetitive circulation of the representations that best serve the narrative of different media ecosystems. It functions somewhat as a choose-your-own-adventure story, with some people on a path to QAnon as savior and others to hopes about an Alexandria Ocasio-Cortez presidential run. Temporality might be a sticking point for narrative theorists in describing "the worst" as a narrative genre—it is disjointed and incohesive in nature. But "the worst" narratives are intensely episodic, filled with cliffhangers and notable events that facilitate the story that some people want to tell about the tragedies of the year and their dreamed-for closure at the end.

Years are constructed as genre in social media framing—they are tragedies, melodrama, black comedies, or disaster films. That "2020 is like a movie" would appear frequently in social media, as people would treat various moments as emblematic of the year or point to films as models. Audiences watched and rewatched the 2011 Steven Soderbergh film *Contagion*, a dystopian thriller about a lethal virus spreading across the globe that began to feel like prophecy.[9] The now-annual terror of California wildfires presented the nightmarish image of drivers on the 405 in Los Angeles as fires awaited to engulf them and seemed straight out of a Roland Emmerich disaster film. The president conducted a press conference in which he suggested that stopping Covid-19 might be possible if there were a way to inject disinfectant into the body or use ultraviolet light internally, and the moment seemed scripted for a satirical political comedy.

Thus "2020 is the worst" is the title of a transmedia story that is a genre mash-up. But it also marks a commitment to a linear trajectory. Because multiple years in a row were designated as "the worst," genre seems a resistance to a realist mode in which we might have to acknowledge that we move forward but stay stuck in place. The pleasure many generic narratives give us is in promising closure, skipping the mundane, glossing over the unrepresentability of trauma. To return to our Black Angel, nothing signifies this more than the moment in which the angel and his interlocutor talk about police murders of Black people. It is this season, and last season, and every season. Killing Black people is "always in season."[10] Part of my discomfort with the "this year is the worst" narrative is about the ways in which so many events can make Black lives the worst, with the promise of an end to suffering as heartbreakingly fantastic.

And yet, when Derek Chauvin murdered George Floyd in Minneapolis on May 25, 2020, it registered with people outside the community that traditionally recognize extrajudicial killings of Black people as an event. Some polls suggested that between fifteen million and twenty-six million people in the United Stated participated in the protest, making it the largest social movement protest in U.S. history.[11] Many people have puzzled over the question of why George Floyd's murder and not the recorded murders of many others produced such a response. Trump, briefly, despite his frequent embrace and defense of white supremacy, said he could not watch the entire video because "it doesn't get any more obvious or it doesn't get any worse than that."[12] As Black Angel stated, "white people mad," and this offered the possibility of a paradigmatic shift. Floyd's death was a creative, productive force—in the Deleuzian sense of creating a political event. The moment of reckoning seemed to have come. Although there had been interracial support before, the widespread discussions of defunding police departments in mass media were unprecedented. A Pew Research Center study reported that approximately 67 percent of adults supported the Black Lives Matter (BLM) movement—there were racial and partisan divisions, but 60 percent of white people were supportive.[13] And yet the past and future were framing the present, preparing consistent supporters of BLM for disappointment. By September, Pew reported that only 45 percent of white Americans supported the movement.[14]

For a moment, some of us may have seen a glimmer of something that could exceed and disrupt anti-Blackness. Black people have the capacity to make and experience the good in life despite trauma, part of what Fred Moten has described as the "magic" and "contrapuntal" practices of Black life.[15] For some Black people, there is a recognition of a perpetual difference between the "Black Good Life" and "the good life" as described by those who feel they have lost the possibility of it in our present but who experienced it as present for themselves and local and larger communities, from family to nation.

But it cannot help but seem like cruel optimism for Africans Americans to imagine—if not the end of anti-Blackness—the possibility that a substantive number of people might feel shame at unapologetic alliance with it. Many of us who identify as progressive may have surprised ourselves by feeling disappointment when seventy-four million fellow citizens voted for a president whose support of white supremacist nationalism was a cornerstone of his presidency. That optimism was an unexpected attachment, not to the good life, exactly, but to expectations that are somewhere above the bottom—a compromised, cruel optimism that is the force required to get you out of bed in the morning.

It is cruel optimism that the claim about the United States becoming minority white in 2045 is treated as an empirical reality and transparently progressive future.[16] This claim ignores the long history of people becoming white in the United States and, in the case of the Latinx population, many people who always identified as white. Many people have spoken to the problem of homogenizing a population whose origins include more than twenty nations, and yet it was perhaps cruel optimism that made people believe that over 30 percent of Latinx would not vote for someone who deported people and families whose circumstances might not be far from their own.[17] Periodically over the last few years, stories have circulated about people who voted for Trump but then felt betrayed when they or a family member became a victim of ICE or had health care struggles. Their optimism was rooted in the experience of many immigrants—a number of whom fled violence and fascism and have indeed experienced the "good life" in the United States. The plot twist of the election—numbers from white women, Latinx, and even some African Americans that surprised the pollsters and the public—were foreshadowed, as the good life that Trump offers successfully constructed his identity politics as worthy of sympathy and other identity politics as worthy of vilification. This success is demonstrated even by leftist condemnations that romanticize the white "forgotten man" as an ideal ally pushed out by protests from Black people, trans people, and feminists. The construction of antagonists to "everyday Americans" was pushed to absurd excesses in 2020 when public health workers who wished to save people's lives became villains attacking freedom in the story some people wanted to tell about the year.

Depending on the melancholic adventure you choose, different people are villains in the "2020 is the worst" plot, but many people might finally describe "2020 is the worst" as a dystopian story that did end with the close of the worst year of their lives. Of course, if it is in the dystopian genre, such conventions suggest there might be cruel optimism embedded there too. For the dystopian plot typically depicts people trying to make the world better, and the protagonists often succeed. The promise of a better world often marks the closure of the plot, even if it is tenuous or incomplete. Worst annum narratives are signs of the dystopian imaginations that are part of our everyday lives, that ironically also can demonstrate a willful resistance to acknowledging omnipresent suffering. Dystopias offer political commentaries, but when the plot is constructed by real-world events, the move toward narrative closure that works for fictions can blunt the force of the criticism.

The narrative closure of worst annum narratives is a comfort—to some. It is a joke—to most of us. But in either case, it speaks to a discursive practice of exclusion to craft national fictions that shore up fantasies of inevitable progress. Perhaps the more capacious sense of something like the long 2020 can let us put annum narratives to bed, then, as an act of solidarity with all those whose perpetual precarity places them out of sync with wished-for futures.

NOTES

1. Frank White (@comedian_frankwhite), "How Angels Watching 'Earth 2020,'" Instagram video, July 28, 2020, https://www.instagram.com/.

2. Lauren Berlant, *Cruel Optimism* (Durham, N.C.: Duke University Press, 2011), 5.

3. Berlant.

4. Jia Tolentino, "The Worst Year Ever, Until Next Year," *New Yorker*, December 14, 2016, https://www.newyorker.com/culture/jia-tolentino/the-worst-year-ever-until-next-year.

5. "Refugee Statistics," UNHCR: The UN Refugee Agency, https://www.unhcr.org/.

6. Brennen T. Fagan, Marina I. Knight, Niall J. MacKay, and A. Jamie Wood, "Change Point Analysis of Historical Battle Deaths," *Journal of the Royal Statistical Society: Series A* 183, part 3 (2020): 909–33.

7. John Gray, "Steven Pinker Is Wrong about Violence and War," *The Guardian*, March 13, 2015, https://www.theguardian.com/books/2015/mar/13/john-gray-steven-pinker-wrong-violence-war-declining.

8. Gray.

9. Jeva Lange, "*Contagion* Is Even More Remarkable after a Year of Pandemic," *The Week*, April 14, 2021, https://theweek.com/articles/977074/contagion-even-more-remarkable-after-year-pandemic.

10. Jacqueline Olive, dir. and prod., "Always in Season," *Independent Lens*, season 21, episode 11, "Always in Season," aired February 24, 2020, PBS.

11. Larry Buchanan, Quoctrung Bui, and Jugal K. Patel, "Black Lives Matter May Be the Largest Movement in US History," *New York Times*, July 3, 2020, https://www.nytimes.com/interactive/2020/07/03/us/george-floyd-protests-crowd-size.html.

12. Jason Silverstein, "President Trump on the Video of George Floyd's Death: 'It Doesn't Get Any Worse than That,'" CBS News, June 18, 2020, https://www.cbsnews.com/news/donald-trump-george-floyd-death-video/.

13. Kim Parker, Juliana Menasce Horowitz, and Monica Anderson, "Amid Protests, Majorities across Racial and Ethnic Groups Express Support for the Black Lives Matter Movement," Pew Research Center, June 12, 2020, https://www.pewresearch.org/social-trends/2020/06/12/amid-protests-majorities-across-racial-and-ethnic-groups-express-support-for-the-black-lives-matter-movement/.

14. Deja Thomas and Juliana Menasce Horowitz, "Support for Black Lives Matter Has Decreased since June but Remains Strong among Black Americans," Pew Research Center, September 16, 2020, https://www.pewresearch.org/fact-tank/2020/09/16/support-for-black-lives-matter-has-decreased-since-june-but-remains-strong-among-black-americans/.

15. Fred Moten, *The Universal Machine* (Durham, N.C.: Duke University Press, 2019), 246.

16. William H. Frey, "The US Will Become 'Minority White' in 2045, Census Projects," Brookings Institution, March 14, 2018, https://www.brookings.edu/blog/the-avenue/2018/03/14/the-us-will-become-minority-white-in-2045-census-projects/.

17. Holly K. Sonneland, "Chart: How US Latinos Voted in the 2020 Presidential Election," Americas Society Council of the Americas, November 5, 2020, https://www.as-coa.org/articles/chart-how-us-latinos-voted-2020-presidential-election.

9 The Obduracy of the Event and the Tasks of the Intellectual

WILLIAM E. CONNOLLY

THE EVENTS OF 2020

The year 2020 has been quite a year, marked merely in America alone by notable events of diverse type, source, and efficacy: the escalation of Trump's Big Lie; a House impeachment of the president based on solid evidence rejected by a Republican Senate; a series of record-setting wildfires devastating large sections of the American West; Putin's bounties to the Taliban to kill American troops; rolling coup attempts by an electorally defeated president and the party he owns; the untimely death of Supreme Court justice Ruth Bader Ginsburg; a videotape of the gruesome police strangulation of George Floyd in Minneapolis, followed by huge multiracial protests in numerous cities; the nobility of courts and election officials in resisting the Trump Big Lie; the intensification of QAnon; the invention of new vaccinations at warp speed; the mutation of Covid-19; a flurry of unseasonal, violent tornadoes; a huge Russian cyberattack on American military and intelligence systems, ignored by an outgoing president; massive hurricanes hitting the Bible Belt; the Zoomification of teaching; a violent insurrection against the Capitol on January 6, the effective end date of 2020; and, through it all, the double-species crossing and rapid human spread of a viral pandemic that threw the world into disarray and was criminally neglected by a U.S. president.

Is it a mistake to lump such diverse happenings together as events? To do so certainly compromises sanctified distinctions between the social and the natural, determined happenings and agentic actions, and life and nonlife. What does it mean to call each an event? What about the idea of the *obduracy* of the event?

To call each an event encourages us, for instance, to range beyond the assumptions of sociocentrism and humanist exceptionalism that have confined much of Euro-American social thought on left, right, and center for far too long. At least five events listed in the first paragraph involved planetary processes intruding into the dynamics of social life. We are now called upon to be governed by the trajectory a problem takes even when it crosses classical divisions of thought. The first assumption— sociocentrism—limits the causes of social change to specific social forces; the second—exceptionalism—confines real agency and striving to human beings, usually conveying as well a hierarchy of agencies that attains its peak in white Euro-America. The two together hamstring attempts to respond to the dictates of the event. They wrap the humanities into a tattered cocoon.

There *are* patterns to ocean currents; aging; death; the racial, sexual, class, and religious inequalities of capitalism; Russian/American low-intensity struggles; electoral democracy; glacier flows; viral transmissions; the seasons; seasonal wildfires; monsoon seasons; and climate change. But each is also subject periodically to rapid changes that intersect with some of the others. Accelerating climate change, triggered by the long march of extractive capitalism, for instance, instigates multiple nonhuman amplifiers that recoil to make the consequences far exceed the force of the triggers. Because that is true, intellectuals need to spend somewhat less time striving to discover socially enclosed patterns of stability and social change and more time becoming worthy of diverse events that periodically pummel, divert, rattle, or turn those patterns.

Before I inspect the constituents of the event more closely, let's review a recent American event whose sources and efficacies did not cross the old natural–social divisions. It did, however, cross a secular–theological line that still governs too many students of political economy. According to that secular creed, religious and spiritual life is either to be bracketed from socioeconomic life or treated as an effect of it. But the creative formation of a white evangelical–neoliberal machine in the United States in the late 1970s and early 1980s confounded such a division. What's more, tacit commitment to the theosecular line of division blocked many intellectuals from addressing consolidation of the new assemblage while it was under way. Once formed, it bestowed a virulent cast to racial–gender–class relations that was unmatched at first by modes of neoliberalism in Europe.[1]

I call the formation of the white evangelical–neoliberal machine an event. It was not determined by a prior regularity or necessity, and it involved a creative consolidation with powerful efficacies. You could say that the cold, deniable racism of high-rolling white neoliberals now began to resonate more with the hot racism and misogyny of white working- and lower-middle-class evangelicals. Each constituency then began to absorb aspects of the political spirituality of the other, until a virulent formation emerged irreducible to either, a spirituality that—in the wake of later events—set the stage for a new movement of aspirational fascism. The first formation constitutes an event partly because it surprised so many; partly because the assemblage between heterogeneous constituencies was not grounded in a lawlike necessity that made it inevitable; partly because it carried profound effects for those demeaned, damaged, and derided by it; and partly because, once consolidated, the defeat of Keynesianism and the welfare state followed. Class, race, and gender hierarchies preceded this formation, but it extended and amplified them. The new formation also set the stage for more obdurate denials of climate change and denialism during the pandemic. Events carry efficacy.

Any theory that does not come to terms with the obduracy of events of multiple types cannot cope with the late modern era, let alone with the long, bumpy year of 2020.

WHAT MAKES AN EVENT?

An event, as a first cut, is any happening that surprises and rattles, turns, amplifies, or decimates a set of previous settlements. An event, that is, both surprises and activates concern in a positive or negative sense. The event of the Anthropocene, rumbling along beneath our feet for a few centuries, both induced shock when it was acknowledged and exposed how seasonal patterns shift over time. It activates concern and denialism in different constituencies and, perhaps, in different chambers of our own souls.

Not all events involve new recognition of things well under way beneath our radar. Sometimes things change fast on their own, as that huge ice shelf did in Antarctica in 2002, when it exploded in three days, or as the pandemic of 2020 did, spreading everywhere a few months after its origin beyond the reach of public attention. Events assume multiple forms and emerge from diverse sources. Attention to the force of an event may compel rethinking, say, about conventional lines of division between the social and the natural, life and nonlife, or secular time and divine time.

One type of event thus unfolds when the dominant focus of attention has been elsewhere. It might have been explicable *in principle,* but either actual theories of the day could not explain its occurrence or its efficacies originated from a place not then on the horizon of attention. The monsoon interruptions that brought famine to India at the end of the nineteenth century outstripped the sciences of the day and the concerns of the British Empire. The former was also the case with the massive drought that helped to decimate the Mayan Empire.[2] Possible monsoon interruptions tomorrow created by a cascade between rapid climate change, intensified El Niños, and a weakening of global wind patterns are more comprehensible today. But the cascading elements hover outside the attention span of many humanists, social scientists, media leaders, elected officials, and citizens. So does a possible closure or turning of the Gulf Stream, an event that has also happened before.

Another type of event occurs when activists and leaders break molds of expectation set by the media and dominant assumptions of the day. Often, timing is crucial. Trump's 2016 victory and his militant dismantling of checks and balances fit that model. So does the fateful death of Ruth Bader Ginsburg. Many have been surprised each time the aspirational fascist has made his next move. Consider also Putin's compromise of Trump, his cyberattacks, and his aspiration to bring America to its knees by indirect means. A more appealing event of this type occurred when cities and towns were flooded with protesters after yet another bout of police brutality resulted in the death of yet another Black man.

These distinctions speak to shining points of emphasis rather than to dichotomies, because the search for dichotomous concepts is one of the problems that discourages people from admitting the obduracy of the event. Thus some events start small and swell to large proportions. They may involve moments of real creativity in the world. The births of Buddha and Jesus took that form. So did the recent pandemic. The creativity of Covid-19 involves evolution of a capacity to jump from one host to another. Of course, the virus does not intend the jump. But are nano-intentions perhaps involved in the attachment of a virion to a new host? Do nano-resonances back and forth between host and suitor enable a crossing to succeed? Or fail? I suspect so.[3] Certainly many biologists now acknowledge that bacteria project nano-purposes, as they also adjust their behavior in response to new obstacles. And bacteria populate human guts as well as the world around humans.[4] On another register, that cop in Minnesota intended to kill George Floyd when he sat on his neck for nine and a half long minutes. The event might have been covered up, as have so many others. But it became a national event when a creative agent videotaped it and millions saw the tape. And it spurred another creative event: whites and Blacks bonded together in multiple cities to renew the movement of Black Lives Matter and to demand police reform in ways that became more difficult to ignore than heretofore.

Many events involve intersections that cross old humanist boundaries. They cascade. Thus rapid planetary warming increases the pace of polar glacier melts; the faster pace creates more melted water on the glacier surface; the lower albedo ratio further enlarges the volume of water; the high volume of water and warmer summers spawn new growth of algae on the glacier surface, further lowering the albedo ratio; that cascade now allows huge volumes of water to pour down moulins to grease a yet faster glacier flow. Much of this may occur behind the backs of investigators until a tipping point occurs, that is, it becomes an event. Similarly, new attempts to flee tropical and semitropical zones in the face of expanding drought and local oppression can incite neofascist drives in temperate states, as disturbed constituencies protect old models of capitalism, sovereignty, and white identity from diversification.

Other examples and types could be cited. But perhaps this list calls attention to the obduracy of the event, amid the porosity and shifting intensities of old regularities. *Obdurat* in Old English means "that which hardens" and "that which endures." I will extend the word to fit a world of events. Events are obdurate in two senses. First, they erupt periodically, assuming diverse shapes and punctuating old regularities. It is thus unwise to project a future world in which events disappear under the province of a sufficient science and/or regime. Second, many events are obdurate in the sense that, once consolidated, their efficacies grow and continue. They become entangled with other events, forging cascades that keep morphing.

Obdurate events are not epiphenomenal and not rare. They find you before you find them. They disorient. And they often carry strange efficacies that persist and become amplified through cascading connections to other processes. It is partly because several conceptions of linear time, hubristic social science, social structure, and human exceptionalism have worked to exorcize the event that its obduracy is so often minimized.

On this last score, some tendencies in Marxism and liberalism reinforce each other, or have done so at least until recently. The first has tended to project the possibility of a unique revolution that ushers into being a smooth future. Such an imaginary can inspire people who are oppressed, and there is ample racial, class, gender, sexual, religious, and intersectional oppression to go around, both within the old, luxurious temperate zone states and between them and nontemperate regions. But you cannot project a smooth future in a rocky world composed of intersecting temporalities of diverse sorts.[5] New forms of critical idealism need to insist on both the elimination of social oppression *and* the transfiguration of vengeful orientations to death and the rocky place of the human estate in the world.

The second ideology—liberalism—has tended to define the future as now, turning too blind an eye to how luxurious states ride on top of downtrodden constituencies within and without and downplaying how events emanating from outside human social processes can rattle or turn those processes. Think, for instance, of how numerous premodern climate emergencies were depressed from liberal historiography until the power of the Anthropocene became too blatant to bypass, or even how the recurrence of plagues in history was obscured until the eruption of Covid-19.[6] The naive sense in the 1970s and 1980s that the invention of antibiotics placed those old plagues in the rearview mirror did not help either.

TASKS OF THE ENGAGED INTELLECTUAL

Some old tasks of intellectuals persist once the obduracy of the event has been given its due. For example, the demand to expose and oppose persistent modes of racial, religious, class, and sexual oppression within and across capitalist states persists. As Georg Simmel reminds us, "this is the tragedy of whomever is on the lowest rung. He not only has to suffer the deprivations, efforts, and discriminations which, taken together, characterize his position; in addition, every new pressure on any point whatever in the superordinate layers is, if technically possible at all, transmitted downward and stops only at him."[7] The task is to expose how those exploitations work, to identify ways to overcome them, and to join movements seeking to do so.

Even here, however, attention to the obduracy of the event becomes pertinent. Accelerating climate change today creates droughts, storms, wildfires, more severe hurricanes, heat waves, floods, unseasonal tornadoes, and monsoon interruptions whose adverse effects disproportionately hit Black and brown peoples, poor urban residents, and the rural poor. Often the burdens of women in these settings are increased disproportionately too. A pandemic, too, threatens the poor most, at first through disease transmission and joblessness, then through cutbacks in state and local welfare, health and education budgets that follow in a neoliberal economy.

Are there, however, distinctive tasks to add to this established set? I think so. In general, intellectuals must strive to become worthy of new events when and as they arise. To do so, we must alter our preparations and spiritualities to some degree. We must, for instance, spend less time searching for the consummate explanatory theory, less time crouched in the disciplines in which we have been trained, and less time seeking an indelible method of explanation. We must more often become willing amateurs, ready to follow the course of an event where it takes us, ready to reach beyond our fields of comfort when an event demands it. For example, virologists, when a pandemic erupts, today follow lab work with anthropological work, combing localities to ascertain how, say, a bat virus crosses into human and other species and asking what actions can be taken to relieve these conditions. Vaccine producers then work at warp speed to create new vaccines. A growing legion of climate scientists, too, previously content to present their evidence to the public and other scientists, now often become activists to dramatize new events more widely. James Hansen, Lynn Margulis, Anthony Fauci, and Naomi Oreskes present shining examples here.[8]

What about those in the humanities, media, and social sciences? Here, too, the obduracy of the event calls upon us to follow the bumpy contours of a problem where it takes us, particularly when those contours stretch beyond the comfort zones of sociocentrism and humanist exceptionalism within which so many of us started our careers and toward which the dictates of old methods point. In the domain of climate change, humanist theorists like Anna Tsing, Dipesh Chakrabarty, Mike Davis, Donna Haraway, Jairus Grove, P. J. Brendese, Deborah Danowski, and Eduardo de Castro increasingly feel pressed to become more attuned to geology, species evolution, climatology, and even volcanology, while remaining attentive to their old provinces. Political theorists now reach into those fields, too, as they expand their strategic repertoire. Some theorists even contest modern Euro-American images of time, doing so to improve our capacities to follow the contours of the event.[9]

I note two other shifts in emphasis needed: the first speaks to a need to refocus efforts to re-form the shape of the neoliberal university, the second to the need for nontheistic intellectuals to forge closer spiritual links with

theopolitical thinkers as both respond to dangerous shifts in the spiritual tone of the right wing. The hierarchical organization of the natural
sciences, the social sciences, and the humanities marking the neoliberal
university hinders it from coping with events. Events repeatedly jump
and bounce across these academic divisions, while guild practitioners too
often stop at their professional borders. Many things enforce such borders, including the priorities of capitalism and neoliberal university administrations. One thing in particular provides cover for neoliberal presidents
of universities as they put the squeeze on the humanities.

The philosophy of linear time that remains hegemonic in physics is at
odds with a world of multiple, intersecting temporalities in which we actually participate. The humanities and social sciences, too, often bracket the
latter image of time. They disable pursuit of the event in doing so. The
intellectual roots of the disconnect sink deeply into the organization of the
Euro-American academy.

If you, coarsely, trace one European image of time as it evolved from
Descartes through Newton to Einstein, you find that Descartes defined
time as a linear series of instants bound together only by the grace of an
omnipotent God. Here is how he put it in 1647: "For the whole duration of
my life can be divided into an infinite number of parts, no one of which is
dependent on the others, and so it does not follow from the fact that I have
existed a short while before that I should exist now."[10] Newton also defined
time as discrete instants. And Einstein, disagreeing with both on several
points, nonetheless defined time in terms of fixed instants anchored objec-
tively in the speed of light, which he took to be demonstrably the fastest
possible speed in the universe. He therefore concluded that the human
experience of duration—the interfolding of past, present, and future in the
protraction of the moment during which creativity sometimes occurs—
was an illusion propagated by what I call entangled humanists, such as
Henri Bergson, William James, and Alfred North Whitehead.

The assumed breach between the humanist illusion of time and Ein-
steinian physics erected an implacable wall against crossings between the
"hard" natural sciences and the "soft" humanistic sciences. That very breach,
however, actually rested on how each party gave priority to a different
human experience of time rather than being divided into a subjective illusion on one side and an objective measure on the other. Einstein bestowed
primacy upon specific techno-math tests of the speed of light, Bergson and
Whitehead upon experiences of duration when the disposition to action

is relaxed. The two large fields of inquiry now either had to ignore one another, or one of them—usually the humanities—was to be subjugated to the other. The debate between these two images—really a struggle persisting at least from the Bergson–Einstein debate in 1922 to today—is beautifully reviewed by Jimena Canales in *The Physicist and the Philosopher.*[11]

And yet the Einstein story of a unique *human* illusion of lived temporality at odds with objective science has for a few decades now been belied by several other nonhuman sciences. There is no longer, if there ever was, a single division between the time of physics and the time of human experience. Bergson in *Creative Evolution* already paid heed to the diverse temporalities of multiple species. Pursued far, his insight opens up exploratory lines of connection between Euro-American experiences of temporality and several Indigenous experiences of intersections between human experiences of temporality and those of several animals and plants. Today we can speak meaningfully of viral temporality, bacterial temporality, whale temporality, glacier temporality, forest temporality, ocean current temporality, capitalist temporality, and so on. The glaciologist Richard Alley, for instance, characterizes a glacier as a "two-mile time machine."[12]

These diverse temporalities, set on different speeds, vectors, and capacities, periodically bump into one another in ways that can rattle and shake established regularities and trajectories. This image of a world of multiple, intersecting temporalities both respects distinctive durations within different processes and demands exploration of how diverse temporalities often intersect through viral crossings, climate changes, species extinctions, volcanic eruptions, new civilizational possibilities, capitalist crises, and so on (i.e., events). It turns out, to note one instance, that during an era of rapid climate warming, the pace and intensity of volcanoes also increase.[13]

Now the stage is set to address problems that sometimes require two or three sciences, as practitioners explore crossings between heterogeneous temporalities, that is, as they come to terms with the obduracy of the event.

SPIRITUAL CROSSINGS AND
AFFIRMATIVE POLITICAL ASSEMBLAGES

Let us distinguish between an existential *spirituality* and an existential *creed.* Catholics, Protestants, Muslims, Hindus, Kantians, Indigenous peoples, and atheists diverge in creed. But a lived spirituality is not entirely reducible to the creed from which it radiates. For example, Catherine Keller, a Protestant theologian of a limited God acting upon a Deep already bubbling at the inception of the world, and I, a nontheistic advocate of a bumpy universe, diverge in *creed*.[14] But we may also express *affinities of spirituality* that jump across those creedal differences, affinities that allow us to participate together in larger assemblages. Charles Taylor, a Catholic philosopher of pluralism, surely diverges from Cornel West in creed, the latter an advocate of prophetic Christianity. But, to me, the two express affinities of spirituality.[15] Such spiritual crossings, when they proliferate between constituencies, help to foment pluralist political assemblages. To bring those kinds of affinities out, to cultivate them, is to pursue possible connections across several creedal (i.e., philosophical, religious, race, class, and ideological) constituencies. It is to pursue enlarged, pluralist assemblages composed of constituencies drawn together partly by affinities of creed, ideology, and social position and partly by affinities of spirituality that spill over the former.

Because we today inhabit states and regions each composed of multiple minorities of many types, cultivation of cultural affinities of spirituality across them forms the glue of actual and possible political movements. Affinities of embodied spirituality are thus profoundly important to a pluralist ethos of collective action. Think, for instance, of how many white, heterosexual males work upon inherited alpha-masculine traits to absorb a pluralization of gender, race, sexuality, and faith, while others intensify patterns of alpha-masculinity to disparage and defeat those same crossings. The latter are pulled by a collective spirituality of alpha-masculinity, an affinity that can help to forge fascist movements drawn (differentially of course) from several social positions.

The modes of care or neglect in child-rearing, educational experience, military life, church assemblies, work life, and encounters with unexpected events have a lot to do with the quality of political spiritualities. To put it briefly, familiar social positions are pertinent to political formations, but so are spiritual dispositions that connect people without being entirely reducible to traditionally defined creeds and social positions.

Today, we encounter a large swath of people in American society drawn from somewhat different positions of race, class, and creed—a spiritual constituency—primed to deny bellicosely the truth of a Republican election defeat, to deny the fact of cultural racism, to deny the pandemic of 2020, and to deny climate change. Think of that minority of Black and Latino males, for example, who voted for Trump. This constellation is bound together in part by affinities of spirituality. Unless the cluster of denialisms drawing it together is somehow redressed, American democracy has little chance of survival. The sources of denialism, of course, are themselves multiple—partly grounded in class grievances too long ignored or neglected by liberalism, partly grounded in long-term demands for white superiority, partly grounded in a host of personal binds irreducible to any traditionally defined social position, partly grounded among the privileged in hubris and extreme demands for entitlement, partly grounded in a right-wing media machine that exacerbates these grievances and feeds the denialism. These multiple sources come together in a right-wing constituency defined in part by spiritual affinities.

It is now timely, then, to take the quality of constituency spirituality seriously as one of the variables that waxes and wanes in political life. One way to put the point is to say that by comparison to the spirituality emanating from labor in the 1960s, the evangelical–neoliberal resonance machine rests to a significant degree upon an alliance *between whites from different classes whose self-definition demands the projection of a hostile spirituality against a large set of other minorities.* There was already ample racism in the white working class, but now it is both more virulent again and more tethered to a distinctive set of other denialisms.

Perhaps one way to address the spiritual dimension of politics, during an age when the obduracy of the event cries for close attention, is for more intellectuals to strive to come to terms themselves in more affirmative ways with the issues of mortality and the precarity of the human estate itself on this planet. We will not reach creedal consensus on these two issues, but perhaps we can amplify our spiritual affinities on them. If you think that *one* spiritual source of multidenialism is prompted, first, by the collective evasion of mortality as a condition of life and, second, by refusal to accept the shaky place of the human estate on the planet, then more of us need to take the *political* efficacies of spiritual assemblages more seriously, to explore how to promote positive spiritual assemblages, and to weave positive spiritualities more profoundly into the political assemblages in which we participate. To pose these issues is not to dismiss the others in play—though many secularists may jump to that very conclusion when the issue is broached. It is to add them to an established list of class grievances, sedimented white racial privilege, and capitalist modes of class entitlement. But, crucially, this addition is not like adding new Lego blocks to an existing stack. It is closer to folding yeast into flour or—dare I say it—a virus into other living tissue. In these latter instances, the effect now permeates a larger constituency rather than being added on top of solid blocks already there. For we inhabit—and are inhabited by—a world of fluids as well as solids and a world in which solids periodically liquefy.[16]

Let me put it this way. Marx's account of the alienation of workers from work and the product of work retains its standing in class-defined capitalist societies. But two other aspects of alienation demand attention too: alienation from mortality and from the shaky place of human beings on a planet susceptible to radical disruptions by new events. If the first two modes urgently need to be *resolved,* the second two need to be addressed and *transfigured* culturally to the extent possible—transfigured into spiritual orientations in which more constituencies strive to overcome resentment of these two conditions of being in one way or another, and thus better able to respond with nobility to events. This becomes a way to draw Marx, James Baldwin, and Nietzsche closer together and, perhaps, even to draw intellectuals in different fields and regions into closer conversations. James Baldwin, facing twin prejudices against Blacks and gays, displayed an acute awareness of how perverse spiritual elements permeate white cultural life when he said that "most people guard and keep; they suppose that it is they themselves that they are guarding and keeping, whereas what they are actually guarding and keeping is their system of reality. . . . One can give nothing whatever without giving oneself—that is to say, risking oneself." Again, "I speak of change not on the surface but in the depths—change in the sense of renewal."[17]

I certainly do not say, recall, that every constituency is in an equally favorable position to pursue these objectives. A society sharply divided by hierarchies of class, race, sexuality, and creed belies that. So, let's focus on a constituency less often so beleaguered: intellectuals during a time when the obduracy of the event urgently demands our attention. The tasks are to follow the event where it cascades, even if that means becoming amateurs drawing upon other fields and academic boundaries to do so; to challenge practices of the neoliberal university that make it more difficult to trace the course of events; and to work on our operative spiritualities so that we periodically overflow professional confinements, are presumptively more receptive to unfamiliar orientations and experiences, and become more worthy of events that keep rolling in. To me, the long 2020 shows that.

NOTES

1. The formation of this machine is explored in William E. Connolly, "The Evangelical/Capitalist Resonance Machine," *Political Theory* 33, no. 6 (2005): 869–86, and Connolly, *Capitalism and Christianity, American Style* (Durham, N.C.: Duke University Press, 2008).

2. The shift in seasonal monsoons and the resulting famines is explored in Mike Davis, *Late Victorian Holocausts* (New York: Verso, 2001). The collapse of the Mayan Empire during the medieval warming period is documented in Brian Fagan, *The Great Warming* (New York: Bloomsbury Press, 2008).

3. For the claim that viruses are living, see Patrick Forterre, "To Be or Not to Be Alive: How Recent Discoveries Challenge the Traditional Definitions of Viruses and Life," *Studies in History and Philosophy of Biological and Biomedical Sciences* 59 (2016): 100–108. For engagements with biological theories of life as purposive and striving, see William E. Connolly, *A World of Becoming* (Durham, N.C.: Duke University Press, 2011).

4. One excellent instance is Stuart Kauffman, *Reinventing the Sacred: A New View of Science, Reason and Religion* (New York: Basic Books, 2008).

5. A superb book that underlines the point is Jairus Grove, *Savage Ecology* (Durham, N.C.: Duke University Press, 2019).

6. For texts that expose such eruptions, see Kyle Harper, *The Fate of Rome* (Princeton, N.J.: Princeton University Press, 2017); Donna Haraway, *Staying with the Trouble* (Durham, N.C.: Duke University Press, 2016); and David Quammen, *Spillover* (New York: W. W. Norton, 2012).

7. Georg Simmel, in Kurt Wolff, ed., *The Sociology of Georg Simmel* (New York: Free Press, 1962), 145.

8. For an account of how state and public refusal aroused one government climatologist to become an activist, see James Hansen, *Storms of My Grandchildren* (New York: Bloomsbury Press, 2014). X and Naomi Oreskes pose similar issues in *Merchants of Doubt* (New York: Bloomsbury Press, 2011). See also Lynn Margulis and Dorion Sagan, *Acquiring Genomes: A Theory of the Origin of Species* (New York: Basic Books, 2002).

9. Besides texts by Grove, Haraway, and Connolly previously noted, see P. J. Brendese, *Segregated Time* (New York: Oxford University Press, 2021); Dipesh Chakrabarty, *The Climate of History in a Planetary Age* (Chicago: University of Chicago Press, 2021); and Bruno Latour, *Facing Gaia* (Oxford: Polity Press, 2017).

10. René Descartes, *Meditations,* trans. Lawrence Lafleur (New York: Library of Liberal Arts, 1952), 105.

11. Jimena Canales, *The Physicist and the Philosopher* (Princeton, N.J.: Princeton University Press, 2013).

12. Richard Alley, *The Two-Mile Time Machine* (Princeton, N.J.: Princeton University Press, 2000). Stephen Gould, similarly, speaks of intersecting "tiers of time" in *The Structure of Evolutionary Theory* (New York: Columbia University Press, 2002).

13. See Bill McGuire, *Waking the Giant* (Oxford: Oxford University Press, 2012).

14. See, e.g., Catherine Keller, *The Face of the Deep* (New York: Routledge, 2003).

15. See Charles Taylor, *Sources of the Self* (Cambridge, Mass.: Harvard University Press, 1989), and Cornel West, *Black Prophetic Fire* (Boston: Beacon Press, 2015).

16. Jane Bennett, in *Influx and Efflux* (Durham, N.C.: Duke University Press, 2020), probes permeable dimensions of personal and cultural life. So does Alfred North Whitehead in *Modes of Thought* (New York: Cambridge University Press, 1938).

17. James Baldwin, *The Fire Next Time* (New York: Vintage Books, 1962), 86, 92.

OIKOS

10 Modern Architecture— Lying Down

BEATRIZ COLOMINA

A grid of empty white beds in a dark cavernous space, waiting for bodies. One architecture inside another. A field hospital is set up within days to accommodate fifty-five hundred patients in two convention center halls in Madrid. Buildings designed for temporary events now host an emergency medical architecture, a space for disease. Sick architecture (Figure 10.1). And it was not just Madrid; all over the world, from Belgrade to New York, similar spaces were set up during the early days of the Covid-19 pandemic in the first months of the long 2020. It was not the first time that this has happened, as can be seen in photographs from the 1918 Spanish Flu pandemic in the United States, showing thousands of beds in field hospitals in cavernous spaces (Figure 10.2).

Sick architecture is not simply the architecture of medical emergency. On the contrary, it is the architecture of normality—the way that past health crises are inscribed into the everyday, with each architecture not just carrying the traces of prior diseases but having been completely shaped by them. Every new disease is hosted within the architecture formed by previous diseases in a kind of archeological nesting of disease. Each medical event activates deep histories of architecture and illness, along with all the associated fears, misunderstandings, prejudices, inequities, and innovations.

In fact, all architecture is sick. Illnesses and architecture are inseparable. It could even be argued that the beginning of architecture is the beginning of disease. As doctor Benjamin Ward Richardson put it when introducing *Our Homes and How to Make Them Healthy,* a compendium of texts by doctors and architects for the 1884 International Health Exhibition in London:

FIGURE 10.1. A field hospital with fifty-five hundred beds and an intensive care unit for patients with Covid-19 at the Ifema exhibition complex in Madrid, March 22, 2020. Photograph copyright Handout/Handout via Getty Images.

Man, by a knowledge and skill not possessed by the inferior animals, in building cities, villages, houses, for his protection from the external elements, has produced for himself a series of fatal diseases, which are so closely associated with the productions of his knowledge and skill in building as to stand in the position of effect from cause. Man in constructing protections from exposure has constructed conditions of disease.[1]

There is no disease without architecture and no architecture without disease. Doctors and architects have always been in a kind of dance, often exchanging roles, collaborating, influencing each other, even if not always synchronized. Furniture, rooms, buildings, and cities are produced by medical emergencies that layer one on top of another over the centuries. We tend to forget very quickly what produces these layers. As soon as the emergency is over, we develop amnesia. We act as if each pandemic is the first, as if trying to bury the pain and uncertainty of the past. And yet it could be argued that the history of cities is the history of disease. Cities represent a kind of accumulation of theories of disease from ancient times

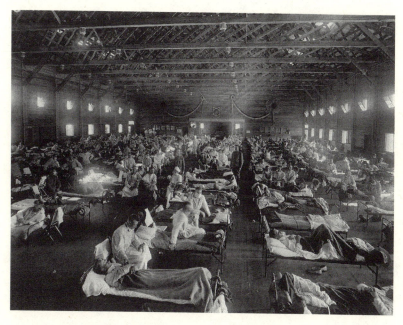

FIGURE 10.2. Emergency hospital during an influenza epidemic, Camp Funston, Kansas. NCP 1603.jpg.

to the present. The pandemics of the nineteenth century brought us the infrastructure we still have today in our cities: clean water systems, sewage systems, urban parks, and so on. And they also revolutionized the design of interiors, furniture, and buildings.

The relationship between architecture and health goes back to the very beginning of architectural theory. In the first century B.C., Vitruvius launched Western architectural theory by insisting that all architects need to study medicine, "healthfulness being their chief object."[2] He devoted a large part of his *Ten Books on Architecture* to the question of health, giving detailed instructions on how to determine the healthiness of a proposed site for a city by returning to the ancient method of sacrificing an animal that lived there and inspecting its liver to make sure it was "sound and firm." Likewise for the health of buildings, he discusses the theory of the four humors, which was the dominant medical theory of the time. Even more interesting, Vitruvius argues, in reverse, that those who are unwell can be cured more quickly through design, rebuilding the system of those "exhausted by disease," including "consumption," an old word for tuberculosis. So already in Vitruvius we encounter the idea of architecture for both the prevention and the cure of disease, something that has persisted through the centuries.

In the Renaissance, for example, the very first school of design, the Academia del Disegno in Florence, founded in 1563 by Giorgio Vasari, placed itself next to the medical academy. Students of design were required to attend dissection in the local hospital Santa Maria Nuova and draw the body for days on end, even as the body putrefied and some students fell ill.

Every subsequent architectural theory added something to this medical paradigm. One could even argue that disease is the real designer of cities. Modern architecture, for example, was produced under emergency conditions. Throughout the nineteenth century and the first half of the twentieth, millions died of tuberculosis every year all over the world. Modern buildings offered a prophylactic defense against this invisible microorganism. All the defining features of modern architecture—white walls, terraces, big windows, detachment from the ground—were presented as both prevention and cure. Yet the medicinal nature of modern architecture and the unimaginable horror to which it was responding have been largely forgotten. The image of white buildings whites out the trauma that gave birth to them.

To produce the idea of modern architecture as healthy, nineteenth-century architecture was demonized as nervous, unhealthy, and literally filled with disease, especially the bacilli of tuberculosis. Decorative excess was itself treated as an infection. Modernizing architecture was first a form of disinfection, a purification of buildings leading to a health-giving environment of light, air, cleanliness, and smooth white surfaces without cracks or crevices where contagion might lurk. Women were advised to leave out petri dishes to see if any bacteria had survived their cleaning routines. The housewife was a bacteriologist and the home her laboratory.

Architecture has always been described in terms of the body, but it is not a healthy body as we usually think about it, particularly with the famous images of athletic male bodies as drawn by Leonardo da Vinci and others, inscribed in geometric systems of proportions. The real body of architecture is a fragile body, prone to sickness or already sick and in need of support. Architecture is a kind of orthopedic support, a kind of crutch or artificial skin for this fragile creature.

Take Alvar Aalto and Aino Aalto and their tuberculosis sanatorium, built in 1929 in Paimio, Finland. With its dramatic terraces in the sky, the building even bears an uncanny resemblance, in canonical photographs, to ribs on an X-ray, the primary diagnostic tool for tuberculosis. Its clean-lined bedrooms, void of ornament, were designed to minimize surfaces where dust could accumulate. Even the intersection of floor and wall beneath the window curved to stop dust buildup. The rooms were equipped with furniture and sanitary fittings designed by the architect, including chairs whose backs were angled to facilitate breathing and expectoration, sinks designed to reduce splashing, and spittoons to minimize sound. Even door handles were carefully designed not to catch the sleeves of the doctors' white coats.

But the building's main equipment was the top-floor terrace, seven stories above the forested landscape, where patients were wheeled out for regular doses of fresh air and sun in the lounge chairs specially designed by Aino Aalto (Figure 10.3). Eventually, the terrace had to be closed off, perhaps because the nurses couldn't keep up with the number of desperate patients throwing themselves from it every time they turned their backs. Modern architecture as a form of assisted suicide? The discovery and success of

FIGURE 10.3. Aino Aalto lying in the lounge chair she designed for the Paimio sanatorium, circa 1934. Alvar Aalto Museum no. 50-003-257. Photograph by Alvar Aalto.

streptomycin in 1944 revealed that there was little scientific basis to the air-and-sun therapy of the sanatorium. Sometimes it even precipitated the end. At Paimio, quite literally.

Tuberculosis made modern architecture modern. It is not that modern architects made modern sanatoria; rather, sanatoria modernized architects. Aalto was a neoclassical architect before his "conversion to functionalism" in the 1927 competition entry for a tuberculosis sanatorium at Kinkomaa, Finland—an unrealized project of horizontal lines and wide terraces for the cure, a design that anticipates Paimio. For Aalto, the sanatorium was not architecture in the service of medicine but a form of medicine in its own right—a medical instrument: "The main purpose of the building is to function as a medical instrument. . . . The room design is determined by the depleted strength of the patient, reclining in his bed."[3]

Aalto himself had been sick at the time of the competition for the building and claimed that having to lie in bed for an extended period of time had been crucial to his understanding of the problem. Architecture was always conceived for the vertical person, but here was a client permanently in the horizontal. The whole design of the room and the building had to change accordingly. Light fixtures could not remain in the ceiling, irritating the eyes of the occupant lying in bed and for whom the ceiling had all of a sudden acquired maximum importance—a new kind of facade, perhaps. The view through the window to the forest outside also had to be calculated from the point of view of the bed. On the terrace, the low parapet and thin rail above allowed the eye of the horizontal person to travel far above the forest.

The colors of the room and the building had to be thought in these terms too. Soothing "quiet, dark hues" of blue for the ceiling. The walls in lighter shades. Bright canary yellow in the reception booth by the entrance and in the linoleum of the lobby, staircase, and corridors evoked "sunny optimism even in cold, cloudy days."[4] Psychological factors were also carefully considered: "An extended period of confinement can be extremely depressing for a bed-ridden patient. . . . A tuberculosis sanatorium is, to all intents and purposes, a house with open windows."[5] The hospital has to be thought as a new kind of house. And in reverse, the generic house needs to be a sanatorium. Aalto later wrote,

I was able to discover that special physical and psychological reactions by patients provide good pointers of ordinary housing. . . . To examine how human beings react to forms and constructions, it is useful to use for experimentation especially sensitive persons, such as patients in a sanatorium.[6]

The bodily and psychological sensitivity of the sick person is used to recalibrate architecture. Even the specialized furniture became ordinary, everyday pieces. If the cantilevered birchwood Paimio chair, for example, was designed to open the chest of the patient, allowing them to breathe easier, soon enough that chair became everybody's chair. Likewise with the rest of the furniture specially designed for Paimio: "The sanatorium needed furniture which should be light, flexible, easy to clean and so on. After extensive experimentation in wood, the flexible system was discovered . . . to produce furniture which was more suitable for the long and painful life in a sanatorium."[7] A workshop was set up with a local company to carry the first experiments, and in 1935, barely two years after completing Paimio, Alvar and Aino Aalto founded the Finnish furniture company Artek, with "the ambition to support and nourish human beings' physical and psychological wellbeing."[8]

The reference point was the seriously ill. Aalto claimed that the architect had to design for the person in the "weakest position." The tuberculosis patient becomes the model for modern architecture. In other words, sickness was seen, no longer as the exception, but as the norm—and varying degrees of sickness define the human condition. The modern subject has multiple ailments, and architecture is a protective cocoon not only against the weather and other outside threats but, in modernity, more notably against internal threats, such as psychological and bodily ailments.

Aalto compared his experiments in Paimio and their application to everyday use to the "exaggerated" forms of analysis that scientists use "in order to obtain clear more visible results," such as "stained bacteria" for microscope examination.[9] He saw design as a form of medical research, with the sanatorium acting as a kind of research lab for modern architecture—a way of testing architecture, looking at what has been hidden, exposing the invisible forces.

The relationship between architecture and the human body is always intimate. With modern architecture, this intimacy deepens as the body now includes invisible microbes. Indeed, the real clients of modern architecture are invisible. Sigmund Freud, X-ray, bacteriology, and the germ theory of disease all emerged in the same short period of time, and they are all about looking inside, acknowledging the invisible: the unconscious, the skeleton, the microelement of the bacterium, and the bacillus of TB.

Architecture, likewise, turns itself inside out. The threat is no longer outside but inside in the invisible. The microscale of the bacterium becomes the base for furniture, houses, and cities—the micro and the macro: the bacterium and the city. Cities were suddenly thought to be teeming with unseen occupants who in that sense became the new clients of modern architecture and urbanism.

The architect became a bacteriologist. Architectural itself became bacterial. As Le Corbusier put it, he needed to do "laboratory work," "isolating his microbe" until it appeared in "undisputable clarity." Those are all his words; then he went on to say that with this, one can make a "diagnosis" and draw up the fundamental principles of modern city planning. Modern architecture goes from microbe to city and back.[10]

Modern architecture lying down is not just the new paradigm of seeing architecture from the point of view of those in the weakest position—the horizontal patient as paradigmatic client—but seeing the human species itself as weak, fragile, vulnerable, and immersed in bacteria. The long 2020 has dramatized how the human is no longer the center of a geometric system but is permanently hospitalized—a complete reversal of Leonardo da Vinci's visualization of the Vitruvian man or even its reincarnation in modern times in figures like Le Corbusier's Modular Man. The clearly defined athletic, vertical, gendered man gives way to a multiplicity of age, sexuality, and physical and mental conditions in multiple combinations and collaborations with other species. Sickness is not the negative term but the generator of new potentials, the very engine of modernity.

NOTES

1. Benjamin Ward Richardson, "Health in the Home," introduction to Shirley Forster Murphy, ed., *Our Homes and How to Make Them Healthy* (London: Cassell, 1883), 5.

2. Vitruvius Pollio, *The Ten Books on Architecture*, trans. Morris Hicky Morgan (Cambridge, Mass.: Harvard University Press, 1914), 20.

3. Alvar Aalto, in a lecture in Italy describing Paimio, 1956, quoted in Schildt, *Alvar Aalto: The Complete Catalogue*, 68–69. Text in the Aalto Archives.

4. Karl Fleig and Elissa Aalto, eds., *Alvar Aalto: Das Gesamtwerk/L'oeuvre compléte/The Complete Work*, vol. 1, *1922–1962* (Basel, Switzerland: Birkhäuser, 1963), 39.

5. Fleig and Aalto.

6. Alvar Aalto, "The Humanizing of Architecture," *Technology Review*, November 1940. Also in *Architectural Forum* 73 (December 1940): 505–6. Reprinted in Goran Schildt, *Aalto in His Own Words* (New York: Rizzoli, 1998), 102–6.

7. Aalto, 104.

8. "The Artek Manifesto," Artek Company, Helsinki. See also Fleig and Aalto, *Alvar Aalto,* 1:43 and 1:66.

9. Aalto, "Humanizing of Architecture," 15.

10. Le Corbusier, *Precisions on the Present State of Architecture and Urban Planning,* trans. Edith Schrieber Aujame (Cambridge, Mass.: MIT Press, 1991), 143. Translation of Le Corbusier, *Précisions sur en état present d'architecture et de l'urbanisme* (Paris: Crès et Cie, 1930).

11 Disabling Environment

DAVID GISSEN

How can "we"—disabled and impaired people—rethink the concept of
the architectural environment through the lens of our and others' impairments? The events of 2020 demonstrate the need for a form of disability
rights that is relevant to the architectural environment. In the past twelve
months, numerous studies examined both the vulnerabilities created by
architecturally engineered heating, ventilation and cooling systems, and
the pervasive experience of these systems within cities. Despite the historic and contemporary links between environments and human physi-
cality, the topic of the environment within and around buildings remains
almost entirely outside contemporary discussions of architecture and disability rights. Most U.S. discussions of justice, rights, and disability focus
on the problems of accessibility to physical space. Curiously, environmental concerns do not easily relate to this traditional disability politics. In an
architectural context, the architectural "environment" generally describes
the immaterial elements within and outside buildings and their surroundings. This includes the climatic, biological, and atmospheric qualities of
spaces from the intensity of sunlight to the sensibilities of indoor air. The
topic of environment rose to become a significant category of architectural
thinking, writing, and designing in the early and mid-twentieth century. Few
topics are more associated with architecture's relationship to the physiology
of human beings and the health of its inhabitants than the environment
harnessed and created by buildings. Thus, in the wake of the long 2020, it
is imperative that we consider how to rethink the architectural environment relative to past and emerging ideas about disability.

ENVIRONMENTAL BEINGS

Environmental thinking about human physiology and architecture emerged from "functionalist" mechanical and deterministic theories that sought to determine the ideal settings for living beings. Architects in the United States and Europe brought studies that were primarily focused on all life to bear on human beings and their ideal conditions. This includes the reaction of human beings to temperature, sunlight, and airflow as well as reactions of the human sensorium to scents, sound, and illumination. In a series of architecturally engineered experiments, a limited range of subjects were exposed to a limited range of stimuli within a carefully designed research space to determine the ideal designed parameters of temperature, air, scent, light, and acoustic responses. Of these studies, one of the most famous is the development of the "comfort zone." This concept emerged from a study, undertaken at Harvard University, to develop universal standards for the use of air conditioning, heating, and ventilation of space. In a window-less, cork-lined laboratory space, young, white, able-bodied men would sit in their underwear while undertaking a series of activities as scientists manipulated the temperature, humidity, and rate of airflow of this space. The goal of this research was to develop standards that could be applied universally in the development of air-conditioning systems and the design of the buildings that house them. The "comfort zone" that emerged from this research describes a parameter for indoor air that is approximately sixty-eight to seventy degrees Fahrenheit and with 50 percent humidity.[1] This standard, one that is distributed almost universally in commercial build-ings today, is most often delivered through forced-air systems that control temperature, humidity, and the rate of airflow.

The study of human environmental parameters within such limited set-tings created unseen dangers and effects. For example, the Harvard study marked a more pronounced shift away from nineteenth-century concepts of health that emphasized access to fresh air. The study completely elimi-nated sunshine and the exposure of interior space to exterior air as factors in the development of a comfort zone. As Michelle Murphy points out, the abandonment of these ventilation practices would have implications fifty years later, when air conditioning in sealed interior rooms became more widely implemented. From the 1970s and on, ailments like Legionnaire's disease and sick building syndrome appeared in fully air-conditioned build-ings. The latter term describes a range of ailments and reactions to sealed, air-conditioned spaces that were first identified by women office workers in the United States in the 1980s. Sick building syndrome was really better described as a product of unhealthy interior *air*—a combination of poor ventilation, the chemical contents of a building's finish materials, and the toxic substances used in office work.[2] In addition to the shift away from "health," the Harvard study further universalized how engineers imagined achieving thermal regulation through architecture—through the entirety of a person's skin and limbs and the person's interactions with a surrounding atmosphere. The architectural engineer Michelle Addington calls this the "dilution" approach to comfort, in which the human body is immersed in a completely mechanically generated atmosphere of conditioned air.[3] The term *dilution* describes how warming air in a space is replaced or refreshed by mechanically generated air of a cooler temperature. The approach relies on the manner in which many people experience heat loss through their limbs—an experience often at odds with how people with disabilities, who are aging, or who sit for most of the day ultimately experience warming and cooling.[4]

The Harvard study was one of many similar studies undertaken in laboratory contexts that would govern the "biometric" guidelines and parameters of architectural environments. This other work includes the development of rooms for studying sound and acoustics, darkened chambers for exploring lighting and illumination, and ongoing explorations of thermal comfort and architectural engineering.[5] These studies of architecture and human physiology were joined by other scientific research on human stimuli, including studies on neurological reactions to the experience of pain and human responses to intensities of light and sound.[6] In tandem with this research into codifying human stimuli and environmental responses, we also see contemporaneous *critiques* of this effort—in some cases through the perspectives of impairment. Among the most influential and relevant examples, the German American neurologist Kurt Goldstein was one of a small number of scientists who argued that the creation of laboratory environments actually impedes knowledge about human physiology, neurology, and stimuli and responses. Goldstein developed his critiques through his studies of stimuli on wounded and traumatized World War I veterans. His concepts gained notoriety because he argued that the way neurologists studied trauma victims—isolating them and observing their responses to various stimuli—only revealed the nature of human responses under highly controlled circumstances. To truly understand human physiology and neurology, Goldstein argued, we must study "the organism" in its entirety. This included self-reflections on the limiting context that scientists use to study people in laboratories; it also included the agency of subjects to adapt and construct environments suitable to their own needs and outside those provided in scientific experiments and studies.

Architects and architectural engineers have certainly been inspired by a more critical and relativistic concept of environment, in an ongoing effort to rethink the limitations of an earlier era's standards. Among the numerous examples, the architectural engineer Michelle Addington has been one of the most vocal in challenging the Harvard study's legacy and impact on architectural engineering. She explored numerous alternative cooling techniques to the dilution model in her research at the Harvard and Yale schools of architecture. In particular, her research examined how the unusual placement of windows or the concentration of much smaller amounts of ventilated air to certain parts of the body can produce sensations of coolness and warmth. For example, in one study that inspired her work, scientists discovered that removing heat from the back of the neck of subjects (by ventilation or conduction) induces a cooling sensation in most people.[7] By concentrating on a more targeted area of the body, such a concept minimizes the dilution and immersive approach to cooling and heating space that requires people to share an environment set to a specific temperature. This technique, and many others like it, offers an inspiring alternative, yet it still relies on standardizing a stimulus and the human reaction to it within architectural space. Nevertheless, the unusual nature of this form of climate control enables us to imagine how environment might be rethought by rethinking how our bodies experience temperature. We can continue this work by introducing other, more aberrant bodies and experiences into the "environment" constructed within buildings, an idea examined at greater length in the following pages.

FROM ENVIRONMENTAL TO ENVIRONMENTALIST BEING

Addington's research is part of a much larger and longer effort by architects and engineers to rethink the enormous energy and health issues of fully conditioned and climate-engineered interior spaces. This "environmentalist" turn in discussions of heating, cooling, and lighting is wide ranging and global in reach, with a history extending back at least to the 1940s and 1950s.

Almost all adherents to an environmentalist architectural approach believe that a building's interior environment must be brought into an engagement with a building's surroundings. This includes, at a very basic level, the role of sunlight, wind patterns, and a general sense of the surrounding climate. This belief, and the pursuit of it, governs a range of practices, from the design of solar and "thermal" architecture to more experimental practices of bioclimatic architecture, explained later. These practices lessen, and in some rare cases eliminate, the need for the use of heating or air conditioning within buildings and at a range of scales. Here we can compare the image of a person, hermetically sealed in a room, and with its origins in the Harvard study explored earlier, with another concept of environmental human-ness. Nevertheless, these alternative "solar," "climatic," or "bioclimatic" concepts of human and environment interaction also rely on similar environmentally determinist ideas and invoke their own concepts of normality and healthfulness.

One of the central features of a European and American architectural environmentalism is the transformed relationship it often cultivates between buildings, inhabitants, and sunlight. The "solarization" of interior and exterior spaces through "radiant" architectural forms emerged as a major program of European urban and architectural planning in the late nineteenth and early twentieth centuries. Not only does sunlight provide light and a form of nonindustrial heat and energy but, since the nineteenth century, it has been imagined to transform the biophysical contents of space and the physiology of its inhabitants. In the late nineteenth century, the scientist Saturnin Arloing argued that sunlight provided a sanitarian effect by killing viral and bacteriological disease, particularly tuberculosis. This desire to increase sun exposure to enhance health and eliminate disease not only influenced the design of sanitoria, hospitals, and institutions; it also extended into large-scale planning and housing strategies.[8] Among the numerous examples, the architect Henri Sauvage proposed to transform sectors of Paris through terraced and open architectural and urban areas. Sauvage viewed his project as part of a longer historical project— beginning with Haussmann's boulevards—of exposing premodern urban spaces to increasing amounts of sun. His realized apartment house on the rue de Amiraux in Paris (1927) represents a vision of solarized hygienic domesticity: the large, terraced apartment house (with a spa-like pool at its center) offers abundant sunlight to each apartment, and most also open to a vitreous white-tiled terrace.[9]

The solarization of space also played a strong role in the concept of a "bioclimatic" architecture, developed by Victor and Alady Olgyay in the late 1950s and early 1960s. Their concepts of the architectural environment offer one of the more totalizing historical and practical theories regarding relationships between a building, its inhabitants, and "environment." Bioclimatic architecture is chiefly a design approach that relates buildings and their surrounding climates through orientation (to light and wind patterns) and the use of natural ventilation, louvers, and other features that negotiate sunlight. Like other functionalist concepts of architecture, the bioclimatic theory of architecture advances a particular and specific image of the human figure. In the Olgyays' *Design with Climate*, which defined this architectural approach, we see a diagram of a standing able-bodied man shown in the manner of a medical journal. Their bioclimatic concept also advanced idealized and universalized environmental parameters of human functioning that resonated with earlier, more explicitly modernist and environmental determinist concepts. For example, in the introduction to his book, Victor Olgyay called out the summer months of Europe, the winter of the hot Mediterranean, and the late spring of Italy as ideal environments—light-filled environments with about 50 percent humidity and average temperatures of seventy degrees Fahrenheit.[10] Thus, even within this more "open" approach to relating buildings and their surroundings, we still see a narrow sense of human environmental needs, a relatively narrow sense of human-ness and its interrelationship with architecture.

Design with Climate represents a broad, midcentury literature that studied the varying ways in which idealized parameters of temperature, airflow, and humidity were architecturally achieved worldwide. This technical study with its global reach was complemented with emerging theories and reflections about the varying *cultural* practices and perspectives that give architectural environments their character. Much of this latter writing brought alternative ideas about climate, environment, and architectural modernization to American and European audiences. This latter writing, which includes books well known among architects, such as Junchiro Tanazaki's *In Praise of Shadows* and Hassan Fathy's *Architecture for the Poor* and *Natural Energy and Vernacular Architecture,* considers the particular national and regional traditions that arise in the lighting, heating, or cooling of a space. The origins of this type of literature often lie in postcolonial reflections on the intrusions of modern, European expertise within specific cultural contexts. For example, Fathy and Tanazaki share a concern with the flattening impact of electrical lighting, thermal control, and modern material sensibilities on the qualities of light, heat, and coolth experienced within North African, Middle Eastern, and Japanese architectural contexts. In response, Tanazaki called for the maintenance of a type of darkened character to traditional Japanese interiors, while Fathy explored how to combine modern planning concepts with historic earthen materials and thermal control.[11] The idea that environmental ideals—very broadly conceived—are related to practices of cultural preservation as much as technical engineering remains an important message from these authors' works.

Finally, another theme in environmentalist literature, and related to the preceding criticisms, questions the value of comfort as a desirable quality—physically built into the architecture of an interior environment. This may sound strange and provocative, but this skepticism about comfort simply argues that the standards for heating, cooling, and illumination have become indulgent, wasteful, and unhealthy. The ventilation, cooling, and illumination standards implemented in many buildings require an enormous embedded and operational use of energy. The consumption of energy in both embedded and operational forms impacts carbon emissions that contribute to the warming of the atmosphere and other forms of climate change. Similarly, the use of air conditioning, in particular, increases the heat loads of urban spaces, because the waste heat from these systems must be expelled into the air.[12] In response to the environmental and social costs of comfort, the historian Daniel Barber asks if the influence of comfort over the design of architectural space should be minimized or eliminated altogether. If comfort is a *concept* about human well-being (vs. an absolute quality of human health), then how might we think after-comfort and in relation to critical histories? Many authors and architects critiquing comfort make little space for questions of impairment or disability in their calculus. For example, in the most militant of these postcomfort concepts, there is sensitivity to how comfort is experienced geographically— between a Global North and a Global South. But we also need to understand how this intersects with vulnerabilities to heat relative to physiological capacity. Considering that the impacts of an altered climate, particularly the experience of heat and humidity, will be felt most intensely by those most compromised physically, this is a significant oversight. In many ways, those exploring a "postcomfort" vision of environmentalist architecture conjure a figure more physically aligned with an earlier era's focus on comfort than not.

AN ENVIRONMENT OF IMPAIRMENT

Numerous scholars of disability have questioned the human norms built into spaces, artifacts, and institutions—from the design of public parks to the physical forms and locations of human-scaled elements. This essay expands this ongoing work by demonstrating how the study and engineering of heat, coolth, ventilation, and light within space relied on a limited range of subjects and a narrow sense of human experience. This environmental disconnect or alienation may seem incidental or even trivial relative to other disability rights issues, but its implications may be as harmful, if not more harmful, than the inaccessibility of space. In many ways, this is because the environmental issue is far more difficult to address. As mentioned, there is enormous pressure on architects and urban planners to rethink the environmental parameters of interior and urban spaces due to the pressures of climate change and urban warming. After this past year, there is a renewed concern regarding the subjection of people to one shared and conditioned environment. In these latter and future studies, I believe we, as disabled people, should find a way to bring our particular perspectives into the redesign of environment as it is architecturally designed and experienced. This involves bringing the physiological experiences of disabled people to the attention of designers within public fora, and it also involves thinking about how these perspectives might be brought into the education of future architects, planners, and designers. Most significantly, it involves confronting various environmental norms—from the qualities associated with health and modernity in urban space to the particular ways architects design connections between human physiology and environment within interior spaces.

Among the examples at the urban scale, in the past five years, numerous municipal governments have questioned the presumed benefits of urban planning strategies and codes that increase the sun exposure of urban and interior spaces.[13] This modern quality of architectural and urban spaces has been debated and questioned because of the transformation of cities due to heat gain. The warming of many urban areas due to climate change, urban deforestation, and increased development produces considerable health risks, particularly in areas without widespread uses of air conditioning. "Vulnerable groups," including disabled people (particularly those with mobility impairments), the very elderly, and young children, face the most significant risks from urban heating and the "heat island effect." In response, a small number of architects and urbanists, I included, have re-visited the uniquely "solarized" character of modern planning strategies and the character of architectural forms that produce an aesthetics in which abundant sunshine in public areas is seen as an automatic good.[14]

As mentioned, the imagined relationship between intense sunshine and health was central to early twentieth-century concepts of planning. In his own writing and visualizations, the architect Henri Sauvage associated his-torical progress with the intensification of sunshine and the elimination of urban darkness over time. Sauvage drew images of his terraced hous-ing schemes in comparison to an earlier medieval urban fabric—the latter visualized as casting streets in permanent shadow. This battle against dark-ness extended into numerous urban plans and codes within any number of cities. For example, in New York City, the transformation of building codes in the early and mid-twentieth century responded to laissez-faire building practices that often set large portions of urban space into shadow. These codes ensured that some amount of light would reach urban streets and interior spaces and fostered an aesthetic of terracing and radiant crystalline forms.[15] In both cities, the intensification of sunlight through building codes often casts enormous areas of urban space in direct sunlight for several hours of the day. Although the original motivation for these urban regula-tions was completely sensible and necessary, today, they need to reexamined.

Those of us who seek to bring darkness back to cities, but as a benevolent and positive addition, must contend with a de facto association between the benefits of sunlight and the future of public and domestic space. Two cities in which I have lived, Vienna and New York, have waged epic battles against darkness that are symbolized within many of each city's most vis-ible and monumental buildings. This extends from the planning of hous-ing to the glass-walled, crystalline aesthetics of office towers and apartment buildings. As these cities' governments are forced to revisit the automatic association between sunlight and health, they effectively rethink basic pre-sumptions about health, history, and the design of urban and interior spaces. This extends to more than just providing shade trees or other landscape ideas to offer people more protection from the sun. For example, in New York City, the municipal government provocatively suggested minimiz-ing the use of glass in tall buildings, while in Vienna, the urban planning department is considering codes that might bring back the narrow and gloomy quality of medieval streets to areas of the city. These architectural concepts are complemented by research in the United States regarding the uneven distribution of trees and shade based on race and class. In response, authors like Nik Heynen and Sam Bloch have called on cities to provide shaded spaces as a human right.[16] These are provocations that are also opportunities to connect disability perspectives and knowledge about the physical effects of solarization within cities and ex-urban areas.

In addition to rethinking the often univocal, illuminated, and sun-filled character of a modern space, the perspective of impairment and disability provides an opportunity to revisit ideas about health and comfort constructed within the interiors of buildings. One of the things that interests me about this topic is that in my own experiences and conversations with other disabled people, I find that we experience and modify temperature in ways out of alignment with the presumptions projected into buildings. I experience this myself because of the way wearing artificial limbs eliminates certain techniques of thermal regulation experienced by most people through their legs and arms. As mentioned, most people lose heat through their limbs, and if one is missing a limb and/or it is encased in prosthetics, one loses this extra capacity to generate coolth.[17] Temperature transformations alone cannot always cool me, but the movement of air around my prosthesis adequately removes the buildup of heat around my encased residual limb. If I experience too much warmth when in a room, I often stand and start moving quickly to cool down—an almost opposite response to how many other people become cooler. I have spent time speaking with people with Parkinson's, with Lou Gehrig's, or who use wheelchairs and have similar experiences or apologize for sweating in rooms with the thermostat set to a cold temperature. Our experiences of temperature are outside the norms around which many spaces are engineered.

My response to these realities as both an architect and a disabled person involves rethinking the larger ways environment is built into spaces. I believe this not only aids disabled people in finding a place within an otherwise indifferent architectural concept of environment; it also provides a lens on how we might rethink the experience of environment in architecture. As the example of Kurt Goldstein and those he influenced demonstrated (examined earlier), an environment is something that is debated by those experiencing it. In other words, an environment is not just a given set of circumstances but something simultaneously reacted against and produced by people in response to given conditions. These ideas upend several things: the determinist argument that an environment is something that "acts" on an "organism," the assumptions that we all react in an identical way to some environmental stimuli, and the acculturated idea that an environment is simply a benign background that can be ignored. I believe Goldstein's and others' concepts provide a pathway to dispense with the grip of the environmental idea often built into spaces and buildings—whether mechanical, bioclimatic, or more radically environmentalist.

A disability perspective suggests that health and comfort are less parameters of a space itself than they are processes achieved by people within a space. A concept of architectural space in which environment is contingent and provisional in this manner disconnects the interior character of a building from the burden of completely managing heat, coolth, and airflow—but as a positive feature. This provocative idea contrasts with the ideas of those environmentalist architects who argue that the structure of a building—its inherent physical and spatial character—must emerge as a response to problems of heat, cooling, and ventilation. As Michelle Addington suggests, we might atomize and distribute the tools that provide comfort. But furthermore, we might atomize and vary such tools in ways that enable people to discover an environment for themselves. Rather than a building's interior providing a single response to a climate or creating a particular physiological environment—imagined as one approach, device, or concept delivering one thing and in equal measure—one imagines any number of things that may (or may not) provide health and comfort. I see this approach as *disabling* environment by both bringing the perspectives of disabled people into dialogue with how buildings' environments are designed and literally turning off (as in "disabling") the controls and features that determine the character of heating, cooling, and ventilation in many spaces. Ultimately, the lens of disability enables us to question the manner in which environmental parameters become the totalizing character of a space that is experienced by collectives of people. A more provisional and contingent quality to the concept of comfort and health offers us another democratic sense of shared built space. Like other types of disability politics, we can dismiss the belief that norms and averages should provide the character of an environment within which people are immersed. Yet, unlike more familiar disability politics, rethinking the architectural environment in the long 2020 requires extending beyond a traditional focus on access and accessibility. Disabling environment involves more than accommodation or integration into a preexisting concept of architecture and space. Rather, it involves excavating another, deeper layer through which spaces predetermine the character of human-ness.

NOTES

1. On the development of the comfort zone and this study, see Gail Cooper, *Air-Conditioning America: Engineers and the Controlled Environment, 1900–1960* (Baltimore: Johns Hopkins University Press, 2002); Michelle Murphy, *Sick Building Syndrome and the Problem of Uncertainty: Environmental Politics, Technoscience, and Women Workers* (Durham, N.C.: Duke University Press, 2006), 20–34.

2. Murphy, *Sick Building Syndrome.*

3. Michelle Addington, "Contingent Behaviours," *Architectural Design* 79, no. 3 (2009): 12–17; Addington, "Good-bye, Willis Carrier," in *The Green Braid: Towards an Architecture of Ecology, Economy and Equity,* ed. Rafael Longoria, 160–70 (London: Routledge, 2007).

4. Colleen E. Reid, Marie S. O'Neill, Carina J. Gronlund, Shannon J. Brines, Daniel G. Brown, Ana V. Diez-Roux, and Joel Schwartz, "Mapping Community Determinants of Heat Vulnerability," *Environmental Health Perspectives* 117, no. 11 (2009): 1730–36; Hiroshi Hasegawa, Hitoshi Makino, Koki Fukuhara, Yukio Mikami, Hiroaki Kimura, and Nobuo Adachi, "Thermoregulatory Responses of Lower Limb Amputees during Exercise in a Hot Environment," *Journal of Thermal Biology* 91 (2020): 102609; Eric Klinenberg, *Heat Wave: A Social Autopsy of Disaster in Chicago* (Chicago: University of Chicago Press, 2015).

5. See the work of Emily Thompson, *The Soundscape of Modernity: Architectural Acoustics and the Culture of Listening in America, 1900–1933* (Cambridge, Mass.: MIT Press, 2004); Laurent Stalder, "Air, Light, and Air-Conditioning," *Grey Room* 40, no. 15 (2010): 84–99; Peter Galison and Emily Thompson, eds., *The Architecture of Science* (Cambridge, Mass.: MIT Press, 1999); and Noam Elcott, *Artificial Darkness: An Obscure History of Modern Art and Media* (Chicago: University of Chicago Press, 2016).

6. Anson Rabinbach, *The Human Motor: Energy, Fatigue, and the Origins of Modernity* (Berkeley: University of California Press, 1992).

7. Addington, "Contingent Behaviours"; Addington, "Good-bye"; and Christopher James Tyler and Caroline Sunderland, "Cooling the Neck Region during Exercise in the Heat," *Journal of Athletic Training* 46, no. 1 (2011): 61–68. Also see the work of Kiel Moe, who was a student of Addington: Moe, *Thermally Active Surfaces in Architecture* (New York: Princeton Architectural Press, 2010). I am indebted to Kiel for these references.

8. On the histories of this, see Luis Fernández-Galiano, *Fire and Memory: On Architecture and Energy* (Cambridge, Mass.: MIT Press, 2000); Margaret Campbell, "What Tuberculosis Did for Modernism: The Influence of a Curative Environment on Modernist Design and Architecture," *Medical History* 49, no. 4 (2005): 463–88; Beatriz Colomina, *X-Ray Architecture* (Zurich: Lars Müller, 2019); Philippe Rahm, "Histoire de l'Architecture," PhD diss. (Université Paris-Saclay, 2019); and Daniel A. Barber, *Modern Architecture and Climate: Design before Air Conditioning* (Princeton, N.J.: Princeton University Press, 2020).

9. François Loyer and Hélène Guéné, *Henri Sauvage: Les immeubles a gradins* (Paris: Mardaga, 1987).

10. This type of thinking is based in the work of Ellsworth Huntington, a geographer who argued for an idealized isotherm through which civilization flourishes and who is quoted in the beginning of Victor Olgyay, *Design with Climate: Bioclimatic Approach to Architectural Regionalism* (Princeton, N.J.: Princeton University Press, 2015), 14.

11. Jun'ichirō Tanizaki, *In Praise of Shadows* (New York: Random House, 2001); Hassan Fathy, *Architecture for the Poor: An Experiment in Rural Egypt* (Chicago: University of Chicago Press, 2010) [the original title of Fathy's book was "Architecture for People"]; and Fathy, *Natural Energy and Vernacular Architecture: Principles and Examples with Reference to Hot Arid Climates* (New York: United Nations University Press, 1986).

12. David Gissen, "Thermopolis: Conceptualizing Environmental Technologies in the Urban Sphere," *Journal of Architectural Education* 60, no. 1 (2006): 43–53; Gissen, *Manhattan Atmospheres: Architecture, the Interior Environment, and Urban Crisis* (Minneapolis: University of Minnesota Press, 2014); Stephen Graham, "Life Support: The Political Ecology of Urban Air," *City* 19, no. 2–3 (2015): 192–215; Eva Horn, "Air Conditioning: A Cultural History of Climate Control," YouTube video, 1:25:46, https://www.youtube.com/watch?v=TQ3ckQtP-IU; Daniel Barber, "After Comfort," *Log* 47 (2019): 45–50; Barber, *Modern Architecture and Climate*; D. Asher Ghertner, "Postcolonial Atmospheres: Air's Coloniality and the Climate of Enclosure," *Annals of the American Association of Geographers* 111, no. 5 (2020): 1483–1502.

13. This includes the "glass ban" proposed by Mayor William de Blasio in New York City and the Hitze project initiated in Vienna by the Academy of Fine Arts in Vienna in consultation with Vienna's Department of Planning.

14. See Nik Heynen, Harold A. Perkins, and Parama Roy, "The Political Ecology of Uneven Urban Green Space: The Impact of Political Economy on Race and Ethnicity in Producing Environmental Inequality in Milwaukee," *Urban Affairs Review* 42, no. 1 (2006): 3–25; Chris Servidio, "Urban Tree Distribution Reveals Neighborhood Inequalities within Cities, Including Houston," Kinder Urban Institute, Rice University, February 2019, https://kinder.rice.edu/; Sam Bloch, "Shade," *Places Journal*, April 2019; Tim Arango, "'Turn Off the Sunshine': Why Shade Is a Mark of Privilege in Los Angeles," *New York Times*, December 1, 2019; Rebecca M. Bratspies, "Seeing New York City's Urban Canopy as a Commons: A View from the Street," in *The Cambridge Handbook of Commons Research Innovation*, ed. Chrystie Swiney and Sheila Foster (Cambridge: Cambridge University Press, 2020); David Gissen, "The Dark Day Returns," *Art in America* 108, no. 5 (2020): 34–39.

15. See the work of Carol Willis on the 1911 zoning ordinance in New York, "'Zoning and Zeitgeist': The Skyscraper City in the 1920s," *Journal of the Society of Architectural Historians* 45, no. 1 (1986): 47–59, and Willis, *Form Follows Finance* (New York: Princeton Architecture Press, 1995).

16. Bloch, "Shade"; Heynen et al., "Political Ecology of Uneven Urban Green Space."

17. See, e.g., Hasegawa et al., "Thermoregulatory Responses of Lower Limb Amputees"; G. K. Klute, G. I. Rowe, A. V. Mamishev, and W. R. Ledoux, "The Thermal Conductivity of Prosthetic Sockets and Liners," *Prosthetics and Orthotics International* 31, no. 3 (2007): 292–99.

12 Ventilation in the Long 2020; or, Open the Window!

DANIEL A. BARBER

VENTILATION

Many underlying social patterns have been revealed and intensified by the long 2020. Alongside dramatic health inequities, ballooning wealth gaps, and systemic racism sits the seemingly more quotidian problem of mechanical ventilation. In the United States, and especially in urban areas, we have become reliant on fossil fuel–fed heating, ventilation, and air conditioning (HVAC) systems, not only for comfort but for the viability of life in interior spaces. Life in our conditioned interiors was even more precious over the last year-plus as the pandemic forced most people around the world, as possible, to spend even more time at home. As schools, universities, and workplaces started to open up, reinhabitation of the spaces fled in March 2020 brought with it heightened attention to the ventilated conditions of the spaces in which we live and work.

While ventilation and conditioning have, of course, long been the concern of building scientists, the pandemic brought these issues into public discourse. Zeynep Tufekci, writing in *The Atlantic* at the end of July 2020, carefully explained the debate around the aerosol nature of viral spread in "We Need to Talk about Ventilation." Transmission of Covid-19, Tufekci explains, is due to the small, aerosol nature of the viral particles. The virus moves through the air like an invisible mist. Interior spaces, in other words, are more threatening than we had previously understood them to be. This aerosol mist can carry enough virus to infect someone when breathed in and can often be suspended far past the six feet of distance that has become a collective mantra. The characteristics of air in interior spaces, already the subject of much analysis for optimizing HVAC systems and optimizing work conditions, took on a new layer of public health resonance. Induced movement of air, mechanical or otherwise, can mitigate or exacerbate the risks of collective life in interior space.

Tufekci's central concern was the return to school. She was, in effect, describing a classroom when detailing the dangers of "super-spreader events." As she wrote, "the super-spreader–event triad seems to rely on three V's: venue, ventilation, and vocalization. Most super-spreader events occur at an indoor venue, especially a poorly ventilated one (meaning air is not being exchanged, diluted, or filtered), where lots of people are talking, chanting, or singing."[1] She expanded this model in an interview on NPR, emphasizing a dastardly characteristic of the virus emphasized by later variants: that in the majority of cases and scenarios, the virus is relatively noncontagious, so it is easy to let down one's guard (or mask). However, some cases (and now we know, some variants) are very infectious, and when such a case emerges under the right conditions (the three Vs), consequent spread can be catastrophic—super-spreader events leading to numerous infections, which then inevitably lead to more infections, and on. Feeling like we are in control, and then not being at all, is how this disease propagates.

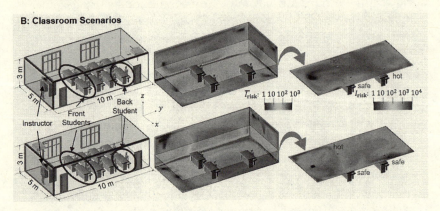

FIGURE 12.1. Suo Yang, classroom scenarios, 2020. Reprinted from Siyao Shao, Dezhi Zhou, et al., "Risk Assessment of Airborne Transmissions of Covid-19 by Asymptomatic Individuals under Different Practical Settings," *Journal of Aerosol Science* 151 (2021): 105661–105661, with permission from Elsevier. Courtesy Suo Yang, Richard and Barbara Nelson Professor in the Department of Mechanical Engineering, University of Minnesota.

As a result of these aerosol dynamics, schools and other institutions began to replace their HVAC filters and, even more frequently, increase the amount of air intake. The American Society of Heating, Refrigerating, and Air-Conditioning Engineers (ASHRAE), the regulatory body that assess HVAC efficiency and promotes comfort standards, encouraged a 100 percent increase in air intake. This was, and is, problematic. Simply turning up mechanical HVAC systems that are left in an unadjusted, pre-pandemic state can cause problems as well as solutions. A study by Jiarong Hong and Suo Wang of the University of Minnesota found that the precise placement of air-conditioning units or ventilation registers is essential to minimizing rather than increasing spread. Left unadjusted, forced-air devices can produce "circulations zones called vortexes, and the aerosols keep rotating in this vortex . . . they are basically trapped." This is not good. Hong and Wang's research shows that the well-intentioned turning up of ventilation units often leads to unwanted results: only 10 percent of the particles are vented out; the rest stay either suspended or attached to surfaces. "Ten percent," the researchers note, "is really a small number."[2] To be clear, mechanical HVAC *can* help diffuse or ventilate out the aerosol particles, but units may have to be rearranged or otherwise targeted to do so. Without careful study, they risk making the problem worse. This further complicates the terms and inputs in the analysis of thermal interiors. As with so many things in our pandemic world, the issues and terms have changed, and citizens and regulatory bodies need to adjust standards and expectations accordingly.

AIR CONDITIONING

These viral vicissitudes of our dependence on machines for ventilation bring up a longer history of our collective reliance on air conditioning. Such a reliance was not inevitable. Over the last seventy years or so, the building industry settled into a cultural and mechanical infrastructure that made air conditioning a necessary fact of contemporary life. A huge carbon budget, as a result, is quite literally *built in* to our buildings and ways of life. This situation is more extreme in the United States but is relevant to cities and suburbs around the world. Air conditioning developed alongside the rise of the curtain-walled skyscraper and the spread of the suburban mansion after World War II; it lies beneath the debates of architectural theory and styles of the last few decades; it presumes and supports the more general imperative toward increasing economic growth.

Air conditioning, and HVAC systems more generally, is intensely carbon dependent. The sealed office tower or mid-rise luxury apartment building, the great room in the suburban manse—a mechanical system for heating, cooling, and ventilation is necessary to make these spaces livable, viable; it provides air to breathe and manages the humidity so materials and systems run smoothly. Of course, our reliance on air conditioning goes far beyond its role in producing comfortable interiors—health systems, industrial supply chains, archives, and museums, much of contemporary life is dependent on the consistency of temperature and humidity that HVAC provides.[3]

In many cases, for example, in hotels, where HVAC costs are carefully optimized, the building envelope is constructed such that the windows don't even open. Contemporary building practices tend toward materials that depend, to varying extents, on a small range of acceptable humidity and temperature variation—without a robust HVAC system, mold or decay would render such spaces unlivable.[4] For a few years before 2020, I taught a course on the history and theory of architecture and climate in a windowless basement room in the University of Pennsylvania's Meyerson Hall; students' first assignment was to analyze the mechanical systems that made our very presence there possible. (Over the long 2020, we made a schematic analysis of the relative hydrocarbon cost of Zoom compared to that basement room. Mostly, students determined that such modeling exercises depend on where one draws the boundaries: Do we take into account the cost of students flying to Philadelphia for the year? Of the coffee purchased in the café versus made at home?)

HVAC systems are powered by mechanical plants that usually draw directly from electrical or gas feeds into the building, and as such, they connect the most distant house or an office in a city center to the penetrating, globalized regime of fossil fuel extraction, processing, and delivery. It is not only the case that this fossil fuel regime is rooted in labor exploitation, devastation of ecosystems, and profit-motivated corporate control; it is also a primary source of carbon emissions. Operational energy in buildings accounts for at least 40 percent of the U.S. carbon budget—a number that increases markedly when taking embodied energy, or car-dependent development patterns, into account. When we, here in the relatively placid United States, turn on the "air-co," we are increasing inequities around the world; we are supporting corporate dominance over millions of lives and livelihoods; we are encouraging further exploitation and environmental degradation—all in addition to the accumulating carbon in the atmosphere. This embedded, infrastructural condition of collective reliance on carbon has led, as Graeme MacDonald puts it, to "acculturation to its hierarchy of material (and, increasingly, immaterial) forms and the manner in which [fossil fuels] dictate fundamental aspects of social life and organization."[5]

Even before the virus, air in interiors was, however slowly and abstractly, killing us, or at least, it was compromising opportunity and equity in the name of optimization and endless economic growth, sacrificing the future prospects of the many for the corporate profits of the few. And yet, to paraphrase whomever Fredric Jameson was paraphrasing, it is easier to imagine the end of the world than the end of air conditioning. Comfort has come to define the parameters of a collective sense of civilization, or aspiration for it. Last summer, stuck inside the northwestern Philadelphia house I shared with my family, in the midst of an ongoing heat wave—maybe not a wave, just near one hundred degrees Fahrenheit (thirty-eight degrees Celsius) every day for weeks—we decided, out of pandemic boredom, not to place our one in-window unit into its summer position. We sweated, complained; we sprayed ourselves with a hose. I struggled to come to terms with a stark reduction of scholarly productivity and to accept the lethargy and discomfort of my teenage children. The pandemic exacerbated this constant discomfort. Occasional rain provided some relief, as we adjusted our patterns and expectations around the intensity of the heat and humidity. Our lives without air conditioning required different rhythms and priorities, different expectations and different values.

A seemingly inexorable global reliance on air conditioning, in other words, on the East Coast and in the South of the United States most intensely, has developed alongside other hallmarks of late capitalism, perhaps especially the persistent pursuit of economic growth, productivity, the optimization of interiors as spaces of work and domesticity—both in production and in the reproduction of the conditions of production. The ironies, if that's what they are, are difficult to avoid: we refuse to compromise on productivity and economic expansion even though we, or our children, and grandchildren, will be, most certainly, devastated by the atmospheric conditions that we are locking in through our daily practices (thereby threatening the productivity, economic expansion, and prospects for self-realization of current and future generations). There is a direct if nonetheless abstract and invisible relationship between the thermal conditions of our built *interiors* and the climatic disruptions of our collective *exterior* conditions; by refusing to let go of comfort *inside,* we are making the world less comfortable *outside.*

Without air conditioning, there would be no skyscrapers as we know them; the sealed curtain wall is just the most visible of a range of design and construction parameters that rely on fossil fuel. Mechanical conditioning systems undergird the design of the built environment. I've demonstrated elsewhere evidence for the tightly entangled development of air conditioning and modern architecture.[6] The skyscraper was seen, especially in the period of economic acceleration right after World War II, as salutary in part because it was a good way to use up the increased energy availability after the industrial war effort was stalled.[7] All the postwar stylistic debates around modernism and postmodernism, perhaps it goes without saying, rest on an assumed foundation of air conditioning; it is the invisible center of architectural avant-gardism—the mechanical plant, hidden in the basement or screened on the roof, that makes programmatic or formalist experimentation possible. At the same time, ASHRAE and other regulatory bodies have set out a field of preconditions with which architects and engineers continue to cooperate—our fossil-fueled thermal interiors are generally not seen as a realm for design experimentation but rather one that requires engineering expertise to best conform to normative guidelines. So-called sustainable architecture, furthermore, simply conforms to these guidelines using more energy-efficient means. The guidelines themselves, conceptually or in detail, are not questioned.[8] Even today, amid increasingly frightening augurs of climate doom, HVAC is assumed by most architects; such interrogations are not a major aspect of professional or student projects in most parts of the world.

Even more striking is the relative one-sidedness of this equation. Designers, engineers, and the building industry provide specific fossil-fueled thermal conditions (speaking generally) on the assumption of a passive resident or user. That is, the normative model is for no demands to be placed on how the building is used, the daily habits and thermal practices—opening a window, a blanket while sitting on the couch, warmer clothes on colder days—that could be encouraged or even designed in. Such considerations could reduce, however slightly, the carbon dioxide emissions of the HVAC system, while also soliciting a broader cultural response, in habits and practices, in affective experience and aesthetic values, that attend to climate instability, or better, an aesthetic or experiential value that takes into account the relative impact of comfort and pleasure today on the possibility of species continuity. Today, even now as the contagion wanes amid the spread of the vaccine, everyday conditioning and ventilation are even more vital, the key to returning to normal and allowing economic activity to continue.

A reconsideration of these buildings, here in the long 2020, invokes one of the more powerful documents from the early days of the global lockdown, when Arundhati Roy insisted, perhaps, initially, counterintuitively, that "the pandemic is a portal, a gateway between one world and the next." Her emphasis was on the inequities that the health crisis and government responses were sharply revealing—a reliance on "essential" laborers, underpaid and at risk; systemic inequities in health care and localized toxicity that placed people of color at higher chance of contracting the virus, in part because of homes and workplaces that were exceptions to a sealed, carbonized interior; the basic reality that those with higher incomes could sit safely sealed in their houses while others were, in effect, forced to work in delivery and service jobs to provide for the formers' well-being. "In the midst of this terrible despair," Roy wrote, the pandemic nonetheless "offers us a chance to rethink the doomsday machine that we have built for ourselves."[9] Again, she wasn't thinking, it seems, about buildings per se, yet the sealed and hardened infrastructure of our built environment, inexorably reliant on fossil fuels, reflects this premise; the sealed skyscraper is at least one model of the doomsday machine that needs rethinking. Buildings today are, in effect, forms of processing hydrocarbon, one of the more prominent cultural means by which we manage, mediate, and render cultural a cycle of resource extraction and distribution, from oil in the ground to carbon dioxide in the atmosphere. They are one of the more prominent cultural sites on these terms: where hydrocarbons enter into aesthetic consideration. These buildings—sealed energetic behemoths, carbon conveyors—are the doomsday machines of the built environment with which we find ourselves, not exactly the one we need. While not the portal that Roy is pointing us toward, perhaps their reconsideration offers a window, a way out that we are trying to squeeze through.[10]

OPEN AIR

Our reliance on mechanical air conditioning was not inevitable. The history of architecture is replete with techniques, styles, materials, and processes that form a building in response to its climatic surround—rather than as a sealed, isolated, conditioned monolith, dependent on hydrocarbon fuels. One can hope that the period for architecture and its theories to be elaborated without attention to carbon dioxide emissions and air conditioning, only really begun in the 1950s, has now passed. It was a relatively short period of unsustainable hydrocarbon intensity during which a specific kind of building practice was facilitated by petroleum-soaked global economic expansion.

Architectural modernism, in this context of climatic management, initially developed through a simultaneous delegitimization and mechanization of preexisting climate-integrative practices. As modern design strategies first developed in a period *without* air conditioning, they developed out of a range of customary technosocial activities and building practices that had, for centuries, adapted social habits to climatic patterns—screens and roof overhangs to block the sun; thick walls of thermally active materials to manage daily temperature shifts. They did so, however, by materially adapting them to so-called (hydrocarbon intensive) modern materials, and conceptually by claiming these strategies as modern. The shading screen became the dynamic brise-soleil, now determined through scientific analysis of the sun's path rather than through tacit knowledge of climatic patterns. Many building scientists and historic preservationists are today returning to these "premodern" practices to assess their viability for contemporary ways of life and, in many cases, to propose novel integrations of such customary means with more recent technologically driven optimizations.

Yet, amid these historical loops and felicitous returns, other practices in the modern period, contemporaneous to the development of air conditioning, focused on how the integration of architectural devices and systems, on one hand, with the potentials embedded in cultural and social dynamism, on the other, could develop an architecture that was both modern and climatically sensitive, technologically driven and attendant to place. Such histories can illuminate cultural pathways to a future, less reliant on air conditioning and the hydrocarbon fuels it demands.

One example is especially potent in the context of today's concerns around the aerosol movement of the Covid-19 virus and the *retour a la normal*: the interior environment of schools. In the 1940s, the Austro-American architect Richard Neutra designed schools and community centers for the U.S. territory of Puerto Rico. Few were built, in large part because the governor, Rexford Tugwell, installed by Harry Truman, faced dwindling power amid an eventual move to governors of Puerto Rican descent.

If not, as will be seen, soaked in petroleum, Neutra's approach was nonetheless emblematic of a colonialist, paternalist approach, evidencing a sort of third layer of coloniality on top of both settler-colonial legacies and the status of the island as a protectorate, without rights of self-determination. On one hand, Neutra saw in the project an opportunity to develop a design method that took into account energy independence, mitigation of climate extremes through design, a sort of operational approach to architectural modernism that sought to manage the population and the landscape. On the other hand, in his 1947 book *An Architecture of Social Concern for Regions of Mild Climate,* Neutra referred to the work as a "planetary test": an attempt to configure the design project as a scaleable approach to territorial occupation—eventually, here, with schools, community centers, hospitals, housing, and other buildings, all self-reliant in terms of cooling and climate management without energy infrastructure, and without substantive input from the communities affected.[11] For Neutra, in the context of an architectural modernism deeply entangled with colonial and endo-colonial ambitions, Puerto Rico was an opportunity to extend the architect's purview beyond the metropolis and to experiment with a new set of skills and

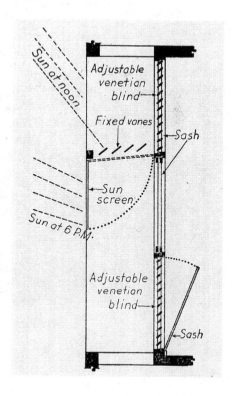

FIGURE 12.2. M.M.M. Roberto, section of the façade of the Edifício Mamãe, Rio de Janeiro, Brazil, 1945. From *Progressive Architecture,* Nov. 1947. Courtesy of the Núcleo de Pesquisa e Documentação, Faculdade de Arquitetura e Urbanismo, Univesidade Federal do Rio de Janeiro. This sectional drawing shows the many different ways the façade could be manipulated to adjust for seasonal and diurnal solar and climatic patterns.

parameters more than it was a thoughtful approach to the autonomous development of the region, also being theorized in this period.[12]

Open-air schools had been an arena for research in northern European modernism in the 1920s and 1930s, appreciated according to theories that valued fresh air as a salutary health benefit in the context of tuberculosis and the flu pandemic, theories that now inform a general reliance on increased mechanical ventilation.[13] Neutra's schools deployed a hinge *wall*, not just a window. The entire wall opens to the yard. This allows the classroom to merge with the atmospheric conditions of the exterior—for the *inside* to be *outside* in terms of air quality and air change—while the remaining three walls protect from some transmission of sound and direct sunlight. The classrooms were arranged in a J-configuration, each with a yard open to others and with lunchrooms at the intersection. The Puerto Rico open schools allowed for fresh air to be a constant part of the school day, in a rural setting and a generally comfortable climate.

FIGURE 12.3. Richard Neutra, school outside San Juan, Puerto Rico, with Rexford Tugwell (left), 1944. Courtesy of Dion Neutra, Architect © and Richard and Dion Neutra Papers, Department of Special Collections, Charles E. Young Research Library, UCLA.

Neutra developed a design formula he referred to as the "continuous subsoffit airchange over lowered spandrel" (CSSA/LS), which attempted to extract from the specifics of Puerto Rico a more general design formula. By inserting an air space between the ceiling and the roof, for which he coined the multilingual term *ventopenings,* breezes could enter deep into the room. As this adapted structural frame was continuous through the building, the breezes could continuously move air through the rooms and corridors. This was offered as a simple and straightforward adjustment to normative building practices at a time, we should note, when such formulas and interventions were still a regular part of modernist architectural discourse. CSSA/LS is a sort of media architecture of the building envelope, framing that envelope—the facade, the roof—as a site for climatic innovation, for the production of comfort, for the facilitation of social adaptability. It is at the opposite end of the spectrum from the sealed, curtain-walled, conditioned office tower; while perhaps just as entangled in geopolitical and global economic frameworks of development and financialization, it suggests a completely different reference point for architectural innovation and the vicissitudes of economic growth, relative in particular to the relationship between hydrocarbon fuels and interior air.[14]

Relatively few locations, in the end, can support an open-walled classroom. The importance of Neutra's experiments is in the demonstration of a nascent technique—an architectural, nonmechanical means of climatic mitigation—intended to be elaborated upon. With the CSSA/LS drawing, Neutra proposed a general approach, a design method prevalent in the period surrounding World War II, before air conditioning was mechanically or economically viable, by which the design and construction techniques for a given building on a given site were informed by an assessment of seasonal and diurnal conditions of the climate. The building was seen as a device to maximize health and well-being. *Design* framed the project of *building* as that of producing a device of climatic adaptability, a mediating system that correlated social needs and desires to the vagaries of the atmospheric surround.

For many architects of the period—again, before a typological orthodoxy of air conditioning more or less took over—this was the promise of modern architecture: a capacity to assess site and infrastructural conditions and to develop techniques and practices according to climatic analyses, focused on a comfortable life in the interior. Just a few years after Neutra's Puerto

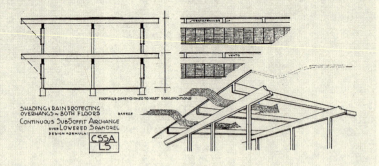

centros de saude urbanos
detalhes da estrutura & do teto

urban health centers
structural design

ventopenings
aberturas para ventilação

shading & rain protection overhangs in both floors
saliencias protetoras contra sol & chuva em ambos os andares

footings dimensioned to meet soil conditions
alicerces adaptados às condições do terreno

$$\frac{CSSA}{LS} = \begin{array}{c} \text{continuous sub-soffit airchange} \\ \text{over} \\ \text{lowered spandrel} \end{array}$$

ventilação contínua entre teto & a viga-mestra abaixada

FIGURE 12.4. Richard Neutra, "continuous subsoffit airchange over lowered spandrel," from *An Architecture of Social Concern for Regions of Mild Climate* (São Paulo: Gerth Todtmann, 1947). Courtesy of Dion Neutra, Architect © and Richard and Dion Neutra Papers, Department of Special Collections, Charles E. Young Research Library, UCLA.

Rico experiments, and with his express encouragement, the Hungarian émigré architects Victor and Aladar Olgyay began to codify methods for designing with climate. Their well-developed techniques may appear naive in the context of more recent computer-driven modeling and simulation software, yet they were innovative in their time.[15]

For example, Aladar Olgyay in 1957 referred to a skyscraper facade as "an environmental filter." Thinking here primarily of light and heat, he encouraged architects and their clients to assess facade and HVAC systems in tandem, that is, to consider the cost of the sealed facade in the context of the mechanical system it necessitated, on the assumption that, given those variables, a shaded, dynamic, bioclimatic facade would provide seasonal cooling and thereby significant economic savings.[16] The Olgyays' experiments with climatic analyses, and with the graphic representation of the same, pushed the logic of the shaded, dynamic facade toward a methodologic approach concerned with the details of the micro-climatic and their possible application. This precomputational, nonmechanical, ventilated, interactive thermal interior was intended to produce a space of climatic adaptability rather than an engineered state of carbon-fueled consistency.

This same space of climate mediation—the "comfort zone" as the Olgyays called it—with aspects of energy and physiological optimization is the target of performance metrics and HVAC efficiencies today. A building's performance, in contemporary parlance, reflects the relative fuel-efficient means by which it can achieve standards of thermal comfort. Those standards remain more or less constant, as contemporary architects experiment with specific solar panels or geothermal heat, multipaned (insulated) curtain walls, attention to the thermal properties of materials, methods of induced ventilation, and other techniques.

Yet here we encounter another seemingly intractable obstacle in the forms and systems by which climatic knowledge is applied in architecture. Performance optimization today tends toward finding means to meet comfort standards with less fossil fuel throughput, while still operating within a hydrocarbon-based design method. Some of these endeavors imagine new ways of living, in new kinds of open, ventilated environments, though this is not the norm. The Passivhaus movement, as one prominent example, is predicated on a fully sealed system, maximized and optimized for health and energy efficiency. The "green building" template is too often just a scaled-down, less energy-intensive version of the sealed curtain wall in the office tower, more attuned to its efficiency potentials.

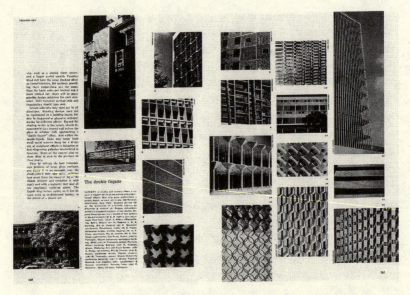

FIGURE 12.5. Aladar Olgyay, "Thermal Economics of Curtain Walls," *Architectural Forum*, Oct. 1957. Reproduced with permission.

OPENINGS

Neutra's examples don't necessarily offer applied solutions to the need today to reopen schools safely. Instead, by presenting one of many alternative technical strategies, they place in relief our collective acceptance of the sealed interior as the model for contemporary social life. And yet, our computation-assisted knowledge of climate patterns and architectural possibilities in the present so far exceeds the devices and methods of the 1940s and 1950s so that we can only reel at the possibilities of a now computationally sophisticated discussion of nonmechanical means of heating and cooling—one that has, in fact, been going on for decades. We have a surfeit of technosocial knowledge to introduce, explore, and render comfortable a building without reliance on hydrocarbon fuels. We don't lack technological knowledge; we lack the cultural aspirations and economic arrangements that could open up to nonmechanical systems and the new ways of life they induce.

In the face of the aerosol nature of the coronavirus, we can expect that carbon emissions of buildings will increase: last August, schools were noting the intensification of their conditioning and ventilation systems, the more frequent changing of filters, and the ascension to higher MERV filtration ratings in demonstrating the safety of reopening. As noted earlier, regulatory agencies recommended a 100 percent increase in air intake, thereby doubling the volume of air that needs to be heated and cooled in any given moment, dramatically increasing the hydrocarbon throughput.[17] The given in this formula is that the built environment has no conceptual or mechanical infrastructure to manage airflow otherwise; in too many cases and climates—in too many schools—this is no doubt the case. They were not built to manage seasonal opening toward the exterior; in other cases, the condition of the air outside is not amenable to unfiltered intake.

As we were stuck inside, isolating ourselves to decrease the vectors of viral transmission, minimizing contact, our built world intensified its reliance on the hard barrier of the building facade. The potential of the facade as "environmental filter" is both an obvious solution to our ventilation challenges and seemingly impossible to enact at a scale that matters, relative to this complication of viral spread and carbon dioxide emissions and given the HVAC reliance built in to our environment. These are not problems

FIGURE 12.6. Ahu Aydogan showing some of the plant matter she experiments with to develop a method of using plant-based systems (rather than increased air intake) to maintain healthy interior conditions. Reproduced with permission.

with easy solutions—increased, targeted ventilation will save lives over the next few months, even as it further ossifies an infrastructural and cultural path dependency that was beginning, just barely, to open toward other conditioning options. It would be difficult to calculate the cost, in health or morbidity, of those lives or lungs saved today by increased mechanical ventilation relative to the lives and livelihoods soon to be compromised or destroyed by the warming climate, rising seas, and other impacts of carbon emissions. Yet these costs exist. In mitigating one public health crisis—the Covid-19 pandemic—we exacerbate another: climate instability. The challenge, in the end, is to push forward on both fronts, managing near-term needs of minimizing viral spread while also recognizing that novel and creative approaches to life in the built interior are increasingly necessary.

The hydrocarbon-fueled conditions of the thermal interior, then, and, to return to Roy, the doomsday machines that have been producing it for the past few decades, are not inevitable modes for attaining comfort. The built environment allows for a plethora of thermal experiences, which open up to different socioclimatic relationships, which have different resonances across and around both design methods and user habits. The thermal interior is a space of politics, of contestation, mitigated by the controls of the air conditioners or the relative insulative capacity of the sealed facade. It is also a space of creative elaboration, for reimagining in the ongoing long 2020 how we might live in interior spaces, without, or with less, reliance on hydrocarbon.

Such creative opportunities might not be "a portal . . . between one world and the next," yet they operate, suggestively, on the terms of porosity: a screen, a window, a chimney, a subsoffit spandrel; louvers, levers, hinges; multiple modes of opening and closing, producing a variety of conditions according to need and desire, according to the vagaries of the climate, adaptable to different regions and cultures. A gateway, then, to build out, build up, a sense of comfort, of thermal comfort, that also takes into account carbon dioxide emissions; a poetics of comfort or, at the limit, an aesthetics that considers not only pleasure, desire, and affect but also how those experiences are inflected by knowledge of the possible continuity of the species. If not a portal, then, at least an opportunity to open a window.

NOTES

This essay is developed out of a series of posts, including a virtual roundtable, on the *Platform* venue for online discussion about architecture and urbanism. Thanks to Marta Gutman, editor of *Platform,* and my fellow discussants Dorit Aviv and Ahu Aydogan for their insights and instigations.

1. Zeynep Tufekci, "We Need to Talk about Ventilation," *The Atlantic*, July 30, 2020, https://www.theatlantic.com/health/archive/2020/07/why-arent-we-talking-more-about-airborne-transmission/614737/.

2. University of Minnesota Research Brief, "New Study Explores How Coronavirus Travels Indoors," July 28, 2020, https://twin-cities.umn.edu/news-events/new-study-explores-how-coronavirus-travels-indoors.

3. On this point, see, e.g., Michael Osman, *Modernism's Visible Hand: Architecture and Regulation in America* (Minneapolis: University of Minnesota Press, 2018); Mal Ahern's recent research on air conditioning and conservation in modern art also illuminates essential aspects of its extension into lives and values.

4. Alan Weisman, *The World without Us* (New York: Picador, 2008), 18.

5. Graeme MacDonald, "Research Note: The Resources of Fiction," *Reviews in Cultural Theory* 4, no. 2 (2013): 10.

6. Aspects of this discussion are drawn from Daniel A. Barber, *Modern Architecture and Climate: Design before Air Conditioning* (Princeton, N.J.: Princeton University Press, 2020).

7. See Daniel A. Barber, "Emergency Exit," *e-flux architecture* (blog), September 2019, https://www.e-flux.com/architecture/overgrowth/284030/emergency-exit/.

8. Susan Roaf, "A Disturbing Reason So Few Buildings Have Windows That Open," *Fast Company*, August 12, 2020, https://www.fastcompany.com/90538499/a-disturbing-reason-so-few-buildings-have-windows-that-open.

9. Arundhati Roy, "The Pandemic Is a Portal," *Financial Times*, April 3, 2020.

10. See also Daniel A. Barber, "Doors and Portals, Revisited," *Architecture Theory Review* 24, no. 2 (2020): 192–97.

11. Richard Neutra, "Regionalism in Architecture," *Plus* 2 (February 1939); see also Richard Neutra, "Planetary Reconstruction," *Journal of the American Institute of Architects* 3, no. 1 (1945): 29–33.

12. Leopold Kohr, *Inner City: Mud to Marble* (Talbont, Wales: Y Lolfa, 1989).

13. Beatriz Colomina, *X-Ray Architecture* (Zürich: Lars Müller, 2019), and see also Colomina's chapter in this volume; Paul Overy, *Light, Air, and Openness: Modern Architecture between the Wars* (London: Thames and Hudson, 2008).

14. See Richard Neutra, *An Architecture of Social Concern for Regions of Mild Climate* (São Paulo: Gerth Todtmann, 1948).

15. Victor Olgyay, *Design with Climate: Bioclimatic Approach to Architectural Regionalism* (Princeton, N.J.: Princeton University Press, 2015), and Aladar and Victor Olgyay, *Solar Control and Shading Devices* (New York: Reinhold, 1957).

16. Aladar Olgyay, "Thermal Economics of Curtain Walls," *Architectural Forum* 106, no. 10 (1957): 154–64.

17. Dorit Aviv, "No Longer an Object: Thermodynamics and New Dimensions of Architectural Design," presented at the 107th ACSA annual meeting, Black Box Proceedings, Pittsburgh, Penn., 2019.

13 Particle Stories

Breathing in the Long 2020

JENNIFER GABRYS

Circulating and recirculating in the atmospheres of 2020 were the residues of viruses and aerosols, air pollution and wildfires, as well as the debris of burning cities and tear gas. Yet these atmospheres also had rare moments of pause from the rain of particles and haze of fumes when cities and transport ground to a halt during pandemic-induced lockdowns. Satellite maps showed marked differences in pollution levels before and after lockdown.[1] Clouds and plumes of nitrogen oxides and particulate matter that usually consumed breathable air space in cities from Beijing to Milan dissipated. Here breathing became a different project and practice, one that registered the tumultuous and transformative events of the long 2020 in the passing of carbon and microbes, toxins and irritants, and their momentary suspension.

How might it be possible to sample this material archive in-the-making to sift through the sediments that are now passing through lungs, bodies, environments, and jet streams? What practices of breathability settle in and attempt to work through these particles? Breathing is not simply a moment of drawing air in and out. It is also an accumulation that informs and changes bodies and environments. It is a process that inherits atmospheric sedimentations and, through exchange, changes them. In this sense, breath is an articulation of duration. Breath centers and excavates the present. It anticipates the next breath to come. But it also contends with highly differential conditions of breathing as they draw together bodies and environments over time. Breath then connects to atmospheres and environments, to crisis and upheaval, to injustice and struggles for breathability.[2]

In this chapter, I consider different ways of breathing in the long 2020 through three particle stories that sift from the debris of this moment: an airborne virus, particulate matter, and wildfire smoke. I craft these particle stories against the backdrop of a nearly decade-long research project, Citizen Sense, that I have been leading.[3] With this work, our research group has investigated how citizens sense air pollution, document particulate matter levels, and, in doing so, work toward more breathable worlds. We have focused on sensing and documenting particulate matter because this is an especially hazardous pollutant and also because it is often less extensively monitored within regulatory monitoring networks. In the context of this research, I consider what potentially surfaces in the circulation and detection of particles. These three stories grapple with the transformative charge of particles that materializes in the relational and world-making exchanges of breath.

PARTICLE 1: AIRBORNE VIRUS (0.125 MICRONS)

The first particle to sift out from these particle stories is the airborne virus, SARS-CoV-2. This microscopic virus particle is only an eighth of one micron (0.125) in size, or seven hundred times smaller than a grain of sand. Similar to all particles that are five microns or smaller in size, this spiky particle can remain airborne for indefinite periods of time in most indoor environments, settling on surfaces and lodging in the respiratory tracts of humans and other mammals. Any particle smaller than ten microns can be inhaled, and so a particle as small as the coronavirus is easily respirable.[4]

Because they are airborne, coronavirus particles are primarily transmitted through vectors of air. They intensify in indoor spaces where particle concentrations increase to deliver a more potent charge. As a virus that attacks respiratory systems, one of the primary Covid-19 symptoms is a shortness of breath and cough. X-ray scans of Covid-19 patients' lungs show a glassy confusion tearing through organs that would filter air and sustain bodies.[5] This viral particle decimates the pathways and processes for exchanging air, breathing, and being in proximity with other bodies.

But these particles do not descend as some cosmic dust transported from another planet. Instead, they are a register of exchanges with environments that are undergoing catastrophic change. With altered land use, warming climates, and shifting habitats, some organisms and microbes are able to proliferate and create new patterns of infection and disease.[6] Breathing is not merely a process of atomized bodies inhaling and exhaling abstract if infectious volumes of air but rather is a lived material and environmental process. This process involves exchanges across plants, animals, microbes, chemicals, and ecosystems that make breathing possible. The likely movement of viral particles across environments, organisms, humans, travel ways, and circuits of commerce is a further indication of how these exchanges generate relations that sustain or constrain breathability.

Just as it has transformed ways of life, Covid-19 has also brought into stark relief patterns of social and economic inequality and environmental destruction that have reached breaking points. Covid-19 has had an outsize impact on Black and brown people, frontline workers, and people living in conditions of economic inequality and deprivation. Published in the spring of 2020, the first obituaries and photos of health workers in the United Kingdom killed by Covid-19 documented this undeniable fact—that many of the people suffering the severest effects from these viral particles were already enduring the interminable stress of inequality.[7] They were not able to breathe in yet another sense, of being able to extend themselves within and through worlds of equity, justice, and livability. The particles that circulated and caused a pandemic in 2020, then, had a longer duration, both in the accumulation of inequality that led to greater vulnerability to Covid-19 and in the enduring residue of illness and lost lives.

PARTICLE 2: PARTICULATE MATTER (1–10 MICRONS)

Particles in the form of ash from burning buildings drifted from the skies of Minneapolis and other cities across the United States. This drift of particles and debris was fallout from the murder of George Floyd by police officers who violently extracted this Black man's breath, but who also had already been extracting his breath for even longer. His plea, "I can't breathe," cut through and defined the long 2020 in yet another way. "I can't breathe" is the same plea enunciated by Eric Garner in 2014, who was also placed in a fatal chokehold by New York City police officers. His words became a recurring phrase and demand throughout the Black Lives Matter movement and protests that have sought an end to the suffocation of so many Black, brown, and poor people. These words raise the question of how it might be possible to breathe and to make more breathable worlds.

As ash and particles rained down from the skies of cities on fire during summer 2020, they carried this charge. Tear gas and pepper spray also filled the air at protests against Floyd's murder. Sprays of particles became a measure of containment against people disputing ongoing conditions of inequality.[8] Thickening and acrid urban atmospheres were a register of the unbreathability of racial, economic, and social inequality. They were also a displacement and reminder of the ongoing conditions of racial, social, economic, and environmental injustice that contribute to the toxic and polluted atmospheres typically experienced by people living in low-income communities, a connection that Lindsay Dillon and Julie Sze investigate in their study of particulate matter and the "mutual constitution of urban environments, social difference, and embodiment—including health outcomes and forms of violence."[9] A rain of particles from burning cities across the United States relocated and surfaced what had been ignored, overlooked, and allowed to continue as impossible and unbreathable conditions in the long 2020.

Particulate matter, usually within the range of particles that are one to ten microns in size, suspended and settled as one register of these conditions of inequality and injustice. As one of the most hazardous forms of pollution, particulate matter is typically at least eight to eighty times larger than the size of SARS-CoV-2 particles but is still able to pass into bodies and lungs, as well as other organs and the bloodstream. In London, as 2020 drew to a close, an inquest concluded that air pollution exposure could for the first time be registered as an official cause of death (along with acute respiratory failure and severe asthma).[10] The landmark case for this ruling was for a nine-year-old Black girl, Ella Kissi-Debrah, who died in Southeast London in February 2013. Her mother, Rosamund Kissi-Debrah, fought for years to draw attention to the impact of air pollution on health.[11] Ella and her family lived on one of the busiest roads in London, nearby to which citizen monitoring had in various places found particulate matter levels at six times the World Health Organization guideline for a twenty-four-hour period.[12] In the second successful inquest, the coroner established that Ella's death certificate could record air pollution as one cause of death.[13] With this ruling, environmental pollution and injustice surface as events that wear away at health and livelihoods but that are also called out and acknowledged so as to work toward other relations across bodies and environments.

Air pollution in the form of particulate matter, as well as nitrogen oxides and ozone, among other pollutants, kills nearly nine million people worldwide.[14] In cities around the world, people have their breath cut short by air pollution, environmental injustice, and inequality, both through everyday attempts to live with polluted air and through the eventual effects of accumulated pollution. Breath and breathable worlds, as shown through these

sedimented particles, again connect here to the lived environments that
contribute to and undergird these inequalities. The inability to breathe
extends to conditions of social inequality and confinement, environmental
injustice and pollution, and relentless pursuits for justice that have erupted
within and continue beyond the long 2020.

PARTICLE 3: WILDFIRE SMOKE (0.4–0.7 MICRONS)

At the same time that viruses, aerosols, particulate matter, tear gas, and
ash drifted through the airways of 2020, a blaze of wildfires converted forests and suburbs into a heady mix of debris, microbes, toxicants, and dust.
Fires made more frequent and intense from climate change engulfed countries around the world, with blood-red skies engulfing cities on the West
Coast of the United States; a vast swath of Australia; and parts of India, the
Canary Islands, China, Ukraine, Poland, Scotland, Cyprus, Greece, Turkey,
the Amazon, the Pantanal wetlands in Brazil, Spain, Algeria, Israel, Lebanon,
and Syria.[15]

Citizen-sensing devices around the world registered the elevated levels
of pollution from these fires.[16] Such pollution could further exacerbate
breathing difficulties for people with preexisting conditions, while leading
to new damage to respiratory health. These sensors would have likely registered pollution in the form of particulate matter within the 1–10 micron
range, but wildfire smoke also circulates as smaller particles between 0.4
and 0.7 microns, along with microbes, including fungi and bacteria, that
can contribute to further illness.[17] Much of what was in the air from wildfire smoke would not register on these digital devices but would nevertheless accumulate in bodies and lungs, soil and air, forming layers of debris
of varying toxicity.

At the same time, in the Australian bushfires alone, nearly three billion
animals were displaced or killed, as charred landscapes and wildfire smoke
created unbreathable conditions not only for humans but for a staggering
number of more-than-humans. Here climate change had a literally incin-
erating effect on environments and organisms. Shifts in land use, fire suppression, and warming climates contributed to ongoing fire cycles that
intensified in 2020 but that had erupted in previous years and will continue for many years to come in what Adriana Petryna refers to as a "pecu-
liar exercise of time reckoning with certain aspects of the global climate
system."[18] The airsheds that humans share with each other and multiple
other organisms are filled with these particles as ongoing, accumulative,

and transformative conditions of exchange and breathability that are marked by urgency and crisis.

CONCLUSION

Many more particles could be assembled here, from microplastics to microbes, sulfur aerosols to lead. It is as though environments and bodies are disintegrating and transforming within the social-political and material demands of living in the long 2020. Breathing practices across bodies and environments carve the routes in and through which these material accumulations and transformations unfold, as materials are exchanged across spans of time from the instant to centuries.

Instead of all that is solid melting into air, could one instead follow the vectors of these three particles to suggest that all that is airborne settles into breath? Or even more, that all that is airborne transforms the conditions for breathable worlds? This is a way of thinking and materializing breath environmentally. The mutual constitution of bodies and environments forms as a breathability of worlds.[19]

Such breathability could be a site of constriction and collapse—or it could anticipate possibilities for more just and livable worlds.[20] These particle stories work through the inherited and accumulated conditions of breathing, the differential hazards of these exchanges, and the possibilities for searching toward more breathable worlds within and beyond the long 2020.

NOTES

1. For a related discussion of air pollution and Covid-19, see Jennifer Gabrys, "Air Pollution," Index of Evidence, https://www.indexofevidence.org/air-pollution.

2. This chapter draws on a longer discussion of struggles for breathability developed in my book *Citizens of Worlds: Open-Air Toolkits for Environmental Struggle* (Minneapolis: University of Minnesota Press, 2022).

3. See Citizen Sense, https://citizensense.net/. Citizen Sense began in 2013 through funding received from the European Research Council (grants 313347 and 779921).

4. Kevin P. Fennelly, "Particle Sizes of Infectious Aerosols: Implications for Infection Control," *The Lancet: Respiratory Medicine* 8, no. 9 (2020): 919–24. As Fennelly writes, "infectious aerosols are suspensions of pathogens in particles in the air, subject to both physical and biological laws. Particle size is the most important determinant of aerosol behaviour. Particles that are 5 μm or smaller in size can remain airborne indefinitely under most indoor conditions unless there is removal due to air currents or dilution ventilation. This same size range of particles (ie, <5 μm) deposits

in the lower respiratory tract in humans as well as in guinea pigs, mice, and monkeys. Particles sized 6–12 μm deposit in the upper airways of the head and neck" (914).

5. In her discussion of transcorporeality, Stacy Alaimo draws attention to yet another particle in the form of silica mining and the silicosis that ravaged Black American miners in 1930s West Virginia, which Murlie Rukeyser describes in her book of poems, *The Book of the Dead* (Morgantown: West Virginia University Press, 2018). The X-rays that documented the snowstorm of particle-induced inflammation in the lungs of miners have stark parallels with X-rays of Covid-19's effects on lungs. See Alaimo, *Bodily Natures: Science, Environment, and the Material Self* (Bloomington: Indiana University Press, 2010).

6. Andrew P. Dobson, Stuart L. Pimm, Lee Hannah, Les Kaufman, Jorge A. Ahumada, Amy W. Ando, Aaron Bernstein, et al., "Ecology and Economics for Pandemic Prevention," *Science* 369, no. 6502 (2020): 379–81.

7. Sarah Marsh, "Doctors, Nurses, Porters, Volunteers: The UK Health Workers Who Have Died from COVID-19," *The Guardian*, May 22, 2020, https://www.theguardian.com/world/2020/apr/16/doctors-nurses-porters-volunteers-the-uk-health-workers-who-have-died-from-covid-19. See also Doctors in Unite, "Black and Asian Deaths from COVID-19 Are Due to Poverty and Racism, Not Genetics, Vitamin D or Lifestyle," https://doctorsinunite.com/race-and-health/black-and-asian-deaths-from-covid-19-are-due-to-poverty-and-racism-not-genetics-vitamin-d-or-lifestyle.

8. For a related discussion of "spray" that addresses crop dusting with insecticides and fungicides for maintaining banana plantations in Martinique, see Vanessa Agard-Jones, "Spray," *Somatosphere*, May 27, 2014, http://somatosphere.net/2014/spray.html. Here lack of control over particles that circulate from aerial spraying techniques becomes a way in which vulnerabilities across bodies and environments are experienced.

9. Lindsey Dillon and Julie Sze, "Police Power and Particulate Matters: Environmental Justice and the Spatialities of In/Securities in US Cities," *English Language Notes* 54, no. 2 (2016): 13–23.

10. Sandra Laville, "Air Pollution a Cause in Girl's Death, Coroner Rules, in Landmark Case," *The Guardian*, December 16, 2020, https://www.theguardian.com/environment/2020/dec/16/girls-death-contributed-to-by-air-pollution-coroner-rules-in-landmark-case.

11. See the Ella Roberta Family Foundation, http://ellaroberta.org/.

12. See Jennifer Gabrys, "Planetary Health in Practice: Sensing Air Pollution and Transforming Urban Environments," *Humanities and Social Sciences Communications* 7, no. 35 (2020), https://doi.org/10.1057/s41599-020-00534-7.

13. Blackstone Chambers, "Inquest into the Death of Ella Adoo-Kissi-Debrah," December 17, 2020, https://www.blackstonechambers.com/news/inquest-death-ella-adoo-kissi-debrah/.

14. This figure is for indoor and outdoor air pollution and is drawn from research that estimates annual deaths from air pollution to be approximately 8.8 million people worldwide. See Jos Lelieveld, Klaus Klingmüller, Andrea Pozzer, Ulrich Pöschl, Mohammed Fnais, Andreas Daiber, and Thomas Münzel, "Cardiovascular Disease

Burden from Ambient Air Pollution in Europe Reassessed Using Novel Hazard Ratio Functions," *European Heart Journal* 40, no. 20 (2019): 1590–96.

15. For example, see Veronica Penney, "It's Not Just the West. These Places Are Also on Fire," *New York Times,* September 16, 2020, https://www.nytimes.com/2020/09/16/climate/wildfires-globally.html.

16. Purple Air and IQ Air are examples of two lower-cost air-quality monitoring devices that also include maps and apps for displaying pollution levels and providing alerts. See https://purpleair.com/ and https://www.iqair.com/. For a related discussion, see Jennifer Gabrys, "Sensing a Planet in Crisis," *Media+Environment* 1, no. 1 (2019), https://mediaenviron.org/article/10036-sensing-a-planet-in-crisis.

17. Joseph Serna, "Wildfire Smoke May Carry 'Mind-Bending' Amounts of Fungi and Bacteria, Scientists Say," *Los Angeles Times,* February 1, 2021, https://www.latimes.com/california/story/2021-02-01/wildfire-smoke-microbes-in-the-air; Leda N. Kobziar and George R. Thompson III, "Wildfire Smoke, a Potential Infectious Agent," *Science* 370, no. 6523 (2020): 1408–10.

18. Adriana Petryna, "Wildfires at the Edges of Science: Horizoning Work amid Runaway Change," *Cultural Anthropology* 33, no. 4 (2018): 570–95.

19. See Gabrys, *Citizens of Worlds.*

20. On this connection between breathability and political possibility, see Alexis Pauline Gumbs, "That Transformative Dark Thing," *New Inquiry,* May 19, 2015, https://thenewinquiry.com/that-transformative-dark-thing/.

14 Air's Inversions

DEHLIA HANNAH

As the doors of society begin to creak open once again as the coronavirus pandemic abates, we encounter one another with a transformed—indeed, traumatized—awareness of *who* and *what* circulate through national borders, transportation infrastructure, architectural spaces, air vents, and locks. Ours is now an explicitly more-than-human society, in which our relations to other beings are registered on our half-covered faces, which declare recognition of the omnipresence of this *Other*—and, implicitly, of a panoply of *others* and their various modes of existence. The notion that we are surrounded and permeated by beings that transcend the foundational categories of modern society—subject and object, living and inert, active and passive—has been well argued in theory, which abounds with accounts of the agency of things, the vibrancy of matter, and the multispecies nature of human identity, informed to no small extent by our microbiomes. Yet what the present pandemic has revealed is the extent to which the contemporary world has been built in denial of these insights. Finally, a single being emerges from the havoc wreaked on ecosystems and the frenzy of capital circulation that is capable of taking advantage of the global ecological niche that we have constructed. One way of understanding the roots of this catastrophic vulnerability is by attending to transformations in concepts of the medium through which this being becomes a global citizen: *air*. In doing so, we can trace the convergence of two great catastrophes of the long 2020—the Covid-19 pandemic and anthropogenic climate change—and entangled hopes for their remediation.[1]

In 2020, the act of breathing became newly fraught. Whereas air has long been imagined as a transparent background condition for human affairs, any question of air's invisibility was put to rest by the necessity of preventing an airborne virus from being shared. Masks, ventilation, and various forms of personal protective equipment expressed an acute awareness of how far particulates and droplets of moisture are transported through "empty" space—*open air* now measured precisely by distances between breathers. A two-meter cushion of air became the most basic demand of interpersonal etiquette, an ongoing choreography of avoidance that signaled care for oneself and others. Quite suddenly, each microcosm became a quantum of a shared state of affairs encompassing the whole world. Borders were closed. Flights were grounded. Air became conspicuous as the fluid medium of all social relations, in which each person's presence radiates outward in spherical waves like a stone dropped into water.

A certain violence attends air's burst into the foreground of attention. In a sense, this pandemic recapitulates a traumatic moment that Peter Sloterdijk dates to a century earlier, to the advent of poison gas warfare during World War I, specifically to its deployment on the battlefields of Ypres on April 22, 1915, where it burned the lungs of soldiers in an overwhelming attack on the habitability of their environment.[2] Thus began a century of what he terms the "explication" of air, in which air pollution, communication, and travel, the militarization and commodification of air space, indoor air conditioning, and climate change emerged as urgent matters of concern. Amid a contagious coughing fit, the Covid-19 pandemic returns us to the immediate issue of air's breathability. Yet, although it is not the first airborne pandemic, nor necessarily the worst threat to the earth's atmosphere, its dependence upon uniquely twenty-first-century global systems calls into question the condition of air in entirely new ways.

As the air between us grew thick and foreboding in the early months of 2020, the skies above cleared, a consequence of an unprecedented drop in transportation and fuel combustion. Spectacular photographs of the Himalayan mountain range towering above cities across northern India—a sight unseen for an entire generation—captivated the world. As wildlife roamed urban landscapes, blue skies appeared over typically smog-choked cities from Paris to Jakarta, allowing residents to glimpse an alternative atmospheric reality.[3] Anxious awareness of the dangers carried by bodily emissions was juxtaposed with previously unimaginable reductions in air pollution. Beyond the visible spectrum, clear skies correlated with equally impressive reductions in invisible pollutants, such as carbon dioxide, nitrogen dioxide, ozone, and methane, which are key drivers of climate change.

In the midst of a global health, economic, and humanitarian crisis, a brief moment of euphoric hope flashed across the airwaves—hope that the climate crisis would finally be attended by a response on the scale of that addressing the pandemic. This hope was not merely that the pandemic response itself would limit CO_2 emissions enough to put a dent in the warming trend, a hope quickly dashed; rather, it was imagined that the experience of rapid mobilization in the face of a shared danger would promote a will to address anthropogenic climate warming like the acute emergency that it is. Bruno Latour compared the pandemic to a dress rehearsal for the climate crisis.[4] "Essentially COVID-19 is the story of anthropogenic global warming on speed," observed an anonymous commenter on the climate science news site RealClimate.org.[5] Comparisons were drawn to the temporary dip in emissions associated with the 2008 financial crisis, only to rebound the following year. Could the present situation, asked the philosopher Eva Horn, offer "an experimental space in which to test out how things might be done differently—proof that it is possible after all to limit travel and transportation, to reorganize work and communication . . . reduce the consumption of fossil fuels, [and] even present an opportunity to reinvent international cooperation in the face of a global threat?"[6] These insights carried a mix of exasperation and relief: *We told you (pointing to charts and appealing to reason)! Now you can see for yourself!*

Why did the pandemic become such a captivating analogy for climate change?

Watching the skies carefully offers visual clues. Thermal inversions in the atmosphere are often visible as a dense layer of hazy air, above which the sky appears clear and bright. Normally, air cools as it rises, driving processes of atmospheric convection, wind and weather patterns. Inversion layers occur when cooler air becomes stuck below warmer air at higher altitude, trapping moisture and particulate matter, as well as ongoing emissions, nearer to the earth's surface. A phenomenon responsible for misty valleys and urban smog islands alike, *inversion* is also suggestive as a new meteorological metaphor. The rapid spread of an airborne virus, via interpersonal contact and international travel, has led to profound transformations not only in the material conditions but also in the discursive terms of air—terms that set the stage for discussions of climate change, pollution, and other airy matters by establishing the parameters of what we notice, care for publicly, and take as actionable. Tracing recent virally induced inversions within the concepts of air, climate, atmosphere, and related terms hints at a postpandemic cultural landscape shaped by different assumptions. Perhaps these changes will also result in different appetites for risk, cooperation, and abrupt transition.

In contrast to slow and invisible greenhouse effects, the sudden assault of Covid-19 on our shared air space fundamentally altered attention to atmospheric conditions in a way that climate change activists could only dream of. Truly global in scope yet local in its effects, the pandemic overcomes the problem of scale that has bedeviled the comprehension of global climate change, the concept of global climate itself a statistical abstraction. Known only indirectly through climate models, statistics, and scenarios, climate change opens up a rift between the temporality of embodied experience and the intensively mediated time of global trends and model projections, what Robert Markley calls "climatological time."[7] Although its effects are increasingly obvious and dramatic today, as temperature records are shattered and wildfires sweep across the Arctic, the comparatively *longue durée* of climate change strains our habits of imagination—more accustomed to cyclical regularities punctuated by dramatic events than gradual yet catastrophic changes. This holds open space for denial. The greenhouse effect was identified in the mid-nineteenth century, when shockingly prescient predictions were made about the global impact of carbon dioxide emissions produced by industrial combustion.[8] The space for denial has been purposefully exploited since the early 1960s, when scientists hired by fossil fuel companies like ExxonMobil and Imperial Oil offered the first compelling scenarios of climate change. Instead of making these findings public, they were suppressed in favor of marketing campaigns aimed at sowing doubt about the validity of scientific research in general—the impact of which extends well beyond climate science.[9] In the American context, the demographics of Covid denialism directly tracks that of climate change, as do the rationales for not taking either problem seriously: from "it's a hoax" to "it's not as bad as they say." Nonetheless, the pervasiveness of the virus and the immediacy of its impact on individual health undermine the plausibility of these arguments far more quickly than the mounting evidence of the reality and severity of climate change—however overwhelming that mountain is.

Bodily vulnerability, though unevenly borne, condensed the time frame of risk from an expansive and indeterminate future into the minutiae of daily life, rending attention to air a constant concern. The so-called *attribution problem*: solved. There is no doubt that the symptoms of Covid-19 are caused by the virus itself—as there is about whether any given storm or wildfire is caused, or merely made more likely, by rising CO_2 levels (and as there was about whether HIV causes AIDS). In the face of a global pandemic that erupted in a matter of months, the slow violence of the Anthropocene (cf. Nixon)[10] tumbles down like an avalanche under the cumulative weight of ignored warnings and predictions: about wildlife habitat loss, industrial farming, air pollution, warming temperatures, disrupted phenological rhythms, frenetic air travel and shipping, high population density, fragile health care systems, and numerous other factors that foster the emergence of new infectious diseases and at the same time render us increasingly vulnerable to them. Even with the safe assumption that the virus mutated from another species with which there was close contact, rather than "escaping" from an infectious disease laboratory, the pandemic is clearly the furthest thing from a natural disaster. As Horn argued, it is the ongoing catastrophe of business as usual that is constitutive of the Anthropocene, which here gives way to a "tipping point"—an *event* that demands immediate action.[11] In this way, Covid-19 inverts the discourses of air to impose radical behavioral changes in how and what air is allowed to circulate through bodies and spaces.

Indeed, what makes the present pandemic so explosive is that, as much as our fleshy bodies, our heavy metallic infrastructure is vulnerable to the effects of the virus. Covid-19 found an incomparably fertile ecological niche in the global technosphere. Stowed away on airplanes and cruise ships, *this virus is one of infrastructure.* To slow its transmission, it has been necessary to shut down large parts of that infrastructure, even at the cost of untold economic hardship and human suffering. To be fine-meshed enough to control the movements of a microscopic entity, a life-form known for just over a century (since 1892), the lockdown necessarily catches people up in its net.

It should come as no surprise, then, that within this social context conspiracy theories and disbelief have proliferated wildly, appealing, in no small part, to circles of society already steeped in manufactured doubt about climate change. Refusing masks and social distance, these fellows insist on breathing together in a cloud of contagion—a literal return to the root of the word conspiracy *(conspirare).* In a certain way, they see the implications of the pandemic clearly: to concede that Covid-19 is serious is to concede that the emergency measures taken by governments are (in principle, if not in particular) justified. To concede the reality of climate change would imply, by the same logic, that drastic changes to social and economic organization are warranted. Indeed, this is precisely what many activists and scientists are calling for to avert a climate catastrophe that now seems imminent. One only hopes that, with the benefit of a half century of foresight on climate change, a Climate Lockdown might be accomplished with somewhat less blunt instruments than the ones on display in 2020—a year in which economies crashed and authoritarian trends were ascendant worldwide.[12]

The pandemic and its aftermaths can be framed as a massive unplanned experiment on numerous aspects of earth systems—a chance to study how the atmosphere behaves and ecosystems respond when humans retreat.[13] At the same time, social scientists may observe how cultures, political structures, and economies fare under the present *state of exception* (cf. Giorgio Agamben).[14] On the climate change front, 2020 saw a drop in global CO_2 emissions of an estimated 6.4 percent, yet the "United Nations Environment Programme estimates that the world would need to cut carbon emissions by 7.6 percent *per year* for the next decade to prevent the globe from warming more than 1.5 °C above pre-industrial levels—a goal set in the 2015 Paris climate agreement."[15] This is an opportunity to take seriously the radical questions, *What if we don't turn the engines back on? What would it look like to sustain such a low-emissions scenario for a decade—or longer? How might we embrace dramatic transformations of social life compatible with radical reductions in emissions?*

Returning to the matter of conceptual inversions, according to the philosopher Luce Irigaray, the *forgetting of air* within a philosophical tradition preoccupied with *groundwork* constitutes a forgetting of embodiment, a luxury not historically afforded to women.[16] Irigaray's *The Forgetting of Air in Martin Heidegger* contests a deep-seated philosophical tendency to take air for granted, in which the philosopher seeks firm ground upon which to erect *his* system. Reason must first breathe before it can think, *she* observes. "Is not air the whole of our habitation as mortals? Is there a dwelling more vast, more spacious, or even more generally peaceful than that of air?"[17] The forgetting of air is a forgetting of thought's inherent corporeality and, implicitly, a repression of bodily differences—and their politics—as elemental to philosophical reflection. Noticing air breathes embodiment into allegedly free-floating ideas. And yet, air does not suddenly become apparent even to the embodied philosopher. For Irigaray, the process of remembering is mediated by vision; "*I opened my eyes and saw the cloud.* And saw that nothing was perceptible unless I was held at a distance from it by an almost palpable density."[18] Air's deceptive transparency is punctured by the sight of a cloud: a *figure* that betrays the thickness of its ground. In this historical moment, our collective coming to awareness of air is not mediated by vision. The long 2020 reminds us that if you are close enough to smell someone's breath, you are close enough to inhale any viral particles they might expel. A cloud envelops each one of us. Even as it remains strictly invisible, Covid-19 has deprived everyone of the luxury of forgetting the air and its connection to embodiment, in effect rectifying a deep elemental bias. If the pandemic inspires hope for the timely remediation of climate change, it is perhaps due to this decisive philosophical inversion of air's meaning.

Even as we long for the freedom to breathe closely once again, we might endeavor to retain the acute memory of breathing within a global atmosphere.

NOTES

A shorter version of this essay was commissioned for a publication that accompanied the art and architecture exhibition *BREATHE—air of our closed world,* curated by Ala Roushan at the Powerplant in Toronto. The essay can be found in Ala Roushan, ed., *BREATHLESS* (Toronto, Ont.: The Power Plant Contemporary Art Gallery, 2021).

1. The title and methodology of this essay are inspired by Tim Choy's "Air's Substantiations," in *Lively Capital: Biotechnologies, Ethics, and Governance in Global Markets,* ed. Kaushik Sunder Rajan, 121–52 (London: Duke University Press, 2012). "By attending to the material practices through which people come to know and politicize the literal atmospheres around us" (121), Choy explains of his study of the material and discursive mediation of air quality in Hong Kong, we come to understand the cultural and political atmospheres through which these material realities are lived. These ways of living and imagining atmospheres of air pollution, airborne pandemic, climate change, and so on have profound implications for the practical responses crafted to address them.

2. Peter Sloterdijk, *Terror from the Air* (Los Angeles, Calif.: Semiotext(e), 2009).

3. See, e.g., Soutik Buswas, "India Coronavirus: Can the Covid-19 Lockdown Spark a Clean Air Movement?," BBC News, April 21, 2020, https://www.bbc.com/news/world-asia-india-52313972.

4. Bruno Latour, "Is This a Dress Rehearsal?," *Critical Inquiry,* March 26, 2020, https://critinq.wordpress.com/2020/03/26/is-this-a-dress-rehearsal/. Originally published in French as "La crise sanitaire incite à se préparer à la mutation climatique," *Le Monde,* March 25, 2020, https://www.lemonde.fr/idees/article/2020/03/25/la-crise-sanitaire-incite-a-se-preparer-a-la-mutation-climatique_6034312_3232.html.

5. Gavin Schmidt, "Coronavirus and Climate," RealClimate, March 20, 2020, http://www.realclimate.org/index.php/archives/2020/03/coronavirus-and-climate/.

6. Eva Horn, "Tipping Points: The Anthropocene and Covid-19," in *Pandemics, Politics, and Society,* ed. Gerard Delanty, 123–38 (Berlin: De Gruyter, 2021).

7. Robert Markley, "Time: Time, History, and Sustainability," in *Telemorphosis: Theory in the Era of Climate Change,* ed. T. Cohen, 43–64 (Ann Arbor, Mich.: Open Humanities Press, 2012).

8. Megan Darby, "Meet the Woman Who First Identified the Greenhouse Effect," *Climate Change News,* February 9, 2016, https://www.climatechangenews.com/2016/09/02/the-woman-who-identified-the-greenhouse-effect-years-before-tyndall/.

9. Naomi Oreskes, *Merchants of Doubt: How a Handful of Scientists Obscured the Truth on Issues from Tobacco Smoke to Global Warming* (New York: Bloomsbury Press, 2011).

10. Rob Nixon, *Slow Violence and the Environmentalism of the Poor* (Cambridge, Mass.: Harvard University Press, 2011).

11. Horn, "Tipping Points," 123.

12. Initiated by the curator and architectural historian Carson Chan, *Climate Lockdown* was offered as a form of "protest-in-place [which] reframes the sheltering in place many of us are doing as a form of protest, of resistance to shortsighted environmental planning while we, as a planetary community, gain resistance to this new coronavirus." See http://www.climatelockdown.com/. The term has also captivated the business sector: "Under a 'climate lockdown,' governments would limit private-vehicle use, ban consumption of red meat, and impose extreme energy-saving measures, while fossil-fuel companies would have to stop drilling. To avoid such a scenario, we must overhaul our economic structures and do capitalism differently." Mariana Mazzucato, "Avoiding a Climate Lockdown," World Business Council for Sustainable Development, October 21, 2020, https://www.wbcsd.org/Overview/Panorama/Articles/Avoiding-a-climate-lockdown.

13. Noah S. Diffenbaugh, Christopher B. Field, Eric A. Appel, Ines L. Azevedo, Dennis D. Baldocchi, Marshall Burke, Jennifer A. Burney, et al., "The COVID-19 Lockdowns: A Window into the Earth System," *Nature Reviews Earth Environment* 1 (2020): 470–81.

14. Giorgio Agamben, *State of Exception* (Chicago: The University of Chicago Press, 2005).

15. Jeff Tollefson, "COVID Curbed Carbon Emissions in 2020—but Not by Much," *Nature* 589, no. 343 (2021).

16. Luce Irigaray, *The Forgetting of Air in Martin Heidegger,* trans. Mary Beth Mader (Austin: University of Texas Press, 1999). For further discussion, see Dehlia Hannah, "The Philosopher against the Clouds," in *Nanna Debois-Buhl—Cloud Behavior* (Milan, Italy: Humboldt Books/Laboratory for Arts and Ecology, 2020).

17. Irigaray, *Forgetting of Air,* 80.

18. Luce Irigaray, *Elemental Passions,* trans. Joanne Collie and Judith Still (New York: Routledge, 1992), 105, emphasis mine.

15 Freedom's Just Another Word . . .

STEFANIE FISHEL

On February 14, 2020, I boarded a plane home after spending the holidays with my family in Oregon. Armed with hand sanitizer and a face mask, I traveled with a heavy sense of resignation that this may be the virus that changes everything. When you study bacteria and viruses, even from a non-science or nonmedical viewpoint, you are aware of the risks that humans face every day at the microscopic level. Dangerous new strains of bacteria resistant to antibiotics from over- and misuse of those antibiotics, ongoing pandemics caused by Ebola and cholera, and, of course, species-jumping zoonotic viruses are some of the most serious and concerning of these risks—AIDS/HIV, H1N1, and previous SARS viruses are cases in point.

Of course, the threat from zoonotic viruses is part of, and overlaps with, other ways in which humanity's destruction, misappropriation, theft, and abuse of the nonhuman natural world and torture and murder of the nonhuman have very real and serious consequences. At a disciplinary and policy level, SARS-CoV-2's appearance as a global actor demonstrates the danger of pushing multiple earth systems to the verge of collapse through human terraforming, unsustainable agricultural processes, urbanization, deforestation, and resource extraction. Disasters, natural and otherwise, are always embedded in a larger story where human injustice and inequity play starring roles. This virus has exacerbated and bared existing inequalities. National and global responses need to reckon with these disparities as much as the medical and public issues.

In addition, as my reflections in this chapter attest, the long 2020 should urge the humanities and social sciences to turn a critical eye to the concepts that found their modern form in the nineteenth and twentieth centuries;

it is essential to link economic and political systems to ecological decline and collapse. As I argued in my book *The Microbial State,* at the theoretical level, a vital reconsideration in the time of Covid-19 is freedom, especially its individualistic and anthropocentric urges. Humans can no longer live in their "tiny skull-sized kingdoms"[1] and expect to survive into the next century. In this chapter, I revisit how my research guided me through this year and what clues it might give for moving forward in a (post-)pandemic world.

SEARCHING FOR WORDS

It has indeed been a long year. In the beginning of the pandemic, I did not contribute to the "hot takes" that came early on. I found myself at a loss for words. In part, it was a fear of overreaching—I am not a virologist or an epidemiologist but a political theorist—but it also felt deeper than just a disciplinary caution about speaking outside of my specialization. My resignation had turned into a twisted set of feelings and affects: fear, dread, exhaustion, worry, nausea, fatigue. I would easily lapse into panic attacks, and it felt impossible to do more than one thing a day. I dreaded and longed for news over social media about family and friends. I quit Facebook and Twitter. Then I reactivated them the next week.

I focused on the security of my team—keeping in touch with family and friends, figuring out how to connect with students in a Zoom room rather than a classroom, and negotiating our shared public spaces with a mask and one and a half meters' distance between myself and others. I dreaded and longed for a hug. While Australia has responded better than some, with our suppression model and strict border control, our collective human experience of this pandemic, and my connections to others elsewhere, had quickly burrowed deep into day-to-day life.

And then, when I did sit down to write, the words for which I reached did not fit what I was experiencing and witnessing, but I also realized that this loss of words was nothing new to me, at least in a disciplinary sense. It felt like a familiar struggle. I started my book *The Microbial State* with this sentence: "International Relations needs a bigger vocabulary."[2] I was quick to add that this doesn't necessarily mean jargon or more specialized language but rather that the intellectual history from which international relations, as a subfield of political science, draws doesn't always see the totality of this complex planet—and not just the seeing of it but the acting in it. This pandemic has only added weight to my original point.

My book took the very small—commensal bacteria in the human gut—
to amplify these tiny creatures and remind the reader how crucial they are
for human health and well-being. The human body is at once a singular
entity and one filled with millions of other beings, living together in sometimes harmonious and sometimes troubled ways. Bacterial communities
aid our bodies in digesting food, controlling immune response, and protecting our skin and mouths from harmful "others." These others are often
ingested and then become "one of us"—making the term *I* a very complex one indeed. The viral and bacterial overlap with the human not only
in terms of danger and risk; they are also filled with wonder, symbiosis,
and care. We need the very small, the bacterium, the virus. Without exposure to these germs, our immune systems are "prone to dysfunction," and
while the germ can cause disease, it is also "part of the body capable of
building new tissue."[3] Eula Biss further points out that the human's adaptive immune system has "borrowed" its essential technology from the virus:
"this technology was viral technology before it was ours."[4]

If we take this complex, lively, and symbiotic system of micro relations
and apply them to our macro systems, how might we understand the body
politic through the flesh and viscera of the human body? This jump took
some imagination and help from an embodied understanding of metaphors and their ability to communicate our bodily understandings to text
and then to politics. It took a few allies in biology, science and technology
studies, and philosophy, but I did this to challenge the metaphor of the
body politic in political theory. I wanted readers to think of politics as
immanent to the biospheric and corporeal rather than the anthropic: we
humans live in many overlapping worlds, human and nonhuman. The politics created from these worlds are involute, composite, often discordant,
but entangled within and supported by the biosphere we share—a biosphere that is quickly becoming unable to support much of the life we see
in it today.[5]

And we are now faced with a different microscopic actor—one that is
certainly not commensal and is even smaller than bacteria—the coronavirus SARS-CoV-2 and the ensuing Covid-19 pandemic. Most likely born
from humankind's disregard for ecosystems and the murder, enslavement,
and trade of nonhuman animals, this turning a deaf ear to the planet only
upped the volume on its response to our violent indifference. As Achille
Mbembe writes in his essay "The Universal Right to Breathe," "we must

answer here and now for our life on Earth with others (including viruses) and our shared fate. Such is the injunction this pathogenic period addresses to humankind."[6] What do we do, more than a year into a pandemic that promises to stretch into another, with what we have experienced and learned?

RETHINKING OUR WORDS

Perhaps a year has given me enough time and space to process what I might think, and write, about SARs-CoV-2. I am certain that my mother, sister, and child receiving their second jabs also helped. Maybe this allowed the words to flow, but I suspect that there is a bigger problem at play: this event has pushed our words and concepts to their limits, and it is not as though we were not struggling before. Sometimes there are no words (lack); there are only the wrong words (translation or experience), or the words bring along too many other things with them. Either words like *wild* and *home* immediately introduce their Other or the speaker must realize that their connection to the word may be different than others' (homes aren't always safe for many of us).

At a conceptual level, Joan Cocks writes that many of our political ideas inherited from the Western tradition are so out of sync with reality that they may as well be only metaphors and, additionally, that they "have helped precipitate many of our current crises in the first place, even as those crises are now undermining the allusive power of those concepts." As I address more at the end of the chapter, rethinking these concepts is at first, as Cocks points out, unthinkable and regrettable, but this "may in fact be an opening to a more promising way of imagining and acting in the world."[7]

Four years before this pandemic, I wrote that freedom is just such a concept, and now the pressing question that has surfaced is, what does—or could—freedom mean in a pandemic? This question took form as I watched the "mask debate" affect the suppression and control of the virus in the United States and elsewhere. This debate over masks and personal liberty in the wake of public health orders is a troubling example of how individual freedom can be a malignancy in the body politic. The individual in this case demands its separateness from all others with personal choice as unrelated to other individuals' interests and safety.

What has become quite clear in this pandemic is that individual freedom must be guided by community needs. As voiced by John Green in his podcast *The Anthropocene Reviewed,* "immunity is not primarily a personal experience but a collective one." We do not care to be personally immune and safe from Covid-19 as much as we desperately desire to hug our loved ones, to eat together, to share our spaces again. We do not desire only to be personally immune but to protect our vulnerable from this disease and its far-reaching health effects, which are only now becoming clearer. To return to Eula Biss's book *On Immunity: An Inoculation,* we need to imagine not only how a vaccine affects a single body but "how it affects the collective body of a community."[8]

Furthermore, it is increasingly clear that it is just as important to recognize that those communities are not only human in composition. In my work, I have argued that attention should rest on collective world-building from something other than the anthropocentric "rational" egoist model that currently pervades our thinking and acting. We must nurture positive attachment and consolidate a belief in the world beyond its use value. This will in turn foster pluralist and generous attachments to a living and non-living earth system where all are dependent on the whole for health and vitality. Not a small ask, of course, but I believe it is one worth fighting for in whatever small way we can. If we all love one thing, to paraphrase Donna Haraway, we can change the world—we live in multiple overlapping worlds that are always in need of attention and love.

Freedom, from both a microbial and an immunological viewpoint, is less about individuality and more about finding connections between human and nonhuman worlds; freedom is about being *more connected,* not cut free from our bonds to others. Our bodies are not inherently disconnected— the health of any one individual is dependent on the health of all others in the community. "We are protected not so much by our own skin, but by what is beyond it. The boundaries between our bodies begin to dissolve here. . . . Those of us who draw on collective immunity owe our health to our neighbors."[9] As Mbembe reminds us, "humankind and biosphere are one. Alone, humanity has no future. Are we capable of rediscovering that each of us belongs to the same species, that we have an indivisible bond with all life?"[10]

Taking these lessons from the pandemic seriously is a way of moving forward through the long 2020. There is no normal to which to return, and this should be a moment to rethink how humans have traveled this dark timeline. We must start anew. We must become something different.

NOTES

1. Stefanie Fishel, *The Microbial State: Global Thriving and the Body Politic* (Minneapolis: University of Minnesota Press, 2017), 69.

2. Fishel, 1.

3. Eula Biss, *On Immunity: An Inoculation* (Minneapolis, Minn.: Graywolf Press, 2014), 17.

4. Biss, 17.

5. Fishel, *Microbial State,* 3.

6. Achille Mbembe, "The Universal Right to Breathe," *Critical Inquiry* 47, no. 52 (2021): 59.

7. Joan Cocks, *On Sovereignty and Other Political Delusions* (London: Bloomsbury Press, 2014), 2.

8. Biss, *On Immunity,* 7.

9. Biss, 6.

10. Mbembe, "Universal Right to Breathe," 62.

16 The Covid Chronicles

The View from the Virus

BERNARD C. PERLEY

What now? This is not a simple question; nor is there a simple answer. We've flipped the calendar on January 1, 2021. Unfortunately, we can neither escape the long shadow of 2020 nor ignore the long histories of structural inequalities leading to the crises of 2020. The co-occurrence of Covid-19 and the tumultuous events leading to and amplifying the social justice movements imbricated with Black Lives Matter, plus the volatile political climate that led to the January 6, 2021, insurrection, bring into focus the entanglement of these social conditions. The slow violence of colonialism, systemic racism, and environmental degradation due to rapacious resource extractive industries became entangled to reveal their mutually reinforcing violence to all citizens of this planet.[1] What now? How do we chronicle the long 2020?

The unfolding of 2020 brought fresh trauma as well as memories of antecedent traumas. As a Native American, I saw ironies in many of the discourses regarding the pandemic. I also saw alliances with the Black Lives Matter movement. I was deeply concerned by the disingenuous political rhetoric that refused to accept the will of the people in the presidential election. How do I make sense of all this and keep my sanity? My strategy was to identify the absurdities so I could highlight and share them with others. I also wanted to provide a visual vocabulary for maximizing interpretive possibilities and aligning multiple reader perspectives. I decided the long 2020 needed some comic relief!

The graphic novella following this introduction is an exploration of how object-oriented ontology might work.[2] The task was to imagine the global pandemic from the point of view of the virus. Everyday discourses from news media to politicians to health experts and citizens across the globe speak in terms that ascribe agency to the virus, as though the virus were a conscious entity with goals in mind. In many respects, it is a form of ventriloquism where humans speak about their fears, uncertainties, and dogged resistance through the virus. "The Covid Chronicles" seeks to decenter the human from the pandemic and imagine pluriverse relations across living entities.[3] The novella begins with a prophecy from Native American writer Leslie Marmon Silko. The excerpt sets a foreboding tone. "The Covid Chronicles" is divided into four sections, which are also composed of four single-page meditations. Finally, the novella concludes with another prophecy, an excerpt from William Butler Yeats's poem "The Second Coming." The organization is intended to tie slow violence, pluriverses, and object-oriented ontology into a mix of satire and irony. Through humor, I offer some small measure of healing.

Prophecy

They will bring terrible diseases
the people have never known.
Entire tribes will die out...*

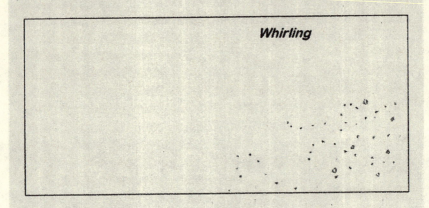

Whirling

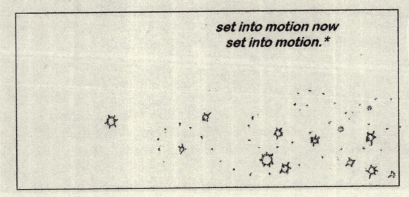

set into motion now
set into motion.*

*Leslie Marmon Silko, *Storyteller*, 1981.

Part 1. Obscure Beginnings

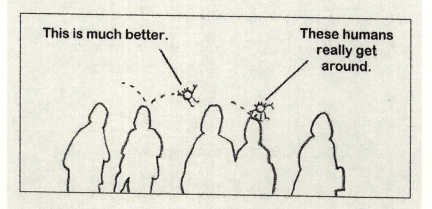

Part 2. American Exceptionalism

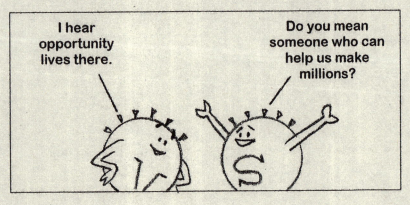

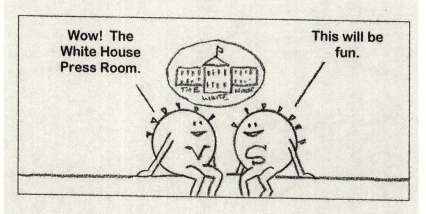

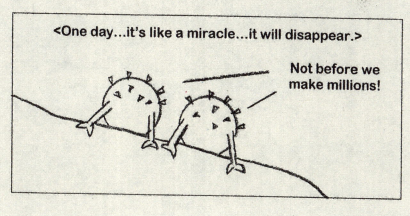

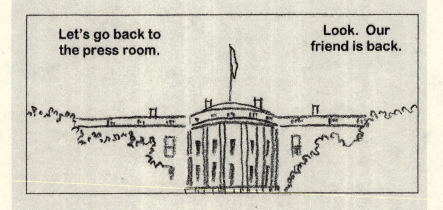

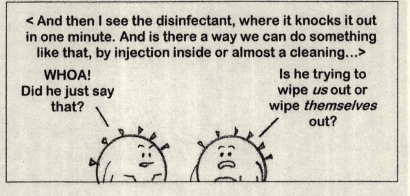

Part 3. Rewriting History

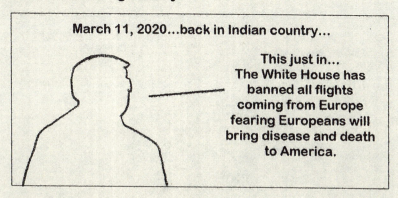

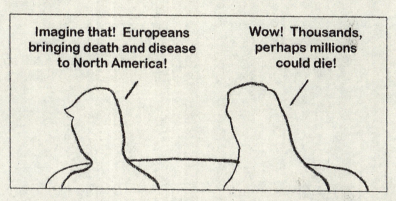

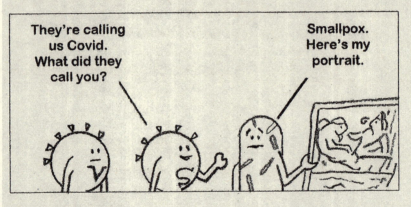
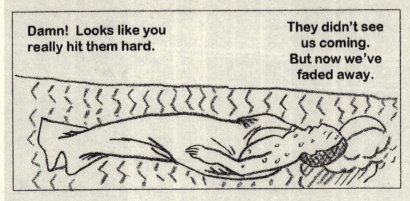

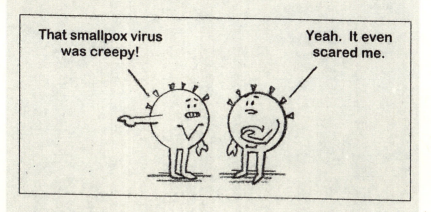

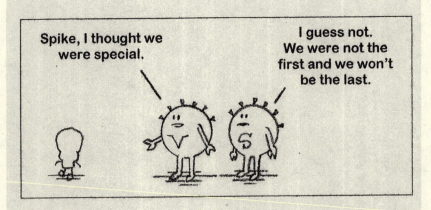

Part 4. Global Domination

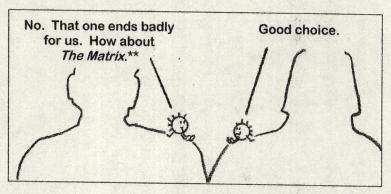

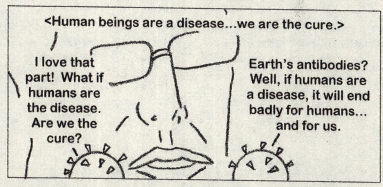

Contagion. 2011. Warner Bros., Participant, Imagenation Abu Dahbi FZ, Double Feature Films, Digital Image associates.

** *The Matrix*. 1999. Warner Bros., Village Roadshow Pictures, Groucho Film Partnership, Silver Pictures, 3 Arts Entertainment.

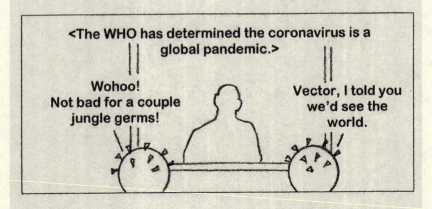

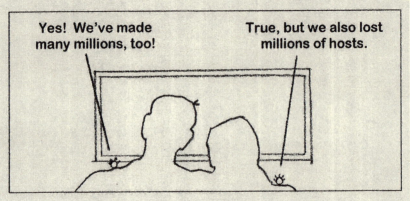

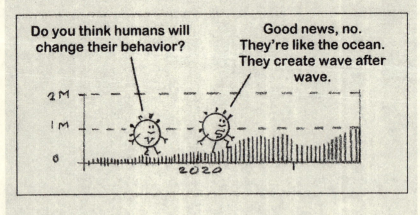

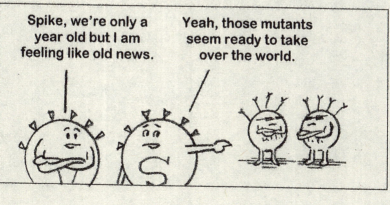

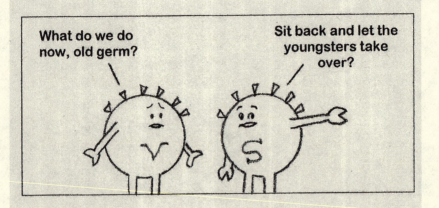

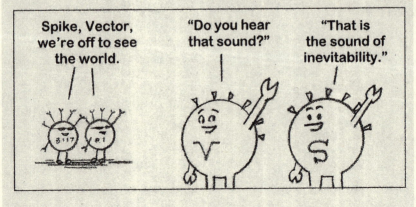

Turning and turning in the widening gyre
The falcon cannot hear the falconer;
Things fall apart; the centre cannot hold.

The darkness drops again; but now I know
That twenty centuries of stony sleep

Were vexed to nightmare by a rocking cradle,

And what rough beast, its hour come round at last,
Slouches towards Bethlehem to be born?*

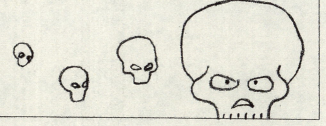

* William Butler Yeats, "Second Coming," in *The Poems of W. B. Yeats*, ed. William York Tindall (Norwalk: The Easton Press, 1976), 108.

NOTES

1. Rob Nixon, *Slow Violence and the Environmentalism of the Poor* (Cambridge, Mass.: Harvard University Press, 2011). Nixon defines slow violence as "a violence that occurs gradually and out of sight, a violence of delayed destruction that is dispersed across time and space, an attritional violence that is typically not viewed at all" (2). The feature that is relevant to this chapter is the "repercussions playing out across a range of temporal scales" (2). The year 2020 was a year in which a multitude of slow violences were manifested in a series of extraordinary upheavals.

2. Timothy Morton, *Hyperobjects: Philosophy and Ecology after the End of the World* (Minneapolis: University of Minnesota Press, 2013). Morton posits a "unique form of realism and nonanthropocentric thinking" (2) that "hyperobjects are real whether or not someone is thinking of them" (2). Apropos to this chapter, Morton argues that hyperobjects end the possibility of transcendental leaps "outside" physical reality. The novel coronavirus is one such hyperobject. It was "in the world" whether or not we were thinking about it. Once its presence was known, all the discourses reflected the myriad thoughts grasping to tame it in our imaginations. The graphic novella attempts to "see" the world from the perspective of the virus.

3. Mario Blaser and Marisol de la Cadena, *In a World of Many Worlds* (Durham, N.C.: Duke University Press, 2018). Blaser and de la Cadena articulate a need to imagine objects in the world as "other-than-human" relations. A "pluriverse," then, is "heterogenous worldings coming together as a political ecology of practices, negotiating their difficult being together in heterogeneity" (4). Instructively, Blaser and de la Cadena are "taking the present as a moment to reconsider the material-semiotic grammar of *the relation* among worlds that dominate the fabrication of the current historical moment" (4). The conceptual stance they offer is "political ontology," whereby "political ontology . . . simultaneously stands for reworking the imaginary of politics (the pluriverse), for a field of study and intervention (the power-charged terrain of entangled worldings and their dynamics), and for a modality of analysis and critique that is permanently concerned with its own effects as a worlding practice" (6). The graphic novella is one such analysis and critique of the long 2020.

17 Viral Agency and Vulnerability

Rethinking Multispecies Entanglements in the Coronavirus Pandemic

EBEN KIRKSEY

Within the space of a few weeks in March 2020, the global systems sustaining human life began to falter. Economic, commercial, social, and cultural activities in all parts of the planet were seriously disrupted by an emergent virus, SARS-CoV-2. Airline fleets were grounded. Carbon emissions were radically reduced. Industrial supply chains struggled to meet the demands for food, medical equipment, even toilet paper. The coronavirus attenuated human agency and action in every nation on earth.

During the long 2020 pandemic, many journalists (and some scientists) conflated the disease (Covid-19) with the viral agent (SARS-CoV-2). Stories about a wet animal market, deep in the Orient, initially grabbed headlines when Chinese researchers first described the emergence of this coronavirus.[1] The media quickly settled on an outbreak narrative that repeated predictable stereotypes that stigmatized particular people, animal populations, locales, and lifestyles.[2] China has long been viewed as a potential pandemic epicenter, as a "natural reservoir" of deadly viruses.[3] It seemed like traditional ecologies, economies, and societies in East Asia once again deserved blame for a disease outbreak.

The very first Covid-19 patients identified in Wuhan never visited the city's now-infamous Hunan Seafood Wholesale Market and had no known contacts with "exotic" animals.[4] A study published by *Nature* reported that no pangolins or bats were actually traded in Wuhan's markets, suggesting that these sites were not "the source of the current coronavirus (COVID-19) pandemic." When experts from the World Health Organization (WHO) visited Wuhan more than a year after initial reports of the outbreak, they further debunked wet market outbreak narratives. An Australian doctor on the WHO mission named Dominic Dwyer reported that the Wuhan seafood market is not the likely source of the outbreak because "none of the animal products sampled after the market's closure tested positive for SARS-CoV-2." Instead, the market was likely the site of a super-spreader event. "When we visited the closed market, it's easy to see how an infection might have spread there," wrote Dwyer. "When it was open, there would have been around 10,000 people visiting a day, in close proximity, with poor ventilation and drainage."[5]

The WHO program manager and mission leader, Peter Ben Embarek, told CNN that the virus was likely widespread in China when it was first detected. "The virus was circulating widely in Wuhan in December, which is a new finding," Embarek said. Because most SARS-CoV-2 infections do not result in severe medical problems, many people could have been asymptomatic carriers. Upward of one thousand people could have harbored the virus in Wuhan in December 2019, even as the severe clinical symptoms of Covid-19 were first being described.[6]

With the Wuhan markets cleared of blame, some insisted that a conspiracy was afoot, that nefarious Asian scientists at the Wuhan Institute of Virology engaged in "gain of function" had released a new super-bug.[7] But careful bioinformatics analysis reveals that there were at least two different strains of SARS-CoV-2 circulating when it was first detected.[8] The genetic evidence suggests that virologists at the Wuhan Institute were heroes who first identified and isolated a novel viral agent of global importance, rather than nefarious villains engaged in a cover-up. The fact that SARS-CoV-2 was first detected in Wuhan may relate to local histories of science— a concentration of world-class coronavirus researchers—rather than the geography of virulent zones.[9] Relatives of the original SARS virus—a member of the same species as SARS-CoV-2—could have been circulating undetected for decades in humans or other animals. At the time of my writing, a definitive multispecies story of viral emergence—or reemergence—remains untold.

VIRAL AGENCY

The agency of SARS-CoV-2 can be understood with help from classic science studies texts about "nonhuman agency." Bruno Latour introduced

the idiom of "co-production" in 1979, to think about how scientific apparatuses produce inscriptions—transforming matter into meaning, substances into written documents.[10] Later, Sheila Jasanoff elaborated the idea
of coproduction to suggest that "the ways in which we know and represent the world (both nature and society) are inseparable from the ways in
which we chose to live."[11]

Agency has been understood in different terms by multispecies ethnographers, who have pushed past ideas about the "nonhuman." Ethnographers who conducted the initial studies of multispecies contact zones
built on insights from Susan Leigh Star, who insisted that "non-human is
like non-white, it implies a lack of something."[12] With the advent of new
approaches to multispecies ethnography in 2010, anthropologists had a
mandate to be *specific* in accounting for how other *species* were entangled
with the diverse political, cultural, and social worlds of humanity. In rethinking the interplay of agency in multispecies worlds, researchers also
turned away from the realm of epistemology (representation) to address
questions related to ontology—or modes of being and becoming in worlds
that people share with plants, animals, fungi, and microbes.[13]

Viruses have been understudied within multispecies ethnography, even
though an essay on "viral clouds" was part of the special issue of *Cultural
Anthropology* that chronicled the emergence of this new field. Celia Lowe
described avian influenza as "a cloud of particles, uncertain ontologies,
multiplying narratives, and apocalyptic dreams."[14] *The Multispecies Salon,*
an experimental art exhibit that explored the intersections of nature and
culture, included a piece by Caitlin Berrigan that used her own hepatitis C
infection to generate ethnographic insights about anxiety, biopolitics, and
interspecies care.[15] Early in the pandemic, Berrigan wrote an essay about
neoliberalism, loneliness, and health care in which she reported, "Living
co-inhabited with a virus for 34 years has taught me that survivance is nego-
tiation, not warfare."[16] Taking an even longer-term view, the art historian
Sria Chatterjee observed that "the natural history of viruses has been a
history of visualization fueled primarily by fear."[17]

Viruses were seen for the first time in 1939, when the electron microscope enabled the direct visualization of infectious particles, or virions.
The name "coronavirus" came from initial electron micrographs of this
viral family showing a spike protein (Figure 17.1) that "soars some 20 nm
above the virion envelope, giving the virus the appearance—with a little
imagination—of a crown or coronet (Latin *corona,* hence the name)."[18]

FIGURE 17.1. A computer image of severe acute respiratory syndrome (SARS).
Created by Alexey Solodovnikov and Valeria Arkhipova. Originally published on
N+1 and available on Wikimedia Commons.

In recent years, new digital tools enabled molecular biologists to form
more vivid images of virion particles. Most of the key viral molecules are
so small that they cannot be seen with electron microscopes. Even as more
knowledge of these tiny viral components accumulates, images of static
viral particles stayed in the public imagination while scientists began to
study dynamic molecular interactions. Advanced laboratory techniques are
just starting to inform artistic renderings of how lively viral proteins interface with host cells. Understanding these interactions with conventional
multispecies methods is challenging, because ethnographers have largely
focused on visible realms as they followed species and the flight of capital

through fragmented landscapes.[19] Multispecies ethnographers and allies in other disciplines are starting to augment their tool kits with the apparatuses of biology—by learning how to use genetic evidence and microscopy to do basic descriptive work.[20]

Because conventional fieldwork and lab work were impractical in the pandemic, I have approached SARS-CoV-2 with the methods of cultural studies. This chapter is based on my own reading of electron micrographs, X-ray images, protein models, and the primary virological literature. In doing this interpretive work, I am indebted to the virologists, historians, anthropologists, geographers, ecologists, sociologists, artists, and philosophers who joined me throughout the pandemic for weekly Zoom meetings with the Coronavirus Multispecies Reading Group.[21]

Sidestepping foundational distinctions between life and nonlife, philosophers John Dupré and Stephan Guttinger suggest that viral ontologies "should be seen as processes rather than things, or substances." On a molecular level, viruses can be understood as "living processes" that interact with other living systems that have "interconnected and collaborating segments of many genetically distinct lineages."[22] If we understand viruses as living processes, rather than as static particles, then it is possible to develop "a relational approach to viral agency."[23] With this approach, we might grasp how agential forces interact as viruses infect host cells. As viral processes interface with other living systems, it is easy to see how they contain tracings of their hosts—like orchid flowers that mimic the form of pollenating wasps.[24]

As virologists and molecular biologists engage in an accelerated program of research to better understand the structure and function of key proteins that make up SARS-CoV-2, their new findings offer an opportunity to further develop conceptual work related to viral agency. Visual representations of the SARS "spike" protein became familiar to members of the public early in the pandemic, who sought to understand how the virus enters host cells via the ACE2 receptor (Figure 17.2). One popular metaphor offers an image of this molecular process: if there is a good fit between the spike and the receptor, then they slot together like a key into a lock. Then the cell and the virus open up into each other. A fusion takes place.

Molecular biologists have produced models of the transformative changes that happen in cells that have been infected by SARS-CoV-2. Once inside the host cell, coronaviruses become a series of distributed processes. The external viral envelope lifts away from the virion, unleashing a tightly packed

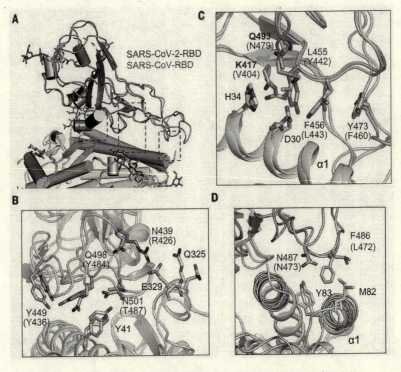

FIGURES 17.2. The spike protein of the SARS virus interfaces with ACE2, a receptor on the surface of many human cells. There are slight molecular variations between the structure of the spike protein of SARS-CoV-2 when compared to the spike of the original SARS-CoV strain. This slight difference in molecular structure results in different rates of infectivity. From "Structural Basis for the Recognition of SARS-CoV-2 by Full-Length Human ACE2" by Yan, Renhong, Yuanyuan Zhang, Yaning Li, Lu Xia, Yingying Guo, and Qiang Zhou, *Science (American Association for the Advancement of Science)* 367, no. 6485 (2020): 1444–48, https://doi.org/10.1126/science.abb2762. Reprinted with permission from AAAS.

bundle of proteins and nucleic acids that become lively inside the cell. These viral molecules might be understood as material-semiotic components involved in the "mutual constitution of entangled agencies."[25] Viruses contain representations of the world. As viruses trace host structures, in iterative intergenerational dances, they illustrate embodied modes of being, knowing, and becoming. Viral epistemologies are entangled with

viral ontologies as infectious agents like SARS-CoV-2 coproduce their own
lifeworlds.

When a coronavirus finds itself inside a "permissive" host, cellular
enzymes initiate the conversation of viral genes into long strings of protein.[26] The suite of proteins expressed in host cells, the transcriptome, is
totally altered by the virus. One of the first viral proteins that emerges
from the process of translation, nonstructural protein 1 (Nsp1), becomes
a "host shutoff factor" suppressing immune functions in the cell. Copies
of the Nsp1 molecule lodge themselves in the host's ribosome, blocking
the host from making new proteins and facilitating the expression of viral
genes.[27]

One of the most important components of all coronaviruses is called
"N," which stands for "nucleocapsid protein." N is key to the structure of
coronaviruses because it "forms complexes" with a long strand of RNA—
where coronavirus genes are encoded. In contrast to the double helix of
DNA, the coronavirus genome is contained in a single strand of RNA that
is looped into a messy structure around long chains of N protein. This
protein is critical to the stability of the viral structure within the cell, and
it also has important functions. During the virus life cycle, multiple copies
of the N protein interact with the loops of RNA to facilitate viral transcrip-
tion (copying the RNA molecule) and translation (turning viral genes into
proteins), according to the definitive paper on the subject.[28]

The N protein works in concert with other distributed viral components
and cellular resources to coproduce new viral particles. Chains of this protein hold a long, unwieldy bundle of RNA in a protective embrace as the
virus drifts around inside the host cell—sometimes making its way to
the cell nucleus, other times just floating free in the cytoplasm.[29] Without the N protein, the viral genetic material in the RNA strand would get
chopped up by the host cell. As viral molecules proliferate, the host tries
to initiate its own cellular defensive processes. Host enzymes try to turn
the material-semiotic elements wrapped up in the viral RNA strand into
nonsense.[30]

As the N protein protects the RNA from degradation, it also facilitates
interactions with generative processes in the host cells. The virus works in
concert with its host to become itself—bending and folding, cutting and
assembling. Many of these parallel processes are oriented toward producing new viral particles, which are released into the world. At the same time,
the virus also becomes polymorphic—translating genetic information into

smaller molecules that interface with the molecular architecture of the host and begin to transform the cell.

Some infected cells become monstrous. The original SARS corona-virus can produce giant cells in human tissue that fuse together with their neighbors, according to a review in the *American Journal of Pathology*.[31] An early report in *The Lancet* found similar giant cells—containing multiple cell nuclei—in the lungs of SARS-CoV-2 patients who were experiencing extreme trouble breathing.[32]

SARS-CoV-2 produces more subtle changes to platelets—the tiny blood cells that form clots to stop bleeding. The p-selectin protein, which makes these cells stick together, is normally stored inside platelet cells. When platelets are infected with SARS-CoV-2, they start expressing the p-selectin protein on their cell surfaces. As the platelets start sticking together, they become hyperreactive and start interacting with white blood cells involved in the immune system response to microbial invaders. Viral and cellular processes start to intersect with processes on other scales—disrupting the predictable functioning of organs and systems.

When another kind of blood cell, the neutrophil, is infected with SARS-CoV-2, a sudden dramatic transformation takes place. Infected neutrophils explode, releasing neutrophil extracellular traps (NETs) into blood vessels. The NETs are made up of long DNA strings, which shoot out from the chromosomes of the exploding neutrophils. A messy jumble of antibodies and enzymes, plus random cellular proteins and viral particles, get tangled in the NETs.[33]

Neutrophil NETs are part of the normal immune system response to infectious microbes. But, in the case of SARS-CoV-2, tissue damage seems to be taking place as neutrophils interact with other kinds of cells. As plate-lets get caught up in the NETs and start sticking together, blood clots start to form, clogging the tiny microvascular blood system.[34] The lungs of COVID-19 patients experience extensive injury and "diffuse alveolar dam-age" that becomes visible in X-rays as "ground glass opacities." In short, studies indicate that "NETs are released in the lung tissue and are associ-ated with lung damage in COVID-19 patients."[35] Blood clots induced by these NETs may also contribute to the damage of tissue in the hearts, kidneys, and brains in severe Covid-19 cases.

While SARS-CoV-2 viruses might be seen as lively processes as they inter-sect with cellular systems, they also become deadly agents in the bodies of some people. An early study of some seventy-two thousand Covid-19 cases

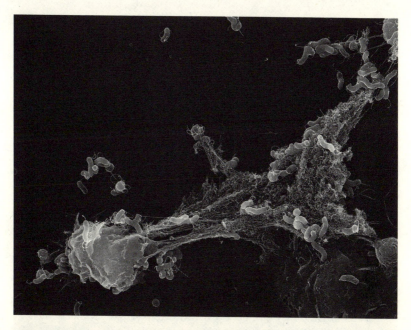

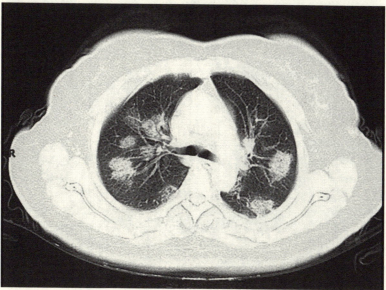

FIGURE 17.3. Above: an image of NETs released by neutrophils infected with SARS-CoV-2. Flavio Protasio Veras et al. Creative Commons License 4.0. Permission courtesy of Dr. Volker Brinkmann, MPI for Infection Biology. Below: ground glass opacities in the lungs of a Covid-19 patient. Ying-Hui Jin Creative Commons Attribution 4.0 International License. *Military Medical Research* 7 (2020), article 24.

in mainland China reported that more than 97 percent of people with infections recovered.[36] The large majority of people who were infected with SARS-CoV-2 during the pandemic never developed serious Covid-19 symptoms. Even still, by May 2022, an estimated 15 million people had died.[37] Many millions of others are now living with the debilitating effects of "long Covid." One in three survivors experience fatigue, breathing problems, or brain fog long after the infection has passed.[38] As biomedical researchers continue to study the molecular interactions of SARS-CoV-2, and the observable pathologies, it is clear that a more distributed form of viral agency has erupted beyond human bodies.

VIRAL VULNERABILITY

In thinking about viral agency, it is possible to keep multiple scales in mind at once. Jumping from the dynamics that take place in molecules and tissues to the scale of species, peoples, institutions, and nations might help us reckon with the speed with which this virus interrupted planetary processes. SARS-CoV-2 spread through airports, international flight paths, and global transportation hubs. Viral agency was amplified by processes of capital accumulation, food production, and global acceleration.[39] The virus diagnosed widespread vulnerabilities in the modern world system.

When capital markets, transportation infrastructures, commodity chains, and agriculture ventures began to falter early in the pandemic, asymmetries in vulnerability and responsibility became readily apparent. "COVID-19 illuminates the stark inequalities along class-race-gender lines, shaping whose lives are considered valuable and whose are not," wrote Carrie Freshour during the intensity of the long 2020 pandemic summer. "Newly recognized as 'essential,' people working in grocery stores, processing plants, day care centers, and hospitals must physically traverse cities and small towns to ensure 'life's work.'"[40] In a similar vein, Anthony Ryan Hatch wrote of the "necropolitical war" that intensified in the pandemic where dominant forces were using "overwhelming technoscientific force to sabotage infrastructures for living." Hatch observed that "the production of mass death" quickly became "a vital part of the national and international economy."[41]

When Donald Trump invoked the Defense Production Act on April 28, 2020—to keep the meatpacking industry in business—the well-being of some was sacrificed so that others might live. By May 6, the U.S. meatpacking industry hit a grim milestone, with more than ten thousand coronavirus cases tied to outbreaks at plants.[42] With patchy record keeping, and industry evasion, the deaths of these sick workers were not carefully tracked. In absence of a coordinated government or industry effort—in the face of a biopolitics of indifference—a Wikipedia page sprang up to account for the hundreds of people who died in the service of the meat industry.[43]

An earlier coronavirus epidemic swept through the hog farms of North America's Great Plains in 2013. This particular coronavirus species, known by the acronym PEDv (porcine epidemic diarrhea virus), was deadly to pigs but benign for people. One major pork producer lost some 190,000 piglets in one week. Alex Blanchette's ethnographic study of this zoonotic outbreak found that corporate leaders designed highly invasive biosecurity regimes that upended the lives of hog farm workers in an attempt to protect the pigs, which have become "fragile capitalist life forms." The meat industry reversed "the typical hierarchy of species"—promoting the life of vulnerable industrial animals over the flourishing of people.[44] Because the PEDv coronavirus species responsible for this deadly epidemic of diarrhea in pigs is a distant relative of SARS-CoV-2, there was some speculation early in the pandemic that the viral hot spots at meatpacking plants were the result of multispecies interactions.[45] But evidence from poultry farms suggests that the early pandemic spread in the United States was an interspecies story (involving the virus, humans, and capital flows), rather than a multispecies story. The biology of chickens is incompatible with SARS-CoV-2. Bird cells have ACE2 receptors with a very different morphology that does not permit this coronavirus strain to enter their cells.[46]

The largest poultry companies—Tyson, Pilgrim's Pride, and Cargill—pushed for faster production lines during the pandemic, even as employees struggled to gain access to or wear effective personal protective equipment (PPE).[47] Line speeds were already running at the astonishing rate of 140 birds per minute—that is 2.33 birds per second—when officials from the Trump administration allowed fifteen gargantuan poultry plants to exceed federal limits on speed. With this acceleration, workers reported that using "protective equipment was like jogging while wearing full head gear."[48] Face shields were quickly deemed impractical because blood spatters forced employees constantly to wipe them off, which exposed them to the virus.

Before the pandemic, the intensity of speed at poultry plants had already produced what Carrie Freshour calls *premature disability*, with forced overtime and no sick leave. In Georgia, where Freshour labored alongside others in poultry plants, she found a form of capital accumulation that was extracting value through organized abandonment, or "stealing time while speeding up lives." Poultry plants have become sites for observing the accelerated velocity and accumulated intensity of racial capitalism—an intergenerational process of wealth accumulation that was rooted in the foundational dispossessions of slavery and colonialism.[49]

Intergenerational processes that have taken place over the *longue durée* of settler colonialism, American imperialism, and plantation slavery have left signatures on bodies that make some people more vulnerable to infectious diseases than others. Structural inequalities in the industrial food system have produced an epidemic of metabolic diseases, such as diabetes, in African American communities. These diseases make people susceptible to Covid-19 complications. In writing about prepandemic inequalities in medicine and metabolism, Anthony Ryan Hatch notes that "racism transforms" as it "seeks to profit from our bodies."[50] As the color of Covid-19 became apparent with the Racial Data Tracker project,[51] Hatch wrote, "When we measure the effects of racism, we are remembering and documenting intergenerational patterns of violence enacted on the bodies of racism's victims."[52]

On a molecular level, we can see durable traces of violence from intergenerational processes—like racism—in human bodies and cells.[53] Metabolic diseases, such as diabetes, result in human cells with more ACE2 receptors than normal.[54] Bodies experiencing metabolic stress seem to make more ACE2 receptors as an adaptive response. The full name of this particular receptor that sits on the surface of the cells is angiotensin-converting enzyme 2 (ACE2), and it normally helps the body regulate blood pressure through a process called vasodilation. The primary literature suggests that ACE2 is part of a "compensatory mechanism" in diabetes that helps patients metabolize sugar.[55] In short, the proliferation of ACE2 receptors is "a physiological defense strategy used to support metabolic health in diabetes [that] may be maladaptive in the context of COVID-19."[56]

Vulnerability to infectious diseases is more a product of configurations than of contagion, as Steve Hinchliffe notes.[57] By quickly jumping scales—bringing insights about molecular configurations together with accounts of intergenerational socioeconomic processes—I hope to catalyze future research.

CONCLUSION

The uncertain ontologies, apocalyptic dreams, and multiplying narratives that proliferated early in the pandemic are starting to resolve into

clearer stories about viral agency and vulnerability. Molecular biologists
and medical practitioners are working to identify the ways that coronavirus agency plays out at a molecular level with the exploding NETs of
DNA that produce blood clots, with the monstrous multinucleated cells
that can be seen in images of ground glass opacities, and with the vulnerability induced by the proliferation of ACE2 receptors in communities
of people impacted by systemic discrimination. By "poaching" emergent
knowledge from the field of biology,[58] this essay is a preliminary attempt
to use the analytical tools of multispecies ethnography to understand how
the coronavirus interrupted commodity chains and played into ongoing
necropolitical wars. A bigger multispecies story, about the disruptive force
of viral agency on a planetary scale, remains to be told.

If viruses are living processes, then it is important to understand how
they are constantly merging with and separating from other processes at
multiple scales.[59] As agential beings, viruses are involved in the coproduction of worlds—from microcosms in cells to the macrocosms of ecosystems
and human social institutions. The modern food system is just one contact
zone that is coproducing a multitude of new microbial worlds with scales,
modes, and tempos that did not exist before the Industrial Revolution.[60]
Some microbes, such as SARS-CoV-2, are just starting to reveal their disruptive potential as they move among worlds, navigate shifting circumstances, and find emergent opportunities.[61]

NOTES

1. Reviewed in Eben Kirksey, "The Emergence of COVID-19: A Multispecies
Story," *Anthropology Now,* June 25, 2020, https://www.tandfonline.com/doi/abs/10.1
080/19428200.2020.1760631.

2. Priscilla Wald, *Contagious: Cultures, Carriers, and the Outbreak Narrative* (Durham, N.C.: Duke University Press, 2008).

3. Carlo Caduff, *The Pandemic Perhaps: Dramatic Events in a Public Culture of Danger*
(Berkeley: University of California Press, 2015), quoted in Lyle Fearnley, *Virulent Zones:
Animal Disease and Global Health at China's Pandemic Epicenter* (Durham, N.C.: Duke
University Press, 2020).

4. Chaolin Huang, Yeming Wang, Xingwang Li, Lili Ren, Jianping Zhao, Yi Hu, Li
Zhang, et al., "Clinical Features of Patients Infected with 2019 Novel Coronavirus in
Wuhan, China," *The Lancet* 395, no. 10223 (2020): 497–506; also discussed in Kirksey,
"Emergence of COVID-19."

5. Dominic Dwyer, "I Was the Australian Doctor on the WHO's COVID-19 Mission to China. Here's What We Found about the Origins of the Coronavirus," *The
Conversation,* February 21, 2021, http://theconversation.com/i-was-the-australian-doc

tor-on-the-whos-covid-19-mission-to-china-heres-what-we-found-about-the-origins
-of-the-coronavirus-155554.

6. Nick Paton Walsh, "CNN Exclusive: WHO Wuhan Mission Finds Possible Signs of Wider Original Outbreak in 2019," CNN, February 14, 2021, https://www.cnn.com/2021/02/14/health/who-mission-china-intl/index.html.

7. See Nicholson Baker, "The Lab-Leak Hypothesis," *Intelligencer,* January 4, 2021, https://nymag.com/intelligencer/article/coronavirus-lab-escape-theory.html; cf. Andrew Lakoff, *Unprepared: Global Health in a Time of Emergency* (Berkeley: University of California Press, 2017).

8. Walsh, "WHO Wuhan Mission"; Jonathan E. Pekar, Andrew Magee, Edyth Parker, Niema Moshiri, Katherine Izhikevich, Jennifer L. Havens, Karthik Gangavarapu et al., "SARS-CoV-2 Emergence Very Likely Resulted from at Least Two Zoonotic Events," *Zenodo,* February 26, 2022, https://doi.org/10.5281/zenodo.6291628.

9. Cf. Fearnley, *Virulent Zones.*

10. Bruno Latour and Steve Woolgar, *Laboratory Life: The Social Construction of Scientific Facts* (Beverly Hills, Calif.: Sage, 1979), 51.

11. Sheila Jasanoff, *States of Knowledge: The Co-production of Science and Social Order* (New York: Routledge, 2004).

12. Quoted in Stefan Helmereich and Eben Kirksey, "The Emergence of Multispecies Ethnography," *Cultural Anthropology* 25 (2010): 555.

13. Donna Haraway, *When Species Meet* (Minneapolis: University of Minnesota Press, 2008).

14. Celia Lowe, "Viral Clouds: Becoming H5n1 in Indonesia," *Cultural Anthropology* 25 (2010): 625–49.

15. Caitlin Berrigan, "The Life Cycle of a Common Weed," in *The Multispecies Salon,* ed. Eben Kirksey (Durham, N.C.: Duke University Press, 2014).

16. Caitlin Berrigan, "Atmospheres of the Undead: Living with Viruses, Loneliness, and Neoliberalism," September 2020, https://march.international/atmospheres-of-the-undead-living-with-viruses-loneliness-and-neoliberalism/.

17. Sria Chatterjee, "Making the Invisible Visible: How We Depict COVID-19," *Impact of Social Sciences* (blog), July 10, 2020, https://blogs.lse.ac.uk/impactofsocialsciences/2020/07/10/making-the-invisible-visible-how-we-depict-covid-19/.

18. M. M. Lai and D. Cavanagh, "The Molecular Biology of Coronaviruses," *Advances in Virus Research* 48 (1997): 2.

19. See, e.g., Anna Tsing, Jennifer Deger, Alder Keleman Saxena, and Feifei Zhou, eds., *Feral Atlas: The More-than-Human Anthropocene* (Palo Alto, Calif.: Stanford University Press, 2021), https://feralatlas.org/; Radhika Govindrajan, *Animal Intimacies: Interspecies Relatedness in India's Central Himalayas* (Chicago: University of Chicago Press, 2018); Alex Blanchette, *Porkopolis: American Animality, Standardized Life, and the Factory Farm* (Durham, N.C.: Duke University Press, 2020).

20. Jamie Lorimer and Timothy Hodgetts, "Methodologies for Animals' Geographies: Cultures, Communication and Genomics," *Cultural Geographies* 22, no. 2 (2014): 285–95; Eben Kirksey, *Emergent Ecologies* (Durham, N.C.: Duke University Press, 2015).

21. Our conversations are archived at https://adi.deakin.edu.au/coronavirus-multispecies-reading-group.

22. John Dupré and Stephan Guttinger, "Viruses as Living Processes," *Studies in History and Philosophy of Biological and Biomedical Sciences* 59 (October 2016): 119.

23. Fearnley, *Virulent Zones*, 11.

24. Gilles Deleuze and Félix Guattari, *A Thousand Plateaus: Capitalism and Schizophrenia* (London: Athlone Press, 1987), 10.

25. Karen Barad, "Invertebrate Visions: Diffractions of the Brittlestar," in *The Multispecies Salon*, ed. Eben Kirksey (Durham, N.C.: Duke University Press, 2014), 238; cf. Donna Haraway, "Situated Knowledges: The Science Question in Feminism and the Privilege of Partial Perspective," *Feminist Studies* 14 (1988): 579.

26. K. Nakagawa, K. G. Lokugamage, and S. Makino, "Viral and Cellular MRNA Translation in Coronavirus-Infected Cells," *Advances in Virus Research* 96 (2016): 165–92.

27. Katharina Schubert et al., "SARS-CoV-2 Nsp1 Binds the Ribosomal MRNA Channel to Inhibit Translation," *Nature Structural and Molecular Biology* 27, no. 10 (2020): 959–66.

28. Ruth McBride, Marjorie van Zyl, and Burtram C. Fielding, "The Coronavirus Nucleocapsid Is a Multifunctional Protein," *Viruses* 6, no. 8 (2014): 2991–3018.

29. McBride et al.

30. Masami Wada et al., "Interplay between Coronavirus, a Cytoplasmic RNA Virus, and Nonsense-Mediated MRNA Decay Pathway," *Proceedings of the National Academy of Sciences of the United States of America* 115, no. 43 (2018): E10157.

31. Jiang Gu and Christine Korteweg, "Pathology and Pathogenesis of Severe Acute Respiratory Syndrome," *American Journal of Pathology* 170, no. 4 (2007): 1136–47.

32. Zhe Xu et al., "Pathological Findings of COVID-19 Associated with Acute Respiratory Distress Syndrome," *The Lancet Respiratory Medicine* 8, no. 4 (2020): 420–22.

33. Flavio Protasio Veras et al., "SARS-CoV-2-Triggered Neutrophil Extracellular Traps Mediate COVID-19 Pathology," *Journal of Experimental Medicine* 217, no. 12 (2020): e20201129.

34. Elizabeth Middleton, "Neutrophil Extracellular Traps Contribute to Immunothrombosis in COVID-19," presented at the Cold Spring Harbor Symposium, July 2020.

35. Protasio Veras et al., "SARS-CoV-2-Triggered Neutrophil Extracellular Traps."

36. Zunyou Wu and Jennifer M. McGoogan, "Characteristics of and Important Lessons from the Coronavirus Disease 2019 (COVID-19) Outbreak in China: Summary of a Report of 72 314 Cases from the Chinese Center for Disease Control and Prevention," *JAMA* 323, no. 13 (2020): 1239–42.

37. Carma Hassan, "Covid-19's Full Death Toll Is Nearly Three Times Higher than Reported, WHO Data Suggests," CNN, May 6, 2022, https://edition.cnn.com/2022/05/05/health/covid-excess-mortality-who-data/index.html.

38. Kate Aubusson, "Sick for the Long Haul: One Third of COVID-19 Patients Have Symptoms for Eight Months," *Sydney Morning Herald*, March 30, 2021, https://www.smh.com.au/national/sick-for-the-long-haul-one-third-of-covid-19-patients-have-symptoms-for-eight-months-20210330-p57fbl.html.

39. See, e.g., Carrie Freshour, "Poultry and Prisons," *Monthly Review* (blog), July 1, 2020, https://monthlyreview.org/2020/07/01/poultry-and-prisons/; Tsing et al., *Feral Atlas.*

40. Freshour, "Poultry and Prisons."

41. Anthony Ryan Hatch, "Two Meditations in Coronatime," *Official Website of the Science, Knowledge, and Technology Section* (blog), May 22, 2020, https://asaskat.com/2020/05/22/two-meditations-in-coronatime/.

42. Sky Chadde, "Meatpacking Industry Hits Grim Milestone of 10,000 Coronavirus Cases Linked to Plants," *Investigate Midwest,* May 6, 2020, https://investigatemidwest.org/2020/05/06/meatpacking-industry-hits-grim-milestone-of-10000-coronavirus-cases-linked-to-plants/.

43. https://en.wikipedia.org/wiki/Impact_of_the_COVID-19_pandemic_on_the_meat_industry_in_the_United_States.

44. Alex Blanchette, "Herding Species: Biosecurity, Posthuman Labor, and the American Industrial Pig," *Cultural Anthropology* 30, no. 4 (2015): 641.

45. The PEDv coronavirus is in the same broad evolutionary "clade" as SARS-CoV-2. Alexander E. Gorbalenya, Susan C. Baker, Ralph S. Baric, Raoul J. de Groot, Christian Drosten, Anastasia A. Gulyaeva, Bart L. Haagmans et al., "Severe Acute Respiratory Syndrome-Related Coronavirus: The Species and Its Viruses—a Statement of the Coronavirus Study Group," bioRxiv, February 11, 2020, https://doi.org/10.1101/2020.02.07.937862; Peng Zhou, Xing-Lou Yang, Xian-Guang Wang, Ben Hu, Lei Zhang, Wei Zhang, Hao-Rui Si et al., "A Pneumonia Outbreak Associated with a New Coronavirus of Probable Bat Origin," *Nature* 579, no. 7798 (2020): 270–73. There is some evidence that an even closer relative of the novel pandemic coronavirus was circulating among pigs in the recent past. After the original SARS outbreak in 2003, a team of leading Chinese scientists found antibodies in two pigs that they tested in the farming villages of Xiqing County, near Beijing. W. Chen, M. Yang et al., "SARS-Associated Coronavirus Transmitted from Human to Pig," *Emerging Infectious Diseases* 11, no. 3: 446–48, https://doi:10.3201/eid1103.040824. Experimental studies with pigs suggest that they are not readily infected with SARS-CoV-2, in contrast to other animal species, such as domestic cats, fruit bats, and mink. Kore Schlottau, Melanie Rissmann, Annika Graaf, Jacob Schön, Julia Sehl, Claudia Wylezich, Dirk Höper et al., "SARS-CoV-2 in Fruit Bats, Ferrets, Pigs, and Chickens: An Experimental Transmission Study," *The Lancet Microbe* 1, no. 5 (2020): e218–25; Bas B. Oude Munnink, Reina S. Sikkema, David F. Nieuwenhuijse, Robert Jan Molenaar, Emmanuelle Munger, Richard Molenkamp, Arco van der Spek et al., "Transmission of SARS-CoV-2 on Mink Farms between Humans and Mink and Back to Humans," *Science* 371, no. 6525 (2021): 172–77.

46. Schlottau et al., "SARS-CoV-2 in Fruit Bats"; Rui Li, Songlin Qiao, and Gaiping Zhang, "Analysis of Angiotensin-Converting Enzyme 2 (ACE2) from Different Species Sheds Some Light on Cross-Species Receptor Usage of a Novel Coronavirus 2019-NCoV," *Journal of Infection* 80, no. 4 (2020): 469–96.

47. Freshour, "Poultry and Prisons."

48. Maywa Montenegro de Wit, "What Grows from a Pandemic? Toward an Abolitionist Agroecology," *Journal of Peasant Studies* 48, no. 1 (2021): 109.

49. Freshour, "Poultry and Prisons"; Cedric J. Robinson, *Black Marxism: The Making of the Black Radical Tradition* (London: Penguin UK, 2021).

50. Anthony Ryan Hatch, *Blood Sugar: Racial Pharmacology and Food Justice in Black America* (Minneapolis: University of Minnesota Press, 2016).

51. The Racial Data Tracker can be accessed at https://covidtracking.com/race.

52. Hatch, "Two Meditations in Coronatime."

53. See, e.g., Hannah Landecker and Aaron Panofsky, "From Social Structure to Gene Regulation, and Back: A Critical Introduction to Environmental Epigenetics for Sociology," *Annual Review of Sociology* 39 (2013): 348.

54. Janelle S. Ayres, "A Metabolic Handbook for the COVID-19 Pandemic," *Nature Metabolism* 2, no. 7 (2020): 572–85.

55. Sharell M. Bindom and Eric Lazartigues, "The Sweeter Side of ACE2: Physiological Evidence for a Role in Diabetes," *Molecular and Cellular Endocrinology* 302, no. 2 (2009): 193–202.

56. Ayres, "A Metabolic Handbook."

57. Steve Hinchliffe, "More than One World, More than One Health: Reconfiguring Interspecies Health," *Social Science and Medicine* 129 (March 1, 2015): 29.

58. For more on the practice of poaching, see Eben Kirksey, Craig Schuetze, and Stefan Helmereich, "Introduction: Tactics of Multispecies Ethnography," in Kirksey, *Multispecies Salon*, 5–7.

59. Dupré and Guttinger, "Viruses as Living Processes."

60. Hannah Landecker, "Antibiotic Resistance and the Biology of History," *Body and Society* 22, no. 4 (2016): 19–52.

61. On this point, see Kirksey, *Emergent Ecologies*.

DEMOS

18 A Tale of Two Protests

Anti-Maskers, Black Lives Matter, and the Specter of Multiracial Democracy

ELISABETH ANKER

The trauma and drama of 2020 wreaked havoc on millions of people's lives, but it also sharpened political visions of freedom. Out of the messy plurality of hopes for freedom always circulating in the United States, two overarching visions came to the forefront. They congealed in the oppositional protests of 2020: the protests against government mandates to wear masks during the Covid-19 pandemic (and their connection to the later insurrection at the U.S. Capitol on January 6, 2021) and the Black Lives Matter protests against police violence and racial injustice, which became the largest protests in American history. The two visions of freedom inherent in the protests disclosed the political stakes of democratic possibility emerging out of the long 2020.

The anti-mask protesters rejected the government's mask mandates to stop the spread of the novel and deadly SAR-CoV-2 virus by requiring face masks in public and commercial spaces. Protesters rejected mandated mask wearing as a principled stance of individual freedom against government paternalism. Their freedom to reject masks, lockdowns, and social distancing, collectively named "health freedom" by its supporters, relied on the principles of individual sovereignty and limited government power over personal decision-making. It included liberal and libertarian values of individual choice-making, a dismissal of community-based considerations for health as tyranny, and an insistence on being unbound by the will or desires of others. It entailed freedom *from* others, from their demands, needs, and sustenance. Mask restrictions, in this vision of freedom, were

an infringement of individual freedom enforced by irrational social con-
formity and government usurpation (Figure 18.1).

Freedom here meant to be free from responsibility to others, to be free
from the burden of others' vulnerability. Indeed, it was to be free from
recognizing one's complicity in making others vulnerable. The refusal to
wear a mask made all other people around the anti-masker much more
vulnerable to a deadly disease, while it actively thwarted public health
measures across the country. Health is a socially interconnected phenomenon that depends on public health measures, environmental regulation,
and economic distribution at a population level. The anti-maskers fanta-
sized away these interconnections, and their individuated refusals to participate in collective containment strategies harmed the entire community
and undid large-scale social measures to stanch the pandemic. Anti-mask
warriors, in this sense, practiced a freedom to exploit others and to be free
from them.[1]

This was freedom as a masculinized performance of invulnerability, an
ability simply to reject interdependence by sheer force of will. Refusing to
wear a mask as a performance of individual sovereignty tried to eradicate
the bodily dependence revealed by Covid-19, as if not wearing a mask meant

FIGURE 18.1. Freedom as exploitation and the refusal of interdependence, 2020
anti-mask protests. Michael Swan via Wikimedia Commons.

that one had ipso facto triumphed over the confines of interdependence. But by making others more vulnerable, it was implicitly but deeply invested in the domination it claimed to abhor. It was tied not only to masculinized investments in the triumph over dependence that actively harms others but also to whiteness as a hierarchy of freedom. White freedom entails not an *ontology* of freedom as an endowment from our creator but a *politics* of freedom tied to racial and gendered hierarchies of desert and capacity. In the popular imaginary of the predominantly white anti-maskers, Covid-19 is a disease that affects Black and brown people the most, not the white people whose freedom comes from disregarding the needs of people of color. In this way, the anti-mask protesters revealed the necropolitics in their vision of freedom, as it necessarily sacrificed public efforts to minimize Covid-19 spread; disregarded the lives of immunocompromised, poor, minority, and immigrant workers; and disavowed the very concept of societal mitigation.

This investment in masculinized, white freedom is where the anti-maskers and insurrectionists intersect and share a conjoined vision of freedom. They may seem to harbor different visions: the insurrectionists harbored a vision of freedom that aims less to escape the state than to dominate it, to force the levers of state power to bend to their whims. Insurrectionists aimed to control state power by installing the leader they believed should helm it, whereas the anti-maskers aimed to rebuff state power altogether to determine their personal decisions. Yet both anti-maskers and insurrectionists reject democracy—as the equal capacities of all people to share in the governance over our collective lives—and their visions of freedom are animated by a two-pronged relationship to state power: one that entails freedom as the ability to escape state violence and a second that entails freedom as the capacity to direct state violence over other people seen as deserving or requiring state control. Freedom includes both escaping state power and directing its violence, most often against nonwhite peoples.

This vision of white freedom tied to racialized hierarchies of power and desert has been part of this country since its earliest moments in Indigenous dispossession and enslavement, in the country's founding in a pro-slavery and pro-conquest freedom. Cristina Beltran describes it as "the opportunity to be the bearer of rights and legal equality while being free to deny those same rights to racialized communities . . . the right to use the law to police other populations, to impose tyranny while participating in forms of violence that feel like freedom."[2] Anti-mask and insurrectionist

protests enacted this vision of freedom, as the capacity to both limit the
state over themselves and direct its exercise against the undeserving, even
when that exercise entails necropolitical neglect.

The figure of Trump that both groups support can help to understand
how their visions of freedom are shared. Trump's popularity rests in his
capacity to enact this double vision of freedom as both antistate over himself and pro–state control over those he considers inferior. His spectacles of domination—whether as a boss on reality TV or as president over
Twitter—demonstrate both control over others and the exercise of power
without consequences. Trump always escapes the strictures of state power
meant for lesser mortals: he never pays taxes, he breaks laws and regulations for housing and real estate, he routinely engages in bribery and cor-
ruption, he flouts constitutional limits of executive power, and he rapes
women without consequence. It is important to remember that his first
foray into public political discourse was taking out a full-page ad calling for
the death penalty for the Central Park Five, Black children falsely accused
of rape—a crime he himself commits without penalty.

Trump's pitch is that the freedom he displays will also accrue by extension to his supporters, the freedom to both control the state and personally escape its reach. He directs state violence over Black and brown people
through police deregulation, "crackdowns" in the inner city, border violence, and racist imagery and, at the same time, promises to reestablish
white Americans' individual sovereignty *from* state power, from the cum-
bersome regulations that force people to consider the environment, racial
and gender disparities, immigrant needs, or the health care of others. His
domination both models and makes possible for individual supporters, at
a smaller scale, a similar domination over those they believe obstruct their
agency or take their things. The insurrectionists of January 6, 2021, aimed
to single-handedly reinstall Trump as president, not merely because they
idolized him, but because implicit in his actions was a promise that some
of the power he wields will trickle down to them—indeed, it was this very
power they thought they could harness to reinstall him. Trump offered them
the promise of trickle-down domination.

Trickle-down domination is an animating vision of American freedom
for both insurrectionists and anti-maskers, inextricably bound up with formations of masculinity and whiteness. It is whiteness as a structure of masculinized power that cultivates feelings of superiority and then grievance if
that superiority is questioned, entitlement and then resentment when that

entitlement isn't fully acknowledged, desert and then umbrage when desert isn't ubiquitously upheld. This is a version of freedom inextricable from masculinity as a performance of power but not necessarily from men as such; its greatest performers at the moment of this writing are Congresswomen Lauren Boebert and Marjorie Taylor Greene, who refuse to wear masks, cosplay with military guns, and verbally attack marginalized peoples as their wildly popular performances of freedom.

In this version of freedom, democracy as the shared practice of collective governance is thoroughly racialized and sexualized, as it entails being forced to consider the needs, desires, and interdependence of people interpreted as weak, dependent, and undeserving. Heather McGhee shows that democracy became thoroughly racialized in the twentieth century, once it stopped serving only white needs and white publics—that is, once the government was forced, in the post–civil rights era, to serve Blacks and people of color.[3] Multiracial democracy threatened whiteness by engaging entire communities in decision-making and providing for everyone's needs, rather than only the needs of white communities. Arlie Hochshild's description of white Trump supporters reveals this relationship to democracy; she writes, summing up their worldview, "It's not your government anymore. It's theirs." I would add that governance as "theirs" also became gendered as feminized, as it emphasized collaborative and interdependent community decision-making, so opposite to the ethos of rugged white masculinity. If anything has summed up the combined racial and gendered stereotype of American democracy that gained traction in the past decades, it is Ronald Reagan's image of the key figure of governmental dependence: the Black welfare mother, an image that has never left those who find democracy as the antithesis of their individual freedom. Democracy is experienced as a form of oppression for those to whom individual freedom is an entitlement most achievable by the strong, deserving, and self-reliant. Freedom thus requires dismantling democracy.

Both anti-maskers and insurrectionists believe, implicitly or explicitly, that government should work only for white people. They share an investment in resecuring the entitlements of whiteness and masculinity as the rightful exercise of a freedom that never entails sharing power. In this vision, if government is directed to democratically serve everyone, it should be undone and work for no one. They aim to destroy democracy by defunding public goods, diminishing state capacity to provide social services, and refusing state regulations aimed at protecting the health and safety of entire communities. This desire to destroy democracy intensified when Trump lost the presidential election. It was symbolized for the insurrectionists not only in their ubiquitous Don't Tread on Me Gadsden flag but also in the Confederate flag, which posits a vision of freedom that is, at once, a refusal to bend to the federal government and an insistence on both dominating and excluding people of color.

The second vision and practice of freedom came into mainstream politics through the Black Lives Matter protests. For the past couple of decades, political theorists and commentators on the left argued that leftist politics—broadly construed as a politics for racial, gender, class, and sexual equality; ending economic inequality; investment in robust publics and commons; and the sharing of political power for all people—was mired in a loss of political vision for achieving a world of real freedom and equality. Scholars like Wendy Brown and Sheldon Wolin identified a lack of galvanizing visions for achieving equality beyond granting individual rights, and Lauren Berlant identified an "impasse" of waning investments in the American Dream's promise of prosperity that rarely came, combined with an exhaustion at failed fights for equality in class, gender, sexuality, race, immigration status, and bodily ability.[4] There seemed to be few large-scale resources for envisioning society-wide desirable futures, and Black and queer freedom dreams were regularly pushed out to the very margins of American culture, far from the center of national politics.[5] I would argue that 2020 saw the emergence from this impasse into a catalyzing and intersectional mainstream moment organized by the embrace of and reliance on racial, gendered, class, sexual, and bodily difference to envision transformative futures for equality and collective freedom.

Black Lives Matter protests throughout summer 2020 called for defunding the police after George Floyd, a Black man, was callously murdered by a white police officer who kneeled on his neck for over eight minutes as Floyd called out to his mother in pain and terror. Protesters in all fifty states and hundreds of individual locations marched against state-sanctioned police violence against Black people and *for* an expansive vision of what a truly free and equal politics might be. The vision of freedom for which they marched has been articulated in generations of abolitionist and intersectional thought and practice throughout U.S. history but seemingly became mainstream through mass protests. Organized under the Black Lives Matter movement and propelled by Black activists and organizers, the protests were the most multiracial, multigenerational, multiethnic,

multireligious, multigendered protests in American history. Millions of
people joined together in the middle of a terrifying pandemic to demand
racial justice—a coalitional and agonistic group articulating a spectrum
of transformations from the end of police violence to full prison abolition to complete social, political, and economic transformation toward full
equality.[6]

Not everyone marching was on the same page or shared the same
tactics for achieving freedom, nor did people need to march in lockstep.
Some called for police reform, some called for the abolition of policing
and mass incarceration, and others called for revolutionary transformation
of all sectors of society, but these differences were agonistically debated as
a crucial part of participation, as part of articulating what solidarity and
mutuality look like on the ground.[7] The protests were tightly aligned with
climate change movements like Sunrise, with gender and sexual equality
movements, and with Latinx immigration movements, as all called for shifting state power from violence against marginalized people to shared control over the mechanisms of collective governance. At their best, the Black
Lives Matter marches performed a solidarity, not of love for all, but of
partnership, shared concern, and the pleasures of difficult alliances amid
community dependencies that cannot be willed away but can be developed
toward mutual flourishing. They performed a call for multiracial democracy as collective freedom.

FIGURE 18.2. Freedom as the fight for multiracial democracy, Black Lives Matter
protests 2020. Felton Davis via Wikimedia Commons.

This vivification of multiracial democratic energies was not captured by the Democratic Party, though even there, for the first time in years, we could find radical democratic visions within institutional form: broad visions of real racial and gender equality, economic redistribution, and a world in which people care for and cooperate with each other rather than threaten and compete with one another. It is embodied in part by new political figures like Alexandria Ocasio-Cortez, Rashida Tlaib, and Ayanna Pressley, as well as elder statesmen like Bernie Sanders, though it was less about them as individuals than it was about the desires of the millions of people who want them to be decision makers in the first place, who demanded that they make the empty shell of congressional representation truly more representative of the will of the people, invested in visions of a society that values difference without hierarchy.

A 2020 cultural event released at the same time as the Black Lives Matter protests performed this vision for multiracial democracy in aesthetic form. The Broadway show *Hamilton* (dir. Thomas Kail) was released on the Disney+ streaming platform in July 2020 just as the Black Lives Matter protests were taking over streets across the United States. On one hand, *Hamilton*'s story of the American founding using actors of color to play white historical figures seemed merely to recapitulate America's founding father fetish for telling history—a story of heroic great men triumphing over tyranny to grant freedom to future Americans, a freedom they achieved for all of us in the past. On this reading, the portrayal of founding fathers by actors of color was a facile attempt to reconcile the country's origins in racist and xenophobic violence with its national ideals of freedom and democracy. Yet I would suggest that *Hamilton* is less a history retold than a *future fabulation* that reimagines what America could look like once it not only grapples with but invests in its truly creolized, multiracial, multiethnic origins. *Hamilton* asks its audience to desire a national vision where people of color are both central to the American story and equal participants in shaping the nation, a vision of freedom that breaks apart the popular founding imaginary of colonial architectures and hallowed gestures of white aristocracy.[8] It envisions immigrants and people of color revolting against injustice and reimagining a better world with all of the authority Americans typically grant to their founding white, male heroes. The lines Hamilton wrote for Washington that they sing together in the show, anticipating "the sweet enjoyment of partaking in the midst of my fellow-citizens, the benign influence of good laws under a free government," is

Hamilton's vision of multiracial democratic pleasures to come, and to fight for now, not those already achieved in the miasma of a mythic and white-washed past.

In this sense, *Hamilton* amplified some of the freedom visions per-formed in the Black Lives Matter protests. The show's famous line "Look around / Look around / How lucky we are to be alive right now!" peti-tioned its 2020 audience—in the midst of a pandemic, illness and loss, anti-Black police violence, anti-immigrant brutality, rousing protest, and rising authoritarianism—to think of *their* difficult moment as a lucky one and to insist that they have the revolutionary potential to change the dire circum-stances in which they find themselves. It would, however, have been per-haps more compelling if George Washington had been played, not by a Black man, but by a Black woman, finding ways to address the core national violence of misogyny as part of the condemnation of white supremacy. Yet the film offers a work of imaginative and affective political theory rather than a revisionist history, one in which multiracial democracy becomes a lived possibility, where agonistic debate over transformative futures plays out to the brash rhymes of hip-hop, where the country is run, not by vitu-perative, xenophobic, and racist leaders, but by people who aim for freedom and equality even within their own ambivalences and contradictions.

The specter of multiracial democracy emerging in 2020, envisioned in film and on the streets, inside and outside institutions, by millions of pro-testers, felt so threatening to the insurrectionists that they tried to take over national politics to stop it. They hoped that by reinstalling their white authoritarian leader, they could once again dominate over the possibility of multiracial democracy. The vision of freedom they found so antagonis-tic, playing out in the 2020 Black Lives Matter protests and on televisions across the United States, forwarded a version of freedom grounded in shared interdependence, collective decision-making, mutual accountability, and a bodily integrity that stands in solidarity with the most vulnerable. Richard Grusin suggests that in contradistinction to the anti-mask movement, mask wearing became a sign of collective care that generated "the radical poten-tiality to mobilize collectivities of resistance or perhaps even revolution through the redistribution of capital and political power"—this seems a precise definition of the pandemic-response energies mobilized by the Black Lives Matter protests up and into 2021.[9] It set in motion the building blocks for a postpandemic near future when community care becomes a shared fight, when the sense of interdependence across and through difference, emerging from the Covid-19 pandemic, offers material building blocks for the galvanizing visions of freedom mobilized by the Black Lives Matter protests. In 2020, amid the horrors and struggles, millions of Americans found the incredibly hard work of crafting a multiracial democracy—the only kind of democracy worthy of the name—a compelling vision of freedom they want to help build, and fight for.

NOTES

1. For more on this analysis of "heath freedom," see Elisabeth Anker, *Ugly Freedoms* (Durham, N.C.: Duke University Press, 2022). On the relationship between masculinity and freedom, see Anker, *Orgies of Feeling: Melodrama and the Politics of Freedom* (Durham, N.C.: Duke University Press, 2014).

2. Cristina Beltran, *Cruelty as Citizenship: How Migrant Suffering Sustains White Democracy* (Minneapolis: University of Minnesota Press, 2020), 89, 104.

3. Heather McGhee, *The Sum of Us: What Racism Costs Everyone and How We Can Prosper Together* (New York: Penguin Random House, 2021).

4. Lauren Berlant, *Cruel Optimism* (Durham, N.C.: Duke University Press, 2011), and Berlant, *The Female Complaint* (Durham, N.C.: Duke University Press, 2008); Wendy Brown, *Politics out of History* (Princeton, N.J.: Princeton University Press, 2001), and Brown, *Walled States, Waning Sovereignty* (New York: Zone Books, 2017); Sheldon Wolin, *Democracy Incorporated: Managed Democracy and the Specter of Inverted Totalitarianism* (Princeton, N.J.: Princeton University Press, 2008).

5. Robin D. G. Kelley, *Freedom Dreams: The Black Radical Imagination* (Boston: Beacon Press, 2003); Fred Moten and Stefano Harney, *The Undercommons: Fugitive Planning and Black Study* (New York: Autonomedia, 2013); José Esteban Muñoz, *Cruising Utopia: The Then and There of Queer Futurity* (Durham, N.C.: Duke University Press, 2009).

6. Deva Woodley Davis, *Reckoning: Black Lives Matter and the Democratic Necessity of Social Movements* (Oxford: Oxford University Press, 2021); Minkah Makalani, "Black Lives Matter and the Limits of Formal Black Politics," *South Atlantic Quarterly* 116 no. 3 (2017): 529–52.

7. Bonnie Honig, *Public Things: Democracy in Disrepair* (New York: Fordham University Press, 2017).

8. On *Hamilton,* see Elisabeth Anker, "*Hamilton* (2020)," in *The Lexicon of Global Melodrama,* ed. Heike Paul, Sarah Marak, and Katharina Gerund, 381–84 (Berlin: Transcript, 2022).

9. Richard Grusin, "Radical Mediation, COVID Masks, Revolutionary Collectivity," *Thinking C21* (blog), April 21, 2020, https://www.c21uwm.com/2020/04/14/radical-mediation-COVID-masks-revolutionary-collectivity/.

19 "Everybody Hates the Police"

On Hatred for the Police as a Political Feeling

JONATHAN FLATLEY

In summer 2020, I saw the police beat, tear-gas, insult, threaten, and arrest my friends, my comrades, my colleagues, and my students.

Filled with rage and grief after the brutal police murder of George Floyd, we had come into the streets of Detroit to protest racist police violence. Even though I knew that the police kill someone in the United States, on average, three times a day, and even though I knew the institution's long history of racist violence going back to its origin in slave patrols, such monstrous indifference to life was a shock. No feeling person could respond to the murder of George Floyd with anything but the strongest sense of rage and revulsion, rebuke and condemnation, I thought. I wondered how the police could feel anything but deep, profound shame for their participation in this murderous institution.

At the same time, it seemed that throughout the long 2020, wherever the latest news directed my attention—Minsk, Moscow, Lagos—the police were there with their shields, their helmets, their masks, their armored vehicles, and their chemical weapons, beating, shooting, Tasering, pushing, gassing, kettling, and arresting. These vivid images of police violence against protesters recalled recent, similar clashes in Santiago, Hong Kong, Quito, Port-au-Prince, Istanbul, and Paris.[1] "It resembles a physical law," the Invisible Committee reminds us. "The more the social order loses credit, the more it arms its police. The more the institutions withdraw, the more they advance in terms of surveillance. The less respect the authorities inspire, the more they seek to keep us respectful through force."[2]

In May 2020, the incapacity of societies like ours to care for its members was already on grotesque display. As Nancy Fraser wrote, "both the pandemic and the response to it represent the irrationality and destructiveness of capitalism. The crisis of care was already evident before the outbreak of COVID, but was greatly exacerbated by it."[3] The rapid spread of illness and breakdown of key infrastructures, including schools, childcare, and health care especially, meant that everyday life changed, sometimes quite dramatically, for most everybody. Many people were socially isolated, maybe sick themselves or knowing people who were, grieving over the death of loved ones, newly unemployed, or overburdened with care of children or parents while still working. Mass evictions loomed as un- or underemployed people struggled to pay rent. By the end of May, there had been time to brood on the egregious inadequacies and failures of public institutions, of the government, of the economy, of our so-called leaders. Things just seemed fucked up. The ongoing spectacle of Trump's sadistic approach to governance, his racism, xenophobia, and misogyny, seemed to announce a new stage in the steady erosion of hard-won publicly funded forms of care already long under way. This erosion had for some time corresponded ("like a physical law") with the steady encroachment of policing into more and more spaces of everyday life (especially schools), with increases in funding (and military equipment) for the police, and with a well-documented expansion of the prison system. Across the range of political positions, the feeling that we were in the midst of a full-fledged crisis of the social order was widespread. All of this contributed to create a certain collective mood, one in which hatred for the police was ready to bloom.

I certainly came to hate the police as never before, a hatred that only grew more intense as the summer went on. While this hatred was my own subjective reaction to the actions of the police, it was also a widely shared feeling. So, on Friday, May 29, 2020, with thousands of others, I came into the streets in front of police headquarters to affirm our common opposition to racist police violence. And it felt good to share, as if the feeling itself *needed* sharing: *Did you see that? Can you believe that shit?* After months of anxious isolation, of not being close to other bodies, our collective hatred was also ebullience. We felt the joy of becoming part of a marching, chanting, demanding collective: *"no justice, no peace, fuck these racist ass police."*

Our judgment of the police was confirmed when the police met our protests against racist police brutality with racist police brutality. The Detroit police seemed to exult in inflicting harm, as if they had been waiting for the opportunity.[4] They clearly regarded the challenge to their authority to hurt any person they wished as a threat to their very existence. Perhaps this is why they directed violence toward protesters with such energy and enthusiasm. They were "expressing their feelings." And then they lied. *It was the protesters who were violent. They were rioting.* But I *saw* police beat and gas peaceful protesters and standers-by. I saw them, along with thousands of others, not only when I was there on the street but on the multiple live-feed broadcasts and rebroadcasts, the hundreds of videos people made on their phones. Indeed, even though the documentation of police brutality seemed to be everywhere, the police continued to lie all summer, with calm, smug confidence. *How could anybody see what we saw*, I thought, *and not hate the police?*

"Everybody hates the police." The slogan, as the Invisible Committee observes, "doesn't express an observation, which would be false, but an affect, which is vital."[5] What does it mean to say that the slogan expresses a vital affect? We know that *not* everybody hates the police. We see the Blue Lives Matter flags in the Detroit suburbs. We read the news, we hear people proclaim their love of the police, or at least, their belief that the police are necessary. And yet, in hating the police, I feel that the hatred *should* be shared by everyone, as if the person who does not hate the police must be lacking in some basic human faculty, as if that person were unable to distinguish bigger from smaller, hot from cold, smile from frown. In this regard, hating the police is akin to aesthetic judgment, especially the judgment of something as beautiful, at least as Immanuel Kant understood it. Kant proposes that an essential part of my own subjective feeling when I judge something to be beautiful is the demand that *everybody* must also see this as beautiful.[6] If, when I say "this is beautiful," I speak with a "universal voice," then so, too, when I say "I hate the police," it feels like I am also saying (or even *requiring* that) "everybody hates the police." And, as with an aesthetic judgment of beauty, hating the police expects confirmation not from a concept (such as justice) but from the agreement of other people.[7]

When I hate the police, "I have issued a demand, made a request, offered a proposal, tendered a solicitation" (to borrow from Michel Chaouli describing aesthetic judgment[8]). Hatred for the police is a feeling that seeks, in its essence, confirmation from others. You feel like all people *should* also share this feeling—you are *asking* them to—but you are not sure they will. This makes such hatred precarious too. For, when others do *not* share the feeling, I can feel like *I* am the one who has been exiled from the realm of the common, the sensible, that maybe it is *my* faculty of judgment that is faulty. If I look at a tree and say "This is beautiful!" and then the people I am with do not agree, that can be alienating, even depressing, because it can spoil the feeling of sharing a world with others. But the recognition that other people do not hate the police but in fact see the same murders, the same lies, the same racism and instead *love* the police produces a more upsetting feeling. It means I have to somehow find a way to accommodate myself to a world governed by people empowered to harm and kill others, people who are hostile to my interests and to the lives of people I love. With thousands of others on the street, this knowledge is bearable. But after the marches have subsided, home alone, with only social media and the daily news about the latest police murder(s) in Palestine or Minneapolis, watching the storming of the Capitol by the Blue Lives Matter crew, I realize that not only is my hatred not met with universal accord but I live in a world run by people who are *against* us and who definitely do not value Black life or Black lives. There is no way for this to be a comfortable feeling.

"Everybody hates the police" is a vital affect because it is a powerful *and* vulnerable demand for universal assent, a demand that only some people meet. Those people are our friends. In bringing people together who share it, hatred for the police creates a collective. It is a form of solidarity, one that draws a line between us and them, that forces the question "Which side are you on?" That is, hatred for the police is also the recognition of an enemy. "An enemy exists," Carl Schmitt writes, "only when, at least potentially, one fighting collectivity of people confronts a similar collectivity."[9] For Schmitt, politics begins with this distinction between friend and enemy; this is not a personal distinction but is about distinguishing one *group* from another. The enemy collective is the one that challenges the very existence and way of life of the collective of friends. This collective quality of hatred—its initiation of political groupings and lines of conflict—is one of several things that distinguishes hatred from anger.

Aristotle observed that hatred was more often directed toward groups or classes of people (he mentions thieves and informers), whereas anger tended to be more specific both in its initial cause—a specific injury or offence—and in its object.[10] Like anger, hatred can be distinguished from other negative affects, such as fear, shame, or sadness, which are mostly about how *I* am feeling, whereas anger and hatred are directed outward at somebody or something else. But just as anger tends to be more specifically focused, it is also more punctual than hatred. Anger, Aristotle asserts, "can be cured by time; but hatred cannot." Indeed, perhaps because it seeks release, it can be difficult to sustain anger for a long time, even if one wants to. That feeling of rage must be turned down to a simmer or redirected or transformed in some way to survive the rhythms and vagaries of everyday life. Peter Sloterdijk makes the case that hatred is a way to contain and store anger for later use.[11] It is like a bank or a battery, preserving anger's energy to be directed at its object when the time is right. And yet, if Sloterdijk is right about that, he is wrong that hatred does not have its own, distinct logic, feeling, and political function. Not only does it tend to be itself collectively felt and to be directed toward a collective, not only can it endure over time, but also—and crucially—hatred does not aim toward revenge. As Aristotle observes, the angry "would have offenders suffer for what they have done." Haters, on the other hand, "would have them cease to exist."[12] In other words, hatred is an abolitionist emotion.

In seeking the abolition of the police, this hatred also moves beyond the object it seeks to abolish. It is, as Lara Cohen and Brian Connolly argue in "Theses on Hating," an "enthusiasm in its own right," with "its own unique possibilities" for solidarity and imagination.[13] Once hatred for the police has brought together a collective, such a collective, like all collectives that last any time at all, must find ways to sustain and refresh itself, to be together, to find that being-together something rewarding in itself. In so doing, the collective that hates the police forms itself into a way of being together from which the police are excluded, a social form that does not need the police. In this way, hating the police also actively imagines a world without the police. When we understand how the police are an obstacle for making Black lives matter, we start to imagine what the world would look like where Black life *is* valued. Detroit Will Breathe is the name of the group that was founded out of the protests here. Like Black Lives Matter, it is affirmative. Right from the beginning, it started to picture how the city could be transformed to value Black life, by halting evictions, abolishing foreclosures, ending cash bail, taking public money from the police and using it instead to fund public schools, and investing in mental health and substance abuse care. The aim was to bolster existing forms of care and to create new ones. Detroit Will Breathe is openly oriented toward a future; it is about the collective creation of a new world. The model and laboratory for picturing that world is first of all the friends who come together in their hatred for the police. And even if that "we" seems to expire after a certain period, if it comes together in what Gwendolyn Brooks called a "package of minutes," that package is portable.[14] It can be carried away, sent to others, saved for a future date. What hate contains, in a package, is the collectivity of friends and comrades and the collective power we can wield when we come together along with the knowledge of what must be removed for us to survive and flourish.[15]

Hatred for the police is hopeful. I don't mean hopeful in the sense of some abstract political hope where we wait for the better future to be delivered to us if we vote for the right person. (I am thinking of Shepard Fairey's famous Obama campaign poster.) It is hopeful in the sense that interested Ernst Bloch: it is expectant, it is actively working for another world, even as it models that world in the collective that has come together to fight for it.[16] Watch the Newsreel film *Black Panther*, for instance, and listen (starting around the seven-minute mark) to the Black Panthers gathered in front of a city building singing and chanting "No more brothers in jail / Off the pigs! / The pigs are gonna catch hell / Off the pigs!" and "No more pigs in our community / Off the pigs!"[17] As the singers bring their voices together, extending and rhyming "hey-ell" and "jay-ell," as they harmonize and call-and-respond, adjusting and recreating as they go, you cannot miss the abundance of joy and of yearning for another world present in the shared opposition to the police. This performance of group formation is not, as Zora Neale Hurston wrote of spirituals, "a final thing" but is instead "a mood."[18] It is itself a way of being with each other. This "group bent on expression of feelings" is finding and making the feeling that is shared. To borrow Bloch's language, we could say that the "fulfillment correlate" of this hatred for the police is much more than the mirror image of police violence. This hatred imagines an "unreal object": that future world without the police, that future world where Black lives matter, and it pictures that unreality in "anticipatory waking dreams," not least in the moment of protest itself.[19]

This expectant hatred of the police, one that is experienced in a group and as a group, produces a kind of emotional flexibility. "What is going on is going on," as Gwendolyn Brooks once put it; the event-ness of it all feels so palpable, and we do not want to miss it.[20] This together-in-the-event feeling seems to bring with it a new friendliness, a new openness, a new willingness to listen, to be moved, to unlearn things we thought we knew. At moments like these, it is possible, at least for a package of minutes, to be open to something else; in such states, with such hatred, we are capable of letting go of former attachments and opening ourselves to an unfolding event. I really felt that in summer 2020. It was not that police abolition was new as an idea in summer 2020, but I think that for very many people, it became a new object of emotional intention; it became something that people started to passionately and enthusiastically want and work toward. It became an object of what Ernst Bloch called educated hope.

As I suggested earlier, the hope that is present in the hatred of the police has, as an essential element, the imagination of a vast, unending solidarity. It imagines "everybody." "Everybody hates the police," like "workers of all countries unite," points to a group that is global, an expansive "more than us." This latter is also the title of a series of large paintings of police and protesters by Moscow-based artist Ekaterina Muromtseva (three of which are reproduced here as Figures 19.1–19.3).[21] These images remind us that, as Walter Benjamin noted, "the collective is a body, too."[22] These bodies suggest forms of duress, such as being lined up against the wall by the police or carried away by them. In the painting here, where police are arresting a protester (Figure 19.1), the protester's single body is a blank space, as if it is the protester's negation that matters here, and the way the body of the

FIGURE 19.1. Ekaterina Muromtseva, from the series *More Than Us*. Watercolor, paper, 234 × 150 cm.

police have formed themselves in relation to a negation. This negation requires isolating a single body. In the protests in Detroit last summer, when confronting police, this was a constant refrain: "shoulder to shoulder," meaning stay together, do not separate, do not run, we will "not back down to bullies with shields." It was a lesson from the long 2020 in how to be a collective body. The police work by containing and then breaking up the collective. They arrest people one at a time. In Muromtseva's paintings, the protesters themselves, by contrast, present a large, collective body with uncertain boundaries (as in Figure 19.2). Even as they are lined up against the wall (Figure 19.3), they seem to verge on ungovernability: they double themselves, fade into the distance, blend into each other. These bodies are also "more" in the sense that they are not just single bodies collected together but seem to be organized and animated by vital shapes

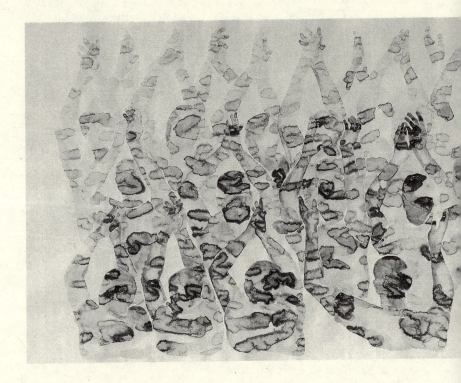

FIGURE 19.2. Ekaterina Muromtseva, *Clapping Hands,* from the series *More Than Us.* Watercolor, paper, 478 × 150 cm.

that look like little floating clouds, or stains, or, when seen all together, like camouflage. These shapes move in and around and through individual bodies like affect itself, moving, joining, and animating. The camouflage character of the pattern these shapes form suggests that perhaps these groups of protesters are trying to "blend in" or hide, like an army in enemy territory, even as the single bodies also blend with *one another*, becoming a unified, and yet unfinished, expanding, collective body.

We see it and feel it in Detroit and Moscow, Minneapolis and Minsk, Lagos and Palestine, Paris and Quito. Hatred for the police seems to include people in "all countries" ("workers of all countries unite"), even if it is not yet "everybody." Indeed, it is one of the few political feelings that translates from one national setting to another. What kind of world might all those who hate the police create together?

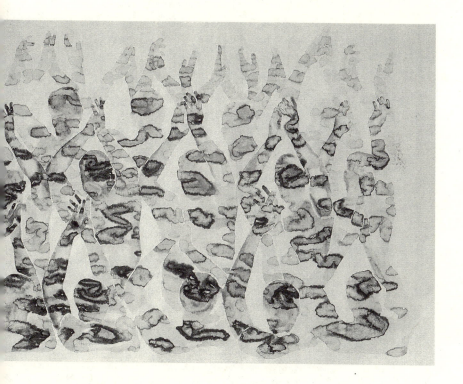

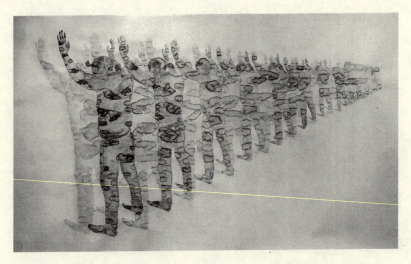

FIGURE 19.3. Ekaterina Muromtseva, from the series *More Than Us.* Watercolor, paper, 150 × 297 cm. Collection of MHKA Museum, Antwerp, Belgium.

NOTES

1. See Joshua Clover's "The Year in Struggles," an impressive account of the very many riots and insurrections that occurred around the world in 2019, in *Commune,* April 3, 2020, https://communemag.com/the-year-in-struggles/.

2. Invisible Committee, *Now,* trans. Robert Hurley (Boston: MIT Press/Semiotext(e), 2017), 65. Zine layout by Ill Will Editions, November 2017. https://libcom.org/library/now-0.

3. Nancy Fraser, "American Interregnum," *New Left Review Sidecar,* April 9, 2021, https://newleftreview.org/sidecar/posts/american-interregnum.

4. Their behavior reminded me of Harriet Jacobs's description of the "musters" of poor white people in the antebellum South, where the "fear of insurrection" provided "a grand opportunity for the low whites, who had no negroes of their own to scourge. They exulted in such a chance to exercise a little brief authority, and show their subserviency to the slaveholders. . . . Those who never witnessed such scenes can hardly believe what I know was inflicted at this time on innocent men, women, and children, against whom there was not the slightest ground for suspicion. . . . All day long those unfeeling wretches went round, like a troop of demons, terrifying and tormenting the helpless. At night, they formed themselves into patrol bands, and went wherever they chose among the colored people, acting out their brutal will. . . . The consternation was universal." Jacobs, *Incidents in the Life of a Slave Girl, Written by Herself* (1861), ed. with an introduction by Jean Fagan Yellin (Cambridge, Mass.: Harvard University Press, 1987), 64.

5. Invisible Committee, "Everybody Hates the Police," in *Now,* 69.

6. Immanuel Kant, *Critique of Judgment,* trans. Werner Pluhar (Indianapolis, Ind.: Hackett, 1987). Kant's argument about the beautiful is intricate and complex, and obviously, I am not doing justice to it here, but I am thinking particularly of formulations like "Beautiful is what, without a concept, is liked universally" (64) or, later, "Beautiful is what without a concept is cognized as the object of a necessary liking" (90), which might suggest, as an analogue, "The police are what, without a concept, is cognized as the object of a necessary hatred." See also "Nothing is postulated in a judgment of taste except such a universal voice about a liking unmediated by concepts. Hence all that is postulated is the *possibility* of a judgment that is aesthetic and yet can be considered valid for everyone. The judgment of taste itself does not postulate everyone's agreement (since only a logically universal judgment can do that, because it can adduce reasons); it merely *requires* this agreement from everyone, as an instance of the rule, an instance regarding which it expects confirmation not from concepts but from the agreement of others" (60, 216). I learned a lot from Michel Chaouli's *Thinking with Kant's "Critique of Judgment"* (Cambridge, Mass.: Harvard University Press, 2017), especially the chapter "Community" (42–75).

7. For a related (and brilliant) representation of hatred for the police, see Sean Bonney's poem "ACAB: A Nursery Rhyme" (2014). This poem is not about everybody hating the police so much as it about such a hatred extending to *everything.* It is within or behind every other thing you could say: "All other words are buried there all other words are spoken there." The poem begins with the line "for 'I love you' say fuck the police," and it continues with this basic structure: "for '*x,*' say fuck the police," where *x* is a phrase like "trotsky" or "the morning commute" or "the moon's bright globe" or "here is my new poem." By listing all these things we could and do say but for which we should instead say "fuck the police," Bonney connects the police to work, to the government, to commuting, to Starbucks, to the environment, to religion, to leftist politics, and to poetry itself. The existence of the police alters every aspect of life. But then, in setting up these metaphorical substitutions (for this, say that), Bonney's poem also indicates what saying "fuck the police" may affirm: to say "fuck the police" is also to say "I love you." Hating the police is an affirmation of all the things the police fuck up, which is everything. See Bonney reading his poem at http://abandonedbuildings.blogspot.com/2014/12/acab-nursery-rhyme.html.

8. Chaouli, *Thinking with Kant's "Critique of Judgment,"* 51.

9. Carl Schmitt, *The Concept of the Political* (1932), trans. George Schwab (Chicago: University of Chicago Press, 1996), 28.

10. As one of the basic human affects or emotions, anger has its own considerable literature, from Aristotle (or, indeed, from *The Iliad,* which begins with Achilles's rage) forward, through all the major theories of emotion. Hate, as Lara Langer Cohen and Brian Connolly note, "has been ceded to reactionary politics, so that we encounter it largely in the all-too-familiar vitriol of those who feel their power threatened." Langer Cohen and Connolly, "Theses on Hating," *Avidly,* June 16, 2015, https://avidly.lareviewofbooks.org/2015/06/16/theses-on-hating/. On hatred, they mention William Hazlitt's "On the Pleasure of Hating" (1826) and D. W. Winnicott's "Hate in the Counter-Transference" (1949). But see also D. W. Harding, "Regulated Hatred: An

Aspect of the Work of Jane Austen," *Scrutiny* 8 (1940): 346–47, reprinted in Monica Lawlor, ed., *"Regulated Hatred" and Other Essays on Jane Austen* (London: Athlone Press, 1998), 5–25, and Wendy Anne Lee, "Resituating 'Regulated Hatred': D. W. Harding's Jane Austen," *ELH* 77, no. 4 (2010): 995–1014.

11. Peter Sloterdijk, *Rage and Time: A Psychopolitical Investigation,* trans. Mario Wenning (New York: Columbia University Press, 2010). "He who wants to remember his rage needs to preserve it in hate containers. . . . In general, the concept of hatred proves analytically unsuitable because it is deduced from the phenomenon of rage and can only be made intelligible as a form of preserving rage" (57).

12. Aristotle, "Rhetoric," in *Basic Works of Aristotle,* ed. Richard McKeon (1941; repr., New York: Random House, 2001), 1389.

13. Langer Cohen and Connolly, "Theses on Hating."

14. The line is "In a package of minutes there is this We." Gwendolyn Brooks, "An Aspect of Love, Alive in the Ice and Fire," in *Riot* (Detroit, Mich.: Broadside Press, 1969), 21.

15. In *When They Call You a Terrorist* (New York: St. Martin's Griffin, 2017), Patrice Khan-Cullors, one of the founders of the Black Lives Matter movement, powerfully describes the forms of affiliation, love, and solidarity that originate in shared experiences of and opposition to racist police violence.

16. "Expectant emotions (like anxiety, fear, hope, belief) . . . are those whose drive-intention is long-term, whose drive-object does not yet lie ready, not just in respective individual attainability, but also in the already available world. . . . Thus the expectant emotions are distinguished, both in their unwish and their wish, from the filled emotions by the *incomparably greater anticipatory* character in their intention, their substance and their object." Ernst Bloch, *The Principle of Hope,* trans. Neville Plaice, Stephen Plaice, and Paul Knight (Cambridge, Mass.: MIT Press, 1995), 1:74.

17. *Black Panther* (aka "Off the Pigs"), Newsreel 19 (San Fransisco: Newsreel, 1968), viewed at https://www.youtube.com/watch?v=IrZIEMrmVrw.

18. Zora Neale Hurston, "Spirituals and Neo-Spirituals," in *Negro: An Anthology,* collected and ed. Nancy Cunard (New York: Continuum, 2002), 224.

19. Bloch, *Principle of Hope,* 110.

20. Gwendolyn Brooks, "The Third Sermon on the Warpland," in *Riot,* 14.

21. Many of Muromtseva's works can be seen on her website: https://www.muromtseva.art/.

22. Walter Benjamin, "Surrealism," in *Walter Benjamin, Selected Writings* (Cambridge, Mass.: Harvard University Press, 1999), 2:217.

20 Who Protects Us from You (Pushing and Pushing and Pushing)

ADIA BENTON

In an oral history interview conducted on April 17, 2017, VB, a self-described junior field epidemiologist from the Centers for Disease Control and Prevention (CDC), told her interviewer about her team's daily foray into Magazine Wharf, a neighborhood in Freetown, Sierra Leone, searching for Ebola cases. It was May 2015, and Sierra Leone had been poised to declare an end to a deadly Ebola outbreak that had begun there a year before. But new cases continued to crop up in the low-lying, informal settlement, dashing all hopes for an end to the death and debility Ebola left in its wake. VB and her team—usually comprising a social mobilizer, an epidemiologist, a clinician, a contact tracer, and an Ebola survivor—were assigned the Magazine Wharf beat. Aggressive contact tracing had become central to efforts to end the outbreak once and for all.

Fast-forward to May 30, 2020, Minnesota, five days after police officer Derek Chauvin murdered George Floyd in Minneapolis, in the midst of escalating protests and the Covid-19 pandemic. Minnesota governor Tim Walz held a press conference with John Harrington, Minnesota's public safety commissioner, to address the protests. When Harrington stepped up to the podium to field questions from the news media, Minnesota Public Radio's Euan Kerr asked, "I mean, who are these people and what's happening right now in terms of . . . you going after them?"

Harrington responded, "As we've begun making arrests, we have begun analyzing the data of who we've arrested, and begun actually doing what . . .

is almost very similar to our Covid. It's contact tracing. Who are they associated with? What platforms are they advocating for? And we have seen
things like white supremacist organizers who have hosted things on platforms about coming to Minnesota. . . . We are checking to see, do the folks
we have made arrests on, and that we have information [on], are they connected to those platforms? . . . We have seen flyers about protests, where
folks have talked about they're going to 'get their loot on' tonight. We've
checked to see, are they part of a criminal organization, and if so, what is
that organization? And how are they organized?"

When Harrington compared police work and contact tracing, it did not
sit well with Epidemiology Twitter. No one wants to be police these days.
Or, at least no one wants to cop to being a cop. An influential young epidemiological modeler whose work has long been supported by the U.S.
Department of Defense shared her thoughts on social media: "This is not
contact tracing! What is described in the video is police work. To see the
two linked jeopardizes the credibility of public health, which needs community trust to work effectively." An enthusiastic defense of public health,
to be sure.

The subtext here is that, at their worst, the police are enemies of the community (i.e., all cops are bastards); at best, they cannot be trusted, and
therefore they do not do their work effectively. (Of course, at that particular moment, in the midst of the long 2020, policing as an institution was
again in the midst of its own reckoning, as evidenced by well-attended
protests against police violence amid a deadly pandemic and widespread
calls to defund and abolish the police.) The subtext here is also that contact tracing is not working effectively because community trust is fickle,
unstable, not guaranteed. Thus, to conflate the two, to confuse police work
and public health work for each other, is to ensure that contact tracing's
legitimacy will always be in question when it comes to "community trust."
(Let's leave aside who constitutes "the community" in the epidemiological
imagination.)

The context here is that public health, and contact tracing as a tool of public health, is very much like police work (ask the pop culture icon "disease
detectives" who work under the formal title of "epidemic intelligence officers"); it often works in concert with police work (ask undocumented sex

workers in the midst of an outbreak of sexually transmitted infections); and it is often experienced as indistinguishable from policing (ask someone who has been interrogated by someone from the public health department). The context here is that public health's legitimacy, irrespective of its cop tendencies, has been undermined by its chronic underfunding at federal, state, county, and municipal levels; its farming out of key functions to private companies (neoliberalism!); its patchwork governance; and the misogyny that accompanies the profession's increasing feminization.

I think again of VB and her team entering Magazine Wharf. I imagine them stepping carefully down the steep pathways, avoiding the debris and puddles that tend to settle in the low-lying areas of the hilly seaside city, with its crumbling water and sanitation infrastructure. Members of the team brush past, sidle by, and rub up against area residents going about their business, as they seek new people with symptoms, as they actively pursue and track the contacts of Ebola patients. They visit the homes and other potential spaces of infectious contact and contagion. VB remarks, "Magazine Wharf has homes that are so close to each other, and this was a disease we're trying to avoid touch and contact and you often had to squeeze by people, sweaty people, and you knew it could be transmitted through sweat, or speculation at the time. We're like, what do we do? And then the homes—you can't invade someone's space when they say this person is not home. You have to verify that there's no one hiding in the room, but how do you do that diplomatically?"

VB asks how to be diplomatic about verifying that no one is hiding. As I scan the oral history transcripts, I look for evidence of whether VB had a hunch about why people would be hiding in the first place. Care and treatment for Ebola had gotten better; more people were surviving an Ebola infection by May 2015; the inhumane holding centers had become less so. Communities had been known to lash out at Ebola workers for their invasiveness, but she was not worried about her safety, she told the interviewer, because her team included a health worker who was from the community and an Ebola survivor, enlisted to help because of their immunity (and membership in the community). VB told us in so many words that the survivor and the community health worker served as intermediaries who allowed for frictionless passage into the homes of Ebola's infected. They were there to help establish trust where it was not guaranteed.

Maybe this brand of public health is trying to shake loose of its cop tendencies. But I cannot get VB's words out of my head, as she's struggling to map all the connections among infections and, by extension, relations and narratives of blame: "Epi[demiologist]s always say this . . . when there's that missing link and you're pushing and you're pushing and you're pushing and you're not getting information, but you know that there's something there that is unresolved."

Pushing and pushing.
And pushing.

Which reminds me of a conversation I had with an acquaintance, LM, a hemorrhagic fever expert who has been living and working in Kenema, Sierra Leone, off and on for years and was especially traumatized by the relentless work, death, and suffering in those early months of the outbreak. LM tells me, of contact tracing efforts, "It was like a police interrogation."

Where have you been? Who were you with? When were you with them?
What did they touch?

Pushing and pushing.
And pushing.

The conversation with LM probably happened when I was writing about the martial politics of epidemic response, where I had been focused on the literal use of national and foreign militaries to manage the Ebola response in the region, and the military metaphors and practices embedded in public health practice—the elective affinity, one might say, between "the" military and public health. Some scholars say "militarization" assumes that, at some point in the recent past, public health and biomedicine were not militarized. (I am one of those scholars.) Other scholars say we need to consider seriously the ways health and other sociobiological concerns infiltrate national security concerns, how security has been medicalized, how the "medical countermeasures" of health security, increasingly pharmaceuticalized, lead to the internalization—the literal embodiment—of biosecurity paradigms.

Biopolitics all the way down.
All the way inside.

I am perhaps one of those scholars, as I write from my basement in Chicago, watching folks on social media describe their efforts to "score" a Pfizer, Moderna, or Johnson and Johnson vaccination against Covid-19.

As people declare themselves newly inducted members of the Pfizer fam or Moderna mafia.

An Ebola survivor whom I met during a visit to southeastern Sierra Leone in 2018—I'll call him Mohammed—is telling me about his work as the leader of a survivor's association, one of several such organizations that were established in the aftermath of the Ebola outbreak, in each of the country's districts. The associations are a way for survivors, and the organizations that (used to) support them, to advocate for the rights of and continued support for people who suffered an Ebola infection and lived. Less is said about the people who lost their family members to the disease. It is an opportunity for them to come together under a common cause: sometimes that cause is better access to health care for post-Ebola syndrome; sometimes it's better access to health care for everyone. But it is also a kind of club whose members speculate on and attempt to reap benefits from a biological affiliation, an immunological membership.

Another survivor, let's call her Binta, interrupts Mohammed to tell me that after he was placed in an "Ebola holding center" to await his test results, Mohammed absconded to another town to escape the terror of the holding center. I thought she was trying to tell me that Mohammed wasn't a "perfect" survivor—and maybe that was OK, and perhaps it was also funny, ironic. A survivor doesn't become a survivor simply by virtue of having survived Ebola but by having embraced it as an identity wholesale. I laughed. Mohammed laughed too. Nervously. He seemed embarrassed. He said, "You have to understand what they were saying about what went on in the holding centers. I was getting WhatsApp messages all the time." Yes, I knew what they were saying in those text messages: if you didn't have Ebola when you entered the holding center, then you contracted it there. The holding centers and the early iterations of Ebola treatment centers were places where people died undignified, excruciating deaths; in those places, temporary residents also saw their compatriots die. Rumors abounded about the kinds of experimentation and extraction occurring in the centers.

One could not know for sure.

But he survived and was one of the earliest of the Ebola patients to have done so. I also heard in his story, in the story that Binta felt compelled to interject into our conversation, that those who failed to comply, those who refused to stay in these sites that inspired terror and fear among their temporary residents, were treated as fugitives.

Fugitivity has its own carceral logics.

Fugitives are hunted. They are tracked. They are brought back to face the consequences of their refusal.

Mohammed survived this too.

Within hours of her plea to dissociate policing and public health in official statements, the influential epidemiological modeler softened her criticism of John Harrington, Minnesota public safety commissioner. "I understand it's an analogy and I'm sure this official had a very long day. But I really don't want public health and police action to get crossed in people's minds. Community trust is paramount." What if the long 2020 shows us that this crossing happened not only in people's minds—in the collective consciousness—but in the organizing logic of "the field" itself? I tread carefully here as an anthropologist for whom "fieldwork" is crucial to professional legitimacy and identity; the field is a place where we anthropologists establish our legitimacy as experts. Field policing methods bear more than a passing resemblance to field epidemiology. Anthropology does not need "field" as a modifier, because that would be redundant; it is not immune from this critique of what constitutes the field, the violence of "the field." Nor is it immune from having its cop tendencies pointed out (e.g., hello, informants).

I nicknamed a former boss, an anthropologist, "mall cop."

It's not the worst kind of cop to be. I guess.

According to the public health ordinance act passed during Sierra Leone's colonial period, and updated in 2014 to reflect changes with Ebola, anyone suspected of harboring an individual suspected of having an Ebola infection could be fined $200 (more than a year's salary for the average Sierra Leonean) or face up to two years' imprisonment. Participating in "illegal" funerals could have warranted similar punishment.

Policing methods bear more than a passing resemblance to epidemiology. Joe McCormick, who investigated Lassa fever outbreaks in Sierra Leone and the first outbreaks of Ebola in Sudan and Zaire in 1976, wrote in his recent memoir, "An outbreak investigation is very much like the investigation of a crime. It consists of detective work, following hunches, and carefully collecting evidence. In epidemiology, however, the criminal is the bug. Find the bug. And then find how it got to its human hosts. The bug's motive? Making a lot more bugs, I guess. But it's not just bugs you're dealing with. You have to deal with people, especially the victims. It requires some effort to explain to them what you're doing, and then to convince them to cooperate."

21 DARVO

The Inversion of Sex, Gender, and
Sexuality in the Era of Trump's Mirror

CARY GABRIEL COSTELLO

I know you are, but what am I?
—schoolyard taunt

The year 2020 was a year that felt to many like it would never end. This was
due partly to the uncertainty and stress of the Covid-19 pandemic. But it
was also just an intensified version of an experience that started with the
inauguration of Donald Trump as president—a strange sense of time dila-
tion endured by many, resulting from the unending stream of crises and
conflicts on which Trump thrived. This produced two things: a sense of
ceaseless chaos and a disconcerting feeling of living in a topsy-turvy world.
In this odd timeline, victims were portrayed as oppressors, social justice as
tyranny, and virtues as vices.

I want to write about how this inversion functioned in the context of
inflicting harm on sex, gender, and sexual minorities in ways that did not
end in 2020, any more than Covid-19 disappeared with the end of the year.
But to do that, I need first to talk more generally about how the upending
of reality relates to the Trump presidency.

Trump was a president who stirred chaos by governing via tweet. For
example, on July 26, 2017, he tweeted, "After consultation with my generals
and military experts, please be advised that the United States government
will not accept or allow . . . transgender individuals to serve in any capacity
in the US military."[1] The Pentagon, decidedly not consulted, had no com-
ment. What was clear was that this tweet proclamation generated fear and
pain among trans Americans and thrilled transphobic Trumpists. What

was not clear is how this would translate into policy, which produced the aforementioned chaos. At that point, just half a year into the Trump presidency, administration officials were still presenting this as a problem that could be solved by better managing the president.

But this was a president who could not be kept on script. Less than three weeks later, white supremacists rallied in Charlottesville, Virginia, and one attendee used his vehicle as a weapon, plowing into a group of counterprotesters and killing one young woman. This incident handed Trump an opportunity to present himself as a reasonable leader who, of course, opposed Nazis killing people. But, stuffing a set of prepared comments from an aide that clearly said just that into his pocket, Trump instead told the press that there were "some very fine people on both sides" and that the press was unfairly focusing on the alt-right instead of the "alt-left" that came "charging at" the white supremacists.[2]

Under Trump, fascists—for decades the cartoon villains of American media—became normalized as just any other political group, and antifascists became framed not as heroes but as dangerous radicals. Many talking heads tsked at those yelping that Trump's statements were unacceptable, claiming that those triggered were making the foolish progressive error of taking the president *literally* but not *seriously*, instead of *seriously* but not *literally*.[3] He doesn't actually mean these things, they chided—he's just having fun pushing the buttons of sensitive liberals for the entertainment of his fans! But by 2020, as Black Lives Matter protests swept across the country, it would be indisputable that Trump was seriously asserting that "antifa is a terrorist organization," and conservative white Americans would equally clearly take him literally. For example, a multiracial family on a camping trip in Washington was accused of being antifa by white men with semiautomatic weapons, who felled trees across the road to trap their bus in an incident that almost ended in tragedy.[4]

This would all culminate in the last days of the Trump presidency, with a horde of the man's supporters—mostly white, mostly men—storming the Capitol and demanding the head of the vice president while calling themselves "patriots." A few days later, my senator Ron Johnson would be falsely claiming on the Senate floor that the insurrectionists were really antifa agents, provocateurs pretending to be Trump supporters.[5] The inversion of reality was complete.

For many Americans, this feeling of inversion set in long before the widespread Covid-19 lockdowns that began in March 2020, though it would swell to appalling intensity during the pandemic. For years, it was as if we were in a *Star Trek* episode where we'd suffered a transporter mishap and wound up in a mirror universe. War was peace and freedom was slavery. Empathy and social justice were declared by the president to be oppressive and censorious political correctness. A land of liberty required giving trans kids no place to pee and locking refugee children in cages. Then, when the pandemic hit, somehow efforts to save people through public health measures were recast by literal Nazis as fascism. People who claimed that they were willing to risk the ultimate sacrifice to protect America from tyranny were unwilling to make the minor sacrifice of wearing a mask to protect their fellow Americans. They were ready to die for what they claimed was a constitutional right to kill their neighbors. It was madness. And Trump fanned the flames, tweeting, "LIBERATE MINNESOTA!," "LIBERATE MICHIGAN!," and "LIBERATE VIRGINIA!"[6]

That's just how Trump is, we were told.

When we say that Trump is who he is, though, what do we mean? A number of factors are regularly raised. Trump is a narcissist; he thrives off chaos and conflict; he is a font of fragile masculinity; he demands loyalty but doesn't give it. All those are true. What I want to focus on here is how he operated as a classic abuser in an era of social media that allowed him to broadcast his abuse. And I want to show how this explains our experience of living in a mirror universe where everything got turned on its head.

What I want to talk about is DARVO, an acronym for "deny, attack, and reverse victim and offender." The term comes out of criminology and the study of sexual violence, which finds that when abusers are held accountable for their actions by some whistleblower, they deny doing anything wrong, attack the whistleblower, and claim that they were the true victims of abuse by the individual they had harmed.[7]

Think about how familiar this sounds. In the first weeks of the Trump presidency, news stories abounded about how false rumors had circulated on social media during the lead-up to the election, presented as "news" but actually produced by Russian troll farms. The reporting on the phenomenon referred to the false stories as "fake news," blowing the whistle on it. Within days, Trump had started referring to mainstream media fact-checking pieces about falsehoods he was asserting as "fake news." All media outlets except for right-wing propaganda sites were dubbed sources of lies, with the media itself being framed as the enemy of truth. Trump referred to the press as the "opposition party" and as utterly dishonest.[8] This reversal of victim and offender and his technique of attacking the whistleblower became mainstays of life under Trump.

Yet the parties we should be worried about most are not the whistle-blowers but the targeted victims of abuse. In a DARVO situation, the abuser claims that he (or she, or they, but most often he) is the "real victim." Victims of abuse are framed as predators and manipulators by the predatory manipulator who has been abusing them. Psychologists might call it "projection." For anyone spending time on social media, it's called "trolling."

Trump was the Troll in Chief. His presidency didn't have a policy plat-form, but it did have a core goal: to "own the libs." This was what endeared him to the online "manosphere"[9] that was essential to the rise of his candidacy. He shared with these misogynists their favorite trolling tactics: to tease and poke and kick their preferred targets—the "social justice warriors"—and, when called out, to feign innocence, to say they were just posing a question or making a joke and were now being attacked for no reason by oversensitive or vicious agents of the culture war. Then they could step back and chortle together, perhaps drinking out of mugs sold on Amazon .com that read "FLAVORED WITH A DELICIOUS DISTILLATION OF LIBERAL TEARS AND MELTED SNOWFLAKES."[10]

This was Trump's main gift: an ability to enflame the culture wars with proclamations causing a wide array of people to howl in sequence: women, people of color, immigrants, LGBTQ+ people, greens, Muslims, disabled people. And he told his base that they no longer needed to feel obliged to empathize with any of these Others. They should enjoy the howling, because those crying out had harmed innocent conservative patriots and deserved to suffer. Empathy was for fools, a prissy progressive shibboleth, a game for losers. Righteous alpha males fought their enemies and cele-brated their victories!

Reversing victim and offender was crucial to this tactic. What was so intoxicating to Trump's base was that he brought them along on his DARVO ride. Not only did he claim that he personally was being unfairly attacked by the whistleblowing press and "un-American" people from every group other than cis straight white conservative Christian men but he validated this worldview for his exhilarated followers. Take the red pill, men: you are victims of feminists! Christians, you are being persecuted! White people are the victims of reverse discrimination! Refugees seeking asylum are really an invading army of criminals and rapists, coming for the good citizens of the United States! Women are being victimized by the trans agenda!

These were DARVO techniques enacted on a mass scale.

What was the effect on sex, gender, and sexual minorities specifically? I am focusing on this population because I am an intersex trans man; my wife is intersex, was surgically assigned male at birth, and also gender transitioned; and both of us are pansexual by orientation. In other words, we are impacted as sex-variant individuals, as trans people, and due to our sexual orientation, and there's nothing like personal experience to make clear how people are impacted by the DARVO gaslighting[11] of a population. In the era of Trump's Mirror, civil rights protections for queer and trans people were cast as attacks on the right to freedom of religion, with Christians framed as suffering persecution by those whose relationships and identities they refused to respect and thus as in need of government protection.

This was hardly the first time that bigotry has been cast in the United States as justified by the Christian faith. For example, in the 1950s and 1960s, desegregation advocacy was opposed by white evangelical Christians, who claimed that God required racial segregation. They based this on Acts 17:26, which reads, "And hath made of one blood all nations of men for to dwell on all the face of the earth, and hath determined the times before appointed, and the bounds of their habitation."[12] White evangelical racists claimed that these words meant that God created all humanity but separated them by race, placing "bounds" around them, and that anyone arguing for desegregation was an agent of Satan opposing God's plan.[13] White evangelical Christian civil rights counterprotesters referred to Dr. Martin Luther King Jr. as the Antichrist.

Nor was Trump first to present LGBTQ+ rights as in conflict with Christianity. That has been around since Anita Bryant's Save Our Children campaign against gay rights ordinances started in 1977.[14] But the posture of Christian claims has changed. Bob Jones referred to integrationists as marginal "infidels."[15] Anita Bryant presented herself as speaking for all parents by framing herself as a Christian mother protecting her children from predatory homosexuals seeking to "recruit" them. In the 1980s, conservative social politics were dominated by white Christian evangelicals calling themselves the "Moral Majority." Christians were presented as the norm and feminists and LGBT people and opponents of school prayer as heretics at society's fringes who must be repressed by the morally righteous.

But the conceptualizations of center and margin were inverted via DARVO tactics under Trump. Now the preferred posture of white evangelical leaders was that Christians were a marginalized group, facing repression at the hands of empowered elites who demand that Christians defer to LGBTQ+ people, trying to force Christians to violate their religious precepts. Their followers have lapped this up. After many decades of framing their "right" to dictate public policy as founded on their position at society's center, presenting those at society's margins as aberrant, evangelicals decided that the people who are "really privileged" are those deemed victims of discrimination by the majority—and that evangelicals were the greatest victims of all. Republican pollster Kristen Soltis Anderson states that "one of the most unifying beliefs of the Trump coalition was the idea that there is religious persecution of Christians in the US these days" and that this explains "why you saw Donald Trump, despite his sort of personal ethical issues, still being quite beloved by evangelicals, [because he] was going to defend their right to practice their religion as they saw fit and not be told by [the government or other institutions] that they couldn't."[16]

This framing of Christian belief and practice is a very strange one in that discriminating against people who are queer, trans, and/or nonbinary is placed at the center of Christian doctrine, when in fact Jesus had absolutely zero to say on those topics (or on abortion) but rather a lot to say about feeding the hungry, welcoming the foreigner, and not casting stones at people you believe to have sinned. But there's no doubt that this posture seized the imaginations of evangelical Christians during the Trump years and has not let go since he left office. In March 2021, as Congress debated the Equality Act—which would prohibit discrimination on the basis of sex, sexual orientation, and gender identity—prominent evangelical preacher Rick Joyner was all over social media referring to the act as a "Bill to Criminalize Christianity."[17] Representative Lauren Boebert declared the Equality Act to be imposing "a supremacy of gays, lesbians, and, uh . . . transvexhikes."[18] The impression given was that Christians were a hair's breadth away from being thrown to the lions in the Colosseum and in dire need of protection from the people persecuting them: trans and queer people and their allies.

This was, of course, the inverse of the reality of who was being victimized, which did not slow at all during the pandemic. In 2020, more than 350 trans people are known to have been murdered.[19] A record number of bills restricting the rights of trans people was introduced in state legislatures around the United States, seeking various combinations of banning trans children and adults from participating in sports in their lived genders, requiring people to use bathrooms of the binary gender listed on their birth certificates, and/or forbidding recognition of gender transitions altogether.[20]

LGBTQ+ people also suffered disproportionately from Covid-19 because of the social marginality that produces unstable and overcrowded housing situations, unsafe employment conditions, poor access to health care, and discrimination by health care providers.[21] Despite this, the Trump administration fought throughout 2020 to eliminate protections for trans people in health care.[22] Providers of Covid-19 testing contracting with the federal government required people being tested to register under their binary sex assigned at birth, though physical sex characteristics have zero relevance to Covid-19 testing. I speak from personal experience, being tested several times at my university by a federally contracted company, which required me to arrange for my own misgendering. I put substantial effort into mobilizing human resources staff to formally point out to the contractor that the university prohibits discrimination against trans people, but the company stonewalled and stated this was federal policy. Contractors providing Covid-19 testing and vaccinations continued to do the same thing through much of 2021, despite the change in administrations.

One of the saddest things about the DARVO approach to denying trans and queer people rights has been the way it has boosted both transmisogynistic hate and concomitant levels of fear experienced by cis women and children in the presence of trans women. During the Trump years, a sex panic about trans women and girls in bathrooms mushroomed, as white evangelical Christian organizations held rallies and "pray-ins" for bills aimed at preventing transfeminine people from using women's bathrooms. These rallies and social media campaigns had titles like #DaughtersOverDollars and #PrivacyOverPredators and generated real fear that an evil cabal of "elites" and corporations was enabling a swarm of "men in dresses" to enter girl's restrooms in elementary schools and women's changing rooms at malls, peeping at and sexually assaulting cis gender victims.

A result of this manufactured sex panic has been increased surveillance of transfeminine people, most especially when it comes to bathrooms and locker rooms. And thus, even though the majority were not enacted, bathroom bills had the desired effect. Many business owners, security guards, and ordinary citizens incorrectly believe that it is currently illegal for trans women to use women's bathrooms unless the government passes a law overtly stating that they have that right. Using a restroom became extremely fraught for trans women and girls, and many stopped attending school, or exercising at a gym, or visiting public parks, or traveling, or doing anything where they might have to pee away from the safety of their homes.

In 2014, *Time* magazine's cover article was titled "The Transgender Tipping Point," and in it, progress toward full societal inclusion was declared to be inevitable and coming soon.[23] Then Trump was elected, and his DARVO tactics metastasized around the nation—and by the time the widespread quarantines began in spring 2020, many trans and nonbinary people, most especially transfeminine ones not living in a big coastal city, were already essentially living in lockdown. I've spoken with numerous trans women and transfeminine nonbinary folks who found life during the pandemic to be a relief, because suddenly their experiences of social isolation at home and a fear of encounters with other people were normalized. The tribulations falling on others like a ton of bricks were ones they'd already had to face, and survive, without others noticing what they were enduring or, worse, blaming them for it, perhaps with bonus unhelpful advice about their clothing or grooming, as if they wouldn't face harassment if they were only to wear skirts instead of jeans, or jeans instead of skirts, or to carry or not carry a cute femme purse.

The rash of transphobic state legislating has not slowed with the end of 2020. In fact, it has accelerated, and in the month in which I am writing, three states have passed laws requiring schoolchildren and college athletes to produce their original birth certificates to participate in sports and only to be allowed to participate with people sharing the gender marker they were assigned at birth.[24] In many other states, similar bills are wending their way through the legislative process.[25] All invert the reality that trans and nonbinary children and adults are subjected to forms of harassment and discrimination that not only keep them from engaging in athletics but prevent them from even trying to access a gym or beach or pool. Everyday trans people's health suffers as a result of this exclusion, but it is cis women athletes who are presented as harmed.

The trans sport bans bring us to a level of DARVO that is even deeper and more insidious but less recognized: the issue of the empirical reality of sex, gender, and sexuality and what exactly constitutes "gender ideology." The term *gender ideology* is used by the pope,[26] by Trans Exclusionary Radical Feminists (TERFs) in Britain,[27] and by Trumpist ideologues in the United States.[28] They define "natural sex" against "gender ideology." According to their description of "natural sex," sex is an eternal binary, established by God or by biology, in which chromosomes determine birth genitals and birth genitals determine destiny. According to the pope and evangelical Christians, genitals reveal God's will for a patriarchal complementarian binary gender arrangement and the place one is to serve in it.[29] For TERFs, genitals determine gender socialization in an oppressive patriarchy and what risks of sexualized violence one is subjected to or enabled to enact. The Christian and TERF visions evaluate patriarchy very differently, but they agree on the following: to deny that sex is a natural binary is "gender ideology." People born intersex are framed as rare, disordered, and desirous of a cure, and to claim otherwise is "gender ideology." To assert that nonbinary sex or gender identity is normal is "gender ideology." In fact, even to assert that gender identity exists and should be respected is "gender ideology." To support gender transition is "gender ideology." Trans and/or nonbinary people are said to be a new and strange group who deny the nature of sex, heretofore unchallenged for millennia—and they are dangerous. Trans women in particular pose a sexual threat to children and cis women, who must be protected from this danger. And parents who adhere to "gender ideology" by respecting the trans and/or nonbinary gender identities of their children are child abusers (according to evangelicals) or pushers of conversion therapies on lesbian and gay children (according to TERFs) who must be stopped.[30]

The strange bedfellows of Christian gender reactionaries and transphobic radical feminists have enjoyed many successes during the Trump years. This is due in no small part to the fact that other, less overtly transphobic people share the biological essentialist assumptions of overt bigots about the nature of sex, gender, and sexuality. But this perception is in fact another inversion of fact and myth. The story of a natural and eternal binary is an ideology that denies both the empirical reality of sex and the world history of gender and sexuality. Empirically speaking, sex is by nature a spectrum, and calling it a binary is ideology.[31] Intersex people (and dogs and goats and chickens and any other animal you can name) have always been born. Nonbinary sex/gender is pervasive in world history; in fact, the most common number of recognized sex/gender categories in world societies is three, and many societies have recognized four, five, or more genders.[32] Binary sex is an atypical gender system that happened to be embraced by Christian Europeans at the time that they imposed their culture by colonial force around the world. It is not gender transition or nonbinary genders or recognizing same-gender relationships or accepting physical sex variance that is new. These things are traditional; they are ancient.[33]

It is not just the victim of discrimination and its perpetrator who have been inverted via DARVO tactics. It is the nature of reality itself. The fact that there have always been intersex people, gender transitioners, and non-binary identities is erased by an ideology that presents the facts of sex, gender, and sexual variance as a novel and dangerous ideology. And what makes it more outrageous is that TERFs and anti-LGBT-obsessed white evangelicals claim that "science" is on their side, because physical sex characteristics are material facts that can be scientifically observed, while gender identity cannot be observed and thus is "not real." This is a mind-boggling argument to come from (1) a group of women who are often lesbians, whose sexual identity can't be observed and are thus called "unnatural" by their evangelical bedfellows, and (2) people whose identity centers belief in God. Science cannot see or measure God, nor can it directly observe someone's religious identity, after all.

Nevertheless, throughout 2020 and beyond, we saw transphobic cis feminists and evangelicals claiming that science demanded that we stop respecting trans people, lest some terrible peril destroy cis women and girls. When Representative Marie Newman, a Democrat with a trans child, hung a trans flag outside her door in support of the Equality Act, Representative Marjorie Taylor Green, Republican and QAnon fan whose office is across the hall, hung up a huge sign in opposition to the Equality Act that read, "There are TWO genders: MALE & FEMALE. 'Trust The Science!'"[34]

And lo! it didn't stop there but, like Covid-19, has persisted and is ever evolving. I will conclude this piece with an example. A few months into the Biden administration, the very-online residents of the manosphere came up with a new gambit. Going instantly viral on Twitter and TikTok, they proclaimed a new sexual orientation: the "superstraight." Supposedly, superstraight people were a newly recognized sexual minority who are only attracted to cis men or cis women and are repelled by trans people. The assertion was that anyone who defends LGBT rights must recognize, respect, and fight for the rights of "superstraights," who are being oppressed by trans people.

Examples of the social media posts in which the "superstraight" campaign was hatched, plotted, and deployed, and samples of the tropes and images employed, can be seen on my blog.[35] To briefly summarize, fascist trolls on 4chan derived a logo mashing the Nazi SS icon with the colors of PornHub and laughed their collective heads off planning a campaign of sending out "SuperStraight SS agents" to attempt to "drive a wedge between trannies and other fag groups" by using "the left's tactics against themselves."[36] That is, their goal was DARVO subterfuge. They conducted a social media campaign framing bigotry as an innate orientation, and anyone who pushed back at the idea that saying "trans people are gross" is more of a sexual orientation than saying "Jews sexually repel me" was accused of "using conversion therapy rhetoric." The trolls mimicked the rhetoric of #MeToo, claiming that "superstraights" were victims of endless sexual harassment by trans women demanding sex from them. This claim was deployed with glee as a great "gotcha," and anyone who pointed out that this was extremely implausible was twitted, "Believe victims!" The dynamics of social power and the empirical reality of who gets sexually abused were not just ignored but inverted by smirking trolls.

As planned on 4chan, the "superstraight movement" was said to have finally united LGB and straight people by revealing their shared dismissal of "trans bullshit." Social media users who decried the blatant transphobia of the #SuperStraight campaign were attacked as "SERFs": "straight exclusionary radical feminists." Post after post claimed that those saying "this is ridiculous, you troll" proved that the left were a bunch of hypocrites who wouldn't let you call *their* gender identities fake but happily denied that *your* sexual orientation was real. Those posts came from people with fascist memes for avatars, posting "superstraight" flags modeled on the Nazi war emblem.

In the two days after the blog post went live, I got to experience the joy of a mass trolling, with more than 250 gleeful bigots coming onto my personal Facebook page, leaving posts accusing me of discriminating against oppressed "superstraights" and calling for me to be "cancelled." Worse things have happened to better people, but it did take me many hours to clean up my Facebook wall and tediously block each snickering bigot one by one.

And this is what life is like under the reign of DARVO. Explanations of how one is being harmed and marginalized are not received with empathy; instead, they are inverted and deployed to cause further harm. As the playground taunt goes, "I'm rubber, you're glue. Anything you say to me bounces off and sticks to you!" Or, more succinctly, with the puerile whine, "I know you are, but what am I?" Cis straight white Christian men name themselves the most persecuted minority on the planet and believe that

this is the ultimate "gotcha," a Super Genius move that will shut up everyone else forever. Sadly, this does seem persuasive to a substantial number
of people or at least renders them speechless. And so the DARVO tactics
remain ubiquitous beyond the long 2020.

NOTES

1. Molly Redden and Sabrina Siddiqui, "Donald Trump Says US Military Will
Not Allow Transgender People to Serve," *The Guardian*, July 26, 2017, https://www.the
guardian.com/us-news/2017/jul/26/trump-says-us-military-will-not-accept-or
-allow-transgender-people-to-serve.

2. Politico Staff, "Full Text: Trump's Comments on White Supremacists, 'Alt-
Left' in Charlottesville," *Politico*, August 15, 2017, https://www.politico.com/story/
2017/08/15/full-text-trump-comments-white-supremacists-alt-left-transcript-241662.

3. This formulation is generally credited to Salena Zito of *The Atlantic* in her
article "Taking Trump Seriously, Not Literally," September 23, 2016, https://www.the
atlantic.com/politics/archive/2016/09/trump-makes-his-case-in-pittsburgh/501335/.

4. David K. Li, "Multiracial Family on Washington State Camping Trip Is Accused
of Being Antifa and Menaced," NBC News, June 9, 2020, https://www.nbcnews
.com/news/us-news/multiracial-family-washington-state-camping-trip-accused-be
ing-antifa-menaced-n1228281.

5. Phil Hands, "Hands on Wisconsin: 'Fake Trump Supporters' Star in Ron Johnson's Latest Conspiracy Theory," *Wisconsin State Journal*, February 5, 2021, https://
madison.com/wsj/opinion/cartoon/hands-on-wisconsin-fake-trump-supporters
-star-in-ron-johnsons-latest-conspiracy-theory/article_4f8a41c4-b196-5a33-9cd9-dfe
8ee9ad641.html.

6. Craig Mauger and Beth LeBlanc, "Trump Tweets 'Liberate' Michigan, Two
Other States with Dem Governors," *Detroit News*, April 17, 2020, https://www.de
troitnews.com/story/news/politics/2020/04/17/trump-tweets-liberate-michigan
-other-states-democratic-governors/5152037002/.

7. The classic description of DARVO that other sources often cite is Jennifer J.
Freyd's "What Is DARVO?," https://dynamic.uoregon.edu/jjf/defineDARVO.

8. Nolan D. McCaskill, "Trump Backs Bannon: 'The Media Is the Opposition
Party,'" *Politico*, January 27, 2017, https://www.politico.com/story/2017/01/donald
-trump-steve-bannon-media-opposition-party-234280.

9. Debbie Ging, "Alphas, Betas, and Incels: Theorizing the Masculinities of the
Manosphere," *Men and Masculinities* 22, no. 4 (2019): 638–57.

10. This mug by Politics Are Funny Shirts Are Serious is just one of a thousand
memetic variants. It can be found at https://www.amazon.com/gp/product/B077
L6V5ZS.

11. Stephanie A. Sarkis, "11 Red Flags of Gaslighting in a Relationship," *Psychology
Today*, January 22, 2017, https://www.psychologytoday.com/us/blog/here-there
-and-everywhere/201701/11-warning-signs-gaslighting.

12. KJV.

13. Justin Taylor, "Is Segregation Scriptural? A Radio Address from Bob Jones on Easter of 1960," *The Gospel Coalition* (blog), July 26, 2016, https://www.thegospel coalition.org/blogs/evangelical-history/is-segregation-scriptural-a-radio-address -from-bob-jones-on-easter-of-1960/.

14. Anthony S. Niedwiecki and William E. Adams Jr., "Thirty Years after Anita Bryant's Crusade: The Continuing Role of Morality in the Development of Legal Rights for Sexual Minorities," *NOVA Law Review* 32, no. 3 (2008): 517–22.

15. In Taylor, "Is Segregation Scriptural?"

16. Ezra Klein interviewing Kristen Soltis Anderson, "Transcript: A Top GOP Pollster on Trump 2024, QAnon and What Republicans Really Want," *New York Times,* March 26, 2021, https://www.nytimes.com/2021/03/26/opinion/ezra-klein -podcast-kristen-soltis-anderson.html.

17. See, e.g., his Facebook post https://www.facebook.com/permalink.php?story _fbid=4371375376228579&id=106368016062691.

18. Sam van Pykeren, "Lauren Boebert Says Equality Act Is 'Supremacy of Gays,'" *Mother Jones,* March 3, 2021, https://www.motherjones.com/mojo-wire/ 2021/03/lauren-boebert-says-equality-act-is-supremacy-of-gays/.

19. Jamie Wareham, "Murdered, Suffocated and Burned Alive—350 Transgender People Killed in 2020," *Forbes,* November 11, 2020, https://www.forbes.com/sites/ jamiewareham/2020/11/11/350-transgender-people-have-been-murdered-in-2020 -transgender-day-of-remembrance-list/.

20. ACLU, "Trans Rights under Attack in 2020," https://www.aclu.org/issues/ lgbtq-rights/transgender-rights.

21. The Human Rights Campaign Fund, "Brief: The Lives and Livelihoods of Many in the LGBTQ Community Are at Risk amidst the Covid-19 Crisis," https:// www.hrc.org/resources/the-lives-and-livelihoods-of-many-in-the-lgbtq-community -are-at-risk-amidst-covid-19-crisis.

22. Ryan Thoreson, "Trump Administration Doubles Down on Trans Discrimi- nation," Human Rights Watch, June 25, 2020, https://www.hrw.org/news/2020/ 06/25/trump-administration-doubles-down-trans-discrimination.

23. Katy Steinmetz, "The Transgender Tipping Point," *Time,* May 29, 2014, https:// time.com/135480/transgender-tipping-point/.

24. Catherine Whelan, "Tennessee Becomes 3rd State This Month to Enact Restrictions for Transgender Athletes," NPR, March 27, 2021, https://www.npr.org/ 2021/03/27/981913132/tennessee-becomes-3rd-state-this-month-to-enact-restrictions -for-transgender-ath.

25. Jeremy W. Peters, "Why Transgender Girls Are Suddenly the GOP's New Tar- get," *New York Times,* March 29, 2021, https://www.nytimes.com/2021/03/29/us/ politics/transgender-girls-sports.html.

26. Robert A. Gahl Jr., "Pope Francis Compares Gender Theory to Nuclear Bomb," Alateia, March 2, 2015, https://aleteia.org/2015/03/02/pope-francis-compares -gender-theory-to-nuclear-bomb/.

27. Katelyn Burns, "The Rise of Anti-trans Radical Feminists, Explained," *Vox,* September 5, 2019, https://www.vox.com/identities/2019/9/5/20840101/terfs-radi cal-feminists-gender-critical.

28. Graeme Reid, "Breaking the Buzzword: Fighting the 'Gender Ideology' Myth," Human Rights Watch, December 10, 2018, https://www.hrw.org/news/2018/12/10/breaking-buzzword-fighting-gender-ideology-myth.

29. Council on Biblical Manhood and Womanhood, "The Nashville Statement," August 29, 2017, https://cbmw.org/nashville-statement/.

30. Sarah Toce, "J. K. Rowling Compares 'Transgender Hormone Therapy to Gay Conversion Therapy,'" New Civil Rights Movement, July 7, 2020, https://www.thenewcivilrightsmovement.com/2020/07/j-k-rowling-compares-transgender-hormone-therapy-to-gay-conversion-therapy/.

31. Liza Bruzman, "Sex Isn't Binary, and We Should Stop Acting Like It Is," Massive Science, June 14, 2019, https://massivesci.com/.

32. Cary Gabriel Costello, "Beyond Binary Sex and Gender," in The Oxford Handbook of the Sociology of Body and Embodiment, ed. Natalie Boreo and Kate Manson, 199–220 (New York: Oxford University Press, 2020).

33. See, e.g., Sharyn Graham Davies, "What We Can Learn from an Indonesian Ethnicity That Recognizes Five Genders," The Conversation, June 16, 2016, https://theconversation.com/what-we-can-learn-from-an-indonesian-ethnicity-that-recognizes-five-genders-60775.

34. Heidi Stevens, "Marjorie Taylor Greene Wants Us to 'Trust the Science' on Transgender Rights. Here's the Science," Chicago Tribune, February 26, 2021, https://www.chicagotribune.com/columns/heidi-stevens/ct-heidi-stevens-marjorie-taylor-greene-transphobia-trust-science-0226-20210226-atqjgfqht5hzjl54qjbeu4hk24-story.html.

35. Cary Gabriel Costello, "The 4chan '#SuperStraight' Troll Campaign," Trans-Fusion (blog), March 6, 2021, https://transfusion.medium.com/the-4chan-superstraight-troll-campaign-ac99ef3b2fdb.

36. I'm not going to direct you to 4chan; see Costello.

22 The Rain of Frogs

MCKENZIE WARK

Much talk during the pandemic circled around the question of "returning to normal." As if this would be desirable. As if there might still be norms to which anyone might return. The word *normal* derives from *norma*, which in Latin is a carpenter's square—a human-made device that approximates a geometric figure, a version of the real that never perfectly appears.

Normativity might then refer to the way human practices oscillate around norms that can never be.[1] And yet what seemed to become of "normal" in the long 2020 was the spectacle of its disintegration. It now takes a truly impressive effort to perceive this climate of fire and flood according to the old norms. And it seems that in political life, no norm is actually sacred when it stands in the way of a ruling class in need of state assistance to maintain a transfer of resources ever upward. The technics in which all our lives are now enmeshed have appeared as unbound by inherited norms of information regulation. It's "rain of frogs" time again.

Panic about the erosion of norms is channeled toward ever more marginal figures. The frogs—the portent, the sign—for much of the long 2020 were the supposed rain of transsexuals, splashing all over the mediasphere. Over the long 2020, I lost count of the states considering legislation to make the lives of transgender people—around 1 percent of the population—considerably worse.[2] It gets hard to practice optimism of the will. Just looking around at my everyday life, the things upon which one might rest, if not optimism, but at least a sense of ongoing-ness, are the practices of love and care and support people are learning for each other, in the absence of what was once normal life. I'll come back to that.

I want to revisit the image of the *norma*, the carpenter's square. The *norma et regular*, the level and the square, from which came *normalis*, that which conforms to the square. The normal is something that is imposed on material through a practice, in the original case here, by the carpenter, sizing up the wood. The norm comes from without. It is not inherent in the wood.

From the crooked timber nothing is ever made straight, as Kant said. That can be read in a conservative way, as Isaiah Berlin did, as a way of dismissing any utopian dream.[3] It's curious how the word *conservative* now has quite the opposite meaning, one that was perhaps always there, latent in conservative desires. Now the conservative is the one who takes the ruler to the human and cuts off any body that isn't, in every sense of the word, straight. The warped body is to be examined, ruled upon, brought into line, or ruled out. The body, after the work of ruling it straight, is then, strangely enough, considered natural. Conservativism really is—as outdated slang has it—for squares.

Tourmaline and others warned a few years ago that trans visibility was an ambivalent thing.[4] To be seen might be enabling, in that other trans people can see us and come out. To be seen might make open-minded cis people understand us better—normalize us as part of their human community. Which is fine, if you are a trans person who wants to be normal. Some of us don't. And in any case, visibility brings with it the possibility of surveillance, which is exactly what happened.

In the bathroom, in the locker room, in school, on the playing field—the trans body, particularly that of the trans woman, became all too visible. That which can be perceived can become an object of the norm—and ruled against. As legislation, many of the bills aimed at imposing norms on us failed. The campaigns to legislate us out of existence do a lot of their work even when they don't become law, however. Establishing the contours of what the right people are supposed to be on the lookout for, upon which to impose the norm of their own volition.

The conservative imposition of a norm responds to a liberal attempt to shape another one. Trans visibility means mostly young, attractive trans women who pass, who are elegantly turned out, who approximate cis womanhood. Who, even when they are not white, can code-switch into the English of "normal" white speech. If they are older, they best be rich. It rarely means trans men. It is highly selective about what the nonbinary body can look and sound like. Not much about this has changed since Christine Jorgensen became a global celebrity in the 1950s.[5]

To be trans in the long 2020 is to be caught between two norms. One is preferable to the other, but not for all of us, and not always. To avoid the straightening gaze of the conservative norm, one has to approximate to the liberal one by showing one is normal in another way, a valid representation in the spectacle and a legitimate subject of the state. Liberalism, too, is for squares.

Liberal and conservative norms appear to differ according to the rule against which one is to be measured: sex or gender. A great deal of mischief enters the language through the distinction between sex and gender. It arose out of sexology, out of the discovery of how wildly nonnormative the sex of the body can be.[6] In frustration, sexology sets up the distinction between the categories of sex and gender so that the nonnormatively sexed body, particularly the intersex one, can be cut to fit what sexology took to be the more rigid binaries of gender.

Oddly enough, this pair of terms is now normally used in the opposite sense, a switch that happened when second wave feminism adopted the concepts for the opposite purposes: sex is now taken to be rigid and inflexible—it is gender that can be changed through the struggles of a social movement. A very white, Western, colonial norm of the sex of a woman was often left in place.[7]

That the collective labor of a social movement could upend norms of gender falls out of a certain kind of feminist discourse. What trans excoriating reactionary feminism has in common with the conservative norm is treating sex as a fixed binary, as "biological," and resisting the mere modification of gender. Even those modifications that might open possibilities for cis women are shut down to exclude trans women. Normal womanhood is defined as weakness, in need of protection, shackled by biological necessity to the uterus.

Liberal discourse points to a different norm, without really challenging this reading of sex and gender. It generally accepts that sex is something fixed but stresses gender as a "social construct" that can be modified. Space can then be made for tolerating the nonnormatively gendered as an act of sympathy, to be bestowed by liberal power in return for conforming to its norms.

The alternative to both might be the path queer theory marked out for us, but that, too, has its traps.[8] This path has two components. The first is to conceptualize the category of sex as a back-formation from the performance of gender. Sex is gender naturalized. It's an interesting reversal of perspective. It's actually not that helpful for trans people, who are then perceived as taking gender too literally, of seeking to cut and shape embodied sex along the lines of the desire to be another gender. The visceral experiences of the trans body, with its own dysphoric flesh, are ruled out of consideration.

The second move doesn't help us much either: that's the celebration of the nonnormative performance of gender as the one that critiques the norm.[9] This just makes the gender nonconformer into an allegory of the norms of the sex gender system itself and queer theory a mere continuation of a certain habit literary modernism.[10] There's no room for actual trans people in it. This nonnormative norm is one of play, difference, the exceptional, the fabulous.

Which is all well and good, except that what are missing are the ordinary and the banal sides of trans lives, which are not about performativity so much as unemployability. And with that exclusion from the norms of labor: poverty, homelessness, violence, incarceration, early death.[11] The conservative norm might be the most harmful to us, but it's not as if the liberal norm or the queer nonnormative norm is all that great either.

I want to return to the image of the carpenter's square, the *norma*. It is an ambivalent figure. What's promising in it is that it is about praxis, about an act of labor, in and against the world. The carpenter takes their square and joins timber at the right angle, to build something that someone can use or inhabit. The carpenter does not work alone. Someone else cut the timber; someone else will paint it.

Metaphysics is the art of forgetting where form comes from. From the carpenter making things square, the metaphysical turn is to make the square more real than the wood, a magical thought made possible by forgetting the labor of making it so. The praxis of collective labor falls from view. The metaphysical essence stands in its place.

The norm, like the commodity, appears shorn of its making. The norm, like the commodity, is both what is proper and someone's property. Through the severing of the ideal of the norm from praxis, the norm itself can become the scene of judgment, for the cop, or the consumer. The liberal and conservative versions of the norm of gender both assert that the state can make proper what best fits the world of property—whether, as trans people, we are included in what's proper, can be exploited as wage labor, can accumulate property and pass it on within the family, can raise children, can order a birthday cake, and so on.

The nonnormative norm of queerness is not all that different. It is performed, but performed to be seen, like a show, to be judged by its consumer. It is performed as an alternative to one or both of these other norms but still oscillates around them. As if the norm were a kind of impossible ideal thing. Queer gender performativity, what is improper, is then the aberration that affirms the norm. Here, too, the norm is reified, rendered metaphysical, and eventually made spectacular. Collective labor falls from view.

What might transsexual lives become, outside of the norm, and even outside of outside of the norm? I use the old-fashioned word *transsexual* deliberately, despite its compromised history. We modify not just the social construct of gender but also our sex. The ambiguities of corporeality of sex as it is felt and gender as it expresses itself with others are not really separable.[12] But if one has to choose an emphasis, let me put it on the modification of embodied sex, that slow, difficult, technical art on which many of us labor in pain.

Which brings me to the three things that did give me, if not optimism, then a way to endure through the long 2020. Things that are not unconnected. It's been a bad time for a lot of trans women whom I know. Some do sex work. Some are performing artists of other kinds. Some tend bar or do other nightlife work. All of that shut down, and for a long time. And yet it was trans people of all kinds whom I saw spring into action to extend the networks of mutual aid.

It's already a thing trans people do. It's in the nature of being a transsexual who transforms the body through technics. That usually requires a collective labor. To raise the money, for one thing. An old joke has it that it's the same twenty dollars that circulates through every trans person's GoFundMe. To prepare someone for surgery and to nurse them through recovery. To gift a spare needle or a shot when supplies ran low during the pandemic. Trans care turned out to be a generalizable set of practices.[13] As civilization falls, my hunch is that we have at least one thing going for us to help us all survive.

To escape the norm is an art, a kind of labor that willfully or experimentally makes things otherwise. I felt the loss of our collective and public arts deeply during 2020. I'd come to rely on a kind of distributed sensory being, together, with other transsexuals. At the rave, at the reading, at the opening. Dancing or looking or listening to expressions of us. Ones that, at their best, played somewhere else, with some other tools than those straight and square. And sometimes we'd go home together. To be without all that was hard—particularly hard for those whose sensory and sensual practices are distributed rather than squared off into something like a family unit.

Over the long 2020, I had to make do with the transsexual arts that can pass along the vector of communication into my quarantine pod. We're good at that, as it happens. A lot of us have been very isolated before. The isolation is hard. But we worked on the collective arts of communication through the internet. Sometimes it turns into the Discourse: that internalization of the policing of norms for ourselves, mimicking in miniature that which excludes us or elects us as its mascots. But not always.

The summer of 2020 was also when BLACK TRANS LIVES MATTER became a slogan within a larger movement. This, together with the care and the art, was a sign of enduring. At Brooklyn Liberation for Black Trans Lives, I saw fifteen thousand people gather under the leadership of Black trans women.[14] It's another praxis, in and against and around the norm.

The most universalizable standpoints are those furthest outside the norm: those ruled out at the point of many intersecting lines. One could see it through the language of intersectionality, although somehow, to me, that seems to leave the lines ruled by the norm intact. You could see it rather as a practice of assemblage, of differences that differ from each other continually, that shade off, have fuzzy edges.[15]

Who knows when the long 2020 will end? Who knows if there can ever be a "new normal"? There's certainly a struggle over it, displaced onto marginal bodies, deflecting from the disintegration of the climate, the polity, and any regulation of the information on which the collective cyborg body of the planet runs.

NOTES

1. Judith Butler, "Performative Acts and Gender Constitution," *Theatre Journal* 40, no. 4 (1988): 519–31.

2. This legislation is tracked online: https://freedomforallamericans.org/legislative-tracker/anti-transgender-legislation/.

3. Isaiah Berlin, *The Crooked Timber of Humanity* (Princeton, N.J.: Princeton University Press, 2013).

4. Reina Gossett, Eric A. Staney, and Johana Burton, *Trap Door: Trans Cultural Production and the Politics of Visibility* (Cambridge, Mass.: MIT Press, 2017).

5. Susan Stryker, *Transgender History* (New York: Seal Press, 2017).

6. Jules Gill-Peterson, *Histories of the Transgender Child* (Minneapolis: University of Minnesota Press, 2018).

7. For a critique of the universality of the Western concept of womanhood as reducible to the observable body, see Oyèrónkẹ́ Oyěwùmí, *The Invention of Women* (Minneapolis: University of Minnesota Press, 1997).

8. A key critique of the way queer theory makes the transsexual the bad object is in Jay Prosser, *Second Skins: The Body Narratives of Transsexuality* (New York: Columbia University Press, 1998).

9. There's a lot to like in Muñoz's writing, but here I'm thinking of the limits to his appreciation of Kevin Aviance in José Esteban Muñoz, *Cruising Utopia: The Then and There of Queer Futurity* (New York: New York University Press, 2009).

10. On the continuity between the allegory of the trans woman in literary modernism and queer theory, see Emma Heaney, *The New Woman: Literary Modernism, Queer Theory and the Trans Feminine Allegory* (Evanston, Ill.: Northwestern University Press, 2017).

11. This difference of agenda is strongly argued in Viviane Namaste, *Invisible Lives: The Erasure of Transsexual and Transgendered People* (Chicago: University of Chicago Press, 2000).

12. Here I'm thinking of the chapter on the phenomenology of the body in Gayle Salamon, *Assuming a Body: Transgender and Rhetorics of Materiality* (New York: Columbia University Press, 2010).

13. Hil Malatino, *Trans Care* (Minneapolis: University of Minnesota Press, 2020).

14. McKenzie Wark, "The Pride Wore White: Black Trans Women Step Out of the Queer Chorus," *Public Seminar* (blog), June 23, 2020, https://publicseminar.org/essays/the-pride-wore-white/.

15. Jasbir Puar, "I'd Rather Be a Cyborg than a Goddess: Intersectionality, Assemblage and Affective Politics," *Transversal*, January 2011, https://transversal.at/transversal/0811/puar/en.

23 The Kids Are OK, Even When Everything Else Is Not

TOM RADEMACHER

I really love teaching middle schoolers. They are ridiculously funny, and they don't have mortgages and ex-husbands, so they have brains with free space to think about important stuff. They very often teach me new ways to see the world, to see problems in the world, and what we should do about them. They give me life and hope, even, or especially, in tough times. Unfortunately, being around eighth graders also makes me reflect on who I was as an eighth grader far more often than I am comfortable with.

When I was in eighth grade, the biggest problem in my life was navigating my simultaneous attraction to and terror inspired by girls. The biggest problem in the world was the death of Kurt Cobain. I wore my own blond hair long like Kurt's, wore the same green flannel every day to school because I didn't want anyone to think I had accidentally worn clean clothes. I was so distressed by his death that I asked for a moment of silence at a middle school dance. The DJ honored the request, and when a few of my classmates used that moment to continue shouting as they chased one another, I went in the hallway and cried real tears. Cobain had been dead for two years already.

That the death of a man I'd never met and definitely shouldn't have idolized was the biggest problem I understood about the world is certainly a result of my being white and middle class but also feels more emblematic of the time.

The scandals of my young years spanned from Milli Vanilli to the Clinton impeachment. Even with the murder trial of O. J. Simpson, we talked about white Broncos and black gloves more than we talked about human victims and domestic violence. I was in health class when the principal came over the announcements to say that the verdict was about to be announced. We were one of the lucky rooms that had a television on a cart that day (to watch some cartoon talk about how pregnancy happens without mentioning sex), so we watched it. We stopped school to watch the verdict of the O. J. Simpson trial.

These days, we don't even pause when there's another mass shooting. Early in the long 2020, when the Covid-19 death toll passed more than a hundred a day, then more than a thousand, then two thousand, students were still told to dutifully check off all the boxes of their daily online assignments.

When George Floyd was murdered less than ten miles from our school, the adults all broke out the language about difficult times—bland and broad hopes for peace and healing. We've gotten pretty good in the last few years at the emails that say nothing. We've had a lot of practice. In the last year, the impacts of global climate change and white supremacy have shown up again and again in catastrophes and atrocities, undeniable and awful. Yet these events, the destruction of lives and property and safety, wink by us in a day or two, sinking to the bottom or the back of our awareness. This year, there has been so much terror competing for our attention.

In the immediate, young people watched their families stock up on food and necessities, preparing for a time in which society would fail to offer food, protection, beds for the sick, and care for the dead.

In years before this, at the worst events in the world, I kept hope in the world by sharing the moments with my students. When Darren Wilson wasn't charged with the killing of Mike Brown, my students came to school that morning. I remember one in particular, Evan, telling me—not asking—"You know we're talking about that today in class." So we did, and students shared their pain and their own experiences and their hopes for a better world. We felt better because we shared it, held it with each other, not because we tried to push it away.

In the years before this, on the worst days of our own lives, we lifted each other up and supported one another. One of the hardest days of teaching I ever had came early in my career. The eighth-grade teachers were brought together and told that one of our student's parents had committed suicide, had only just been found at home. The other parent was on the way to pick the kid up and tell her. The school gave the conference room to that parent and child the rest of the day, had our school counselor and psychologist available to them, brought up friends of the student from their classes to sit with her, brought in food and drink and gave them a place to be while they couldn't go home. For the remaining months of the school year, every student and adult in the building showed up for that kid however we could, because that's what people do for each other when they can.

This year. This last school year, there was just too much. Loss after loss after loss we were victim or witness to. We did for each other what we could, which was far less than required. None of us had the help we needed carrying this last year, and we kept adding weight, bit by bit, that we had to carry alone.

Any time I checked in with my eighth graders this year about their burdens, these twelve- and thirteen-year-olds talked about how scared they were that things would never get better. In the years we start to really see the world, we tend to assume a degree of permanence: that what is important then will always be, as true for our crushes as for how the world sees us and works for or against us.

I struggle to think of a single foundational sector of our society that has not openly shown its failings over the last year: education, democracy, health, policing. It will take a lot of work before young people build any trust that the world is trying to take care of them.

If I'm honest, I don't remember most of what I've learned during professional development, and the stuff I remember has rarely helped me. One notable exception is a session on trauma I attended six or seven years ago. The presenter, a psychologist who worked specifically with groups of young people who were victims of generational trauma (like much of the student body of that school), was using the tried-and-true "oxygen mask in an airplane" metaphor. In an event of an emergency, you're supposed to put your mask on first. Take care of yourself so you can take care of others. I've heard it, I've understood it, I've devoted myself to a profession that glorifies never doing it.

Maybe the presenter saw in our eyes that none of us were going to worry about oxygen masks. So he switched tactics: "Look, if you're a pig farmer, and you're shoveling shit all day, you're going to bring some home on your boots." He was making a point of what it means to be someone not experiencing trauma but working with and for those who have. When we take it with us, we can't help but be impacted in some way. By extension, then, this year, we've all had more shit to shovel than we can handle, and we're tracking it everywhere we go. Sounds right.

As we hit the third or fourth or four hundredth month of distance school (it's very hard to keep count), we started hearing about how 2020 will be a "lost year." Students, it was believed, were not learning enough of anything they were supposed to be learning. They were so far behind.

It was a worry that, quite honestly, had kept me up at night through the first half of the year. I have their precious little brains for one year (actually more like nine months, and really more like five months' worth of actual school days), and distance learning meant moving slower than usual. And they had to be ready for high school, they *had* to be. I worried so much about whether they'd write enough or read enough.

It took me a lot longer to get to know these kids over Google Meets and email than it would have in a classroom, which I think is why I worried so hard for so long. As I got to know them, got to see their work and their brains and their humor, I started to worry more about them as people, about what they were missing not getting to be around each other, about the worry and sadness of living through this year. I started to mourn the time we didn't get to work together. I stopped worrying about whether they'd be ready for high school. I stopped worrying about whether they'd be ready for the world.

So much has been asked of young people this year. Without so many of the relationships that make school worth it on the bad days and powerful on the good ones, we asked them to keep working, to hold all the weight of the world and all the weight of their worlds and still find some space to keep themselves organized and motivated and productive. I've got a really good feeling about what these kids are going to do when we finally get them back into buildings full time. I don't really care how much work they got done this year. I don't. We always confused work with learning anyway. We always confused a lot of things with learning.

We had a staff meeting where we divvied up phone calls to students we were most concerned about. I called the mom of one kid who hadn't been doing his reading homework, hadn't been practicing his band instrument, who had been an ideal student in the years before, whom we worried, I suppose, we were losing.

His mom was worried too, having had years of only hearing how good at school her kid was, suddenly to see failing grades, missing assignments. When I called her, she told me that he was reading a few hours a day but not doing his reading homework. He hadn't been practicing the flute, but he had taught himself to play piano. He was working, thinking, creating, exploring, and learning more hours a day than ever before, but leaving a stream of unchecked boxes in his wake. Really, he had skipped all the silly stuff we try to get kids to do and, with school out of the way, had gone right to the learning.

Somewhere in the mess of what they learned this year living through this, and what they learned from whatever school was for them, these kids are going to come back ready to do amazing things, with brains so much more ready to be pushed, to push through things that before would have pushed them away.

I'm old enough to have my own child. They're ten, but they sigh and yell "what?!" when I knock on their door, like a fifteen-year-old. They're a smart kid and have always been pretty good at school. A few years back, we moved them to a school program for gifted students, and they really took off. School came easy to them in a way it doesn't for a lot of kids, in a way it never did for me. At parent conferences, teachers often said something along the lines of "if I could just have a few more kids like Ollie."

Then we hit distance learning. Ollie was already a kid who preferred to spend as much time as possible in their room and on their computer, so it seemed like distance learning wouldn't be so bad.

It was so bad.

Without the context of the classroom around them, Ollie struggled to focus and started to rush, which is a not-great combination of things. Assignments started being missed, and the messages that they were missing started being missed. Most subjects had at least one item a day to be completed, and a typical week sometimes had twenty or more items due. Not all those things took very long, but Ollie was overwhelmed by the amount of stuff they had to keep together.

The struggle felt like failure, and Ollie went through a time feeling like they had suddenly become "bad" at school. Like my musical eighth grader, Ollie was doing most of their real learning outside of school hours (or during school hours when they were supposed to be doing their grammar worksheety website thing). Ollie was learning Japanese, was teaching themselves to 3D model and code, was building things on Minecraft on a server with friends, was drawing and animating, was nearly always doing something, and yet was being told they were very behind.

It took some hard months of work from Ollie and what felt like a second full-time job from both already-working parents, but Ollie started to turn it around. Unfortunately, this involved many conversations about doing things that weren't going to teach them anything and playing the game of school more efficiently so they could keep doing the real brain work they loved. But we got there.

And yes, I hate online word programs and wish schools were a whole lot less focused on completion, but even in doing all those things that didn't seem to teach much, Ollie learned a lot about how to do things that are hard, how to do things they don't want to do, about accomplishment and resilience. We've seen those lessons spill out into other parts of Ollie's life, seen them grow into a more capable and flexible kid, one who is that much more ready for whatever comes next.

Ollie isn't alone. I have about 140 students this year, and contact with hundreds more whom I've taught recently. This will be a generation of young people on fire, who will come back from this "lost year" and not accept a school that looks like the one from years before it, who have shown what they can do under some of the worst conditions and that they are ready to do more if we get out of the way.

We won't be ready for them, but I hope we'll be ready to try.

In the worst parts of this year, we tried to recreate school without learning. There were lots of worksheets to do, tasks to check off, things that showed time spent and little else. In the best parts of this year, we gave our students space and support to learn. We were flexible with how it looked, and when it happened, we led with compassion, and we treasured our connections.

I hold the weight of this long 2020, unable to put down any of it yet, but I carry with me the strength of these students alongside all the sadness and pain and worry.

I know there are students who have flourished under distance learning, who love to work at their own pace and in their own space. I carry one student who has learned what I most care about, who will send me quick messages to ask "is it OK not to do all the worksheet stuff? I'm ready to start the project" and then is off writing an essay comparing James Baldwin's "Nobody Knows My Name" to the Black Panther Party's Ten-Point Program that is every bit as good as the best essays of years past.

I know the student who couldn't always make it to class during the day because she was taking care of her younger siblings. The other student who took a job during the day because their family needed it.

I know the students who have written novels, whole novels, and others who have filled sketchbooks with art more moving than ink and paper has any right to be.

I know students who have, while living through a year of compounded and concentrated tragedy, continued to be kids. Who made dumb jokes with their friends over group texts while they were supposed to be listening to an online class I was teaching. Who showed more resilience than should ever have been asked of them. The kids are OK. The kids are incredible.

Without them in our classrooms, we missed all the pieces that make them people, their brains and not their obedience. When they return, we will have no excuse not to be better for them, to get out of their way now that they've learned the skills to go on their own.

24 Democracy and the Dignity of Work

BONNIE HONIG

The idea of the dignity of work traverses the twentieth century and has had an unexpected impact on the twenty-first. Although the "dignity of work" has been appealed to in the context of right-wing antiwelfare politics, it had a different impact, I will argue here, on the long 2020 election, which began in fall 2020 (with early and mail-in voting) and ended, months later, with a failed effort to abort it in January 2021.[1] Up until that final failed effort, which comprised the Stop the Steal rally and the violent white riot at the Capitol, efforts by then President Trump and his allies, followers, and lawyers to discredit the 2020 election results had explicitly or implicitly disparaged the hard work of election management and vote counting. The disparagement meant that many of those who worked on the election, whether Trump-supporting Republicans or Democrats, felt compelled to resist its overthrow. Pride in their work was one important source of the pushback. Attending to the work dimensions of democracy's electoral processes highlights the metonymic transfer of pride in one's work to pride in democratic institutions and processes. It also highlights the important but often neglected electoral work done by Black political actors, from minimum wage earners to state representatives and movement leaders, on behalf of democracy.

The idea of the dignity of work had pride of place in the agenda of American Progressives in the early twentieth century. Taylorism and the assembly line's division of labor had revolutionized the workplace, which could now provide cheap industrial goods for a new age of mass consumerism. But, Marc Stears says, these innovations also degraded the experience of work, and this worried Progressives, who were "deeply concerned about the dramatic mismatch between their democratic ideals and the experience of everyday life in the workplace."[2] With many Americans subject to "the arbitrary powers of [their] employer," Progressives worried that absolutism at work groomed people for absolutism in politics.[3] Forced deference to authority in one sphere would surely teach undemocratic habits of deference to authority in others.

Writing in the 1950s, Hannah Arendt worried about the effect of new work arrangements too. She noted how the division of labor separated people from their skills. "Every activity," she says, "requires a certain amount of skill, the activity of cleaning and cooking no less than the writing of a book or the building of a house."[4] But, under capitalism, such activities are broken down into simple, discrete tasks: each task is "unskilled" (or deskilled), and so, too, are "those expected to perform them." What were once tasks "assigned to the young and inexperienced" are now frozen "into lifelong occupations," Arendt says ("as Marx rightly predicted").[5] One casualty of this ever-increasing widgetization of work (to borrow a figure, if not a term, from Adam Smith) was the very idea of the dignity of work, attached to pride in one's labor or craft, the idea that the work of one's hands was connected to one's own singularity, imagination, and skill—part of a unified life.

Twenty years later, Robert Dahl argued that the modern corporate worker was alienated: "compelled to perform intrinsically unrewarding, unpleasant, and even hateful labor in order to gain money to live on."[6] Compelled, also, to follow directives given by anonymous corporate directors, corporate workers were deprived of the "intrinsic rewards" of work: no pride, no sense of empowerment, accomplishment, or capability.

Many of the proposed solutions to the problem of industrialized and corporate work involved democratizing the workplace. If only democracy could lend its dignity to work, work could regain its dignity. Unions, participatory workplace practices, and community ownership were all measures intended to make work a rehearsal for democracy, not its antithesis.[7] But accelerationism, which has many of us work as cogs in ever-faster-moving machines, has only further undone the power of democracy to elevate work as well as the power of work to elevate those who do it. We are now in a more precarious economy. As Russ Muirhead observes, workers must now "stand ever-ready to change employers and industries, [and] the *experience* of work *cuts* against the gradual accumulation of ability, renders expertise irrelevant, and makes it hard to conceive of our careers (and perhaps our lives) as possessing any unity."[8] Once, the bonds that might underwrite democracy were developed in the workplace. Now, without them to count on, democracy, too, has become precarious.

And yet, in the winter season of the long 2020 election, we saw a glimmer of possibility in a new and reversed relation between democracy and work. Rather than democracy lending its dignity to the workplace, workers lent their dignity to democracy. They kept their heads down and refused to be distracted by all the noise. Where once the concern was that degraded labor would degrade democracy, we saw in the determination of embattled election workers and Capitol caregivers a sign that maybe a now-degraded democracy could be ennobled by workers who personified dignity in their conduct and gave new life to, and imagistic evidence of, the "dignity of work." Maybe such workers were essential in even more ways than the pandemic was already teaching us?

Watching them count, especially in Detroit and Lansing, Michigan, we saw how work, dignity, and democracy might be connected, and not just in the sense of nondegradation or rehearsal noted here by way of the Progressives and Dahl. In Michigan, as in many other states, minimum-wage workers counted ballots under adverse work conditions, with politicized Republican poll watchers loudly and aggressively challenging their every move, especially so in majority minority precincts. Because of these challenging circumstances, the fortitude of election workers was on particular display.

They counted votes. They transported ballots from polling places to counting centers. They matched signatures; they took part in recounts. They worked long hours, and some were subjected to personal risk when misleading videos accused them of malfeasance and went into social media circulation, sometimes with their home addresses posted. Still, vote-counting workers, many of them Black, kept their focus and did the work. It was during a pandemic, and some of those poll watchers were not masked, which meant that not just the health of *democracy* but also that of the election workers was on the line.

There is no dignity in the lack of choice at work. Those vote counters were not free to leave, and they undoubtedly needed the pay they would have sacrificed were they to do so. But if we attribute their constancy to powerlessness, we assume they were unaware of the stakes of the moment and ignorant of the history to which it, and they, belonged. And that is not right, surely. The issue was addressed by the Reverend Steve Bland, senior pastor of Detroit's Liberty Baptist Church, who was outside Detroit's TCF center as part of a group of "poll chaplains" there to encourage voters and to help make sure the votes were counted. He was asked by a reporter if he knew who *were* the protesters trying to stop the count. He answered, "These are persons who are passionate and they are consistent. They've been saying all along they're going to suggest that it's rigged, it's flawed or fake, they've been saying that before now. We just need to be persistent, to make sure our voice gets counted. . . . And I will say, the Black vote in Detroit is higher than it's ever been, and we will determine the outcome because we've gone from picking cotton to picking presidents."

What we saw in the long 2020 election was how much *work* is involved in elections and, by extension, in the larger functioning of democracy, and we saw how essential, and hands-on, such work indispensably is. We also saw, in the weeks that followed, how pride in such work can harden resistance to its overthrow. Standing in the way of a powerful—if not entirely competent—effort to overturn the result of the 2020 election was people's pride in their work, a pride born of their material proximity to the counting of ballots or to a yearlong defense of electoral processes from intrusion or manipulation (Figure 24.1).

FIGURE 24.1. Michigan election officials count ballots in Lansing. Photograph by John Moore, via Getty Images.

Certainly when Georgia's Republican secretary of state Brad Raffensperger was importuned by Trump to find the exact number of votes needed to flip the state to Republicans, Raffensperger refused. When some in the news and entertainment media interpreted that refusal as suggesting we had a new voting rights hero to celebrate, Stacy Abrams was quick to correct them: "Lionizing Brad Raffensperger's a bit wrong-headed," she said. "This man is not defending the right of voters. He's defending an election that he ran." He was defending his work, though he had voted for Trump and, as a Georgia Republican, had worked on restricting access to voting in Georgia.[9]

Responding to Georgia's blue wave, which, in January 2021, sent two Democratic senators to Washington to represent Georgia, Georgia's governor, Brian Kemp, signed a ninety-five-page bill in March 2021 that limits access to the ballot in Georgia in ways old and new. If the bill is implemented, many more people will have to wait many more long hours to vote. This means they will need water and nutrition or they will be forced to leave the line. But the bill makes it a crime to give out bottled water at polling stations. That provision echoes the prohibition against providing food and water to migrants in the deserts of the United States. In 2019, four members of the humanitarian group No More Deaths were found guilty of this charge in Arizona. "If giving water to someone dying of thirst is illegal," one said in a statement, "what humanity is left in the law of this country?"[10] It's a good question. The use of this same provision in Georgia does more than just restrict voting; it positions Georgia's Black voters as migrants, as if they, too, are just lawlessly passing through and are not part of the cacophony of democratic voice in the United States.

It was another man's pride in his electoral work that brought him to the attention of former President Trump, who quickly fired Chris Krebs after Krebs reassured the American public that the 2020 election had been free of interference and fraud. Krebs was director of the Cybersecurity and Infrastructure Security Agency (CISA) in the Department of Homeland Security from November 2018 to November 2020. A former Microsoft cybersecurity executive, Krebs led "state and local officials from both Republican- and Democratic-led states to boost cybersecurity surrounding their election infrastructure and to cooperate with one another and the federal government."[11]

When Trump said the election was rigged, Krebs had to contradict him, not only because the charge was false but because its falsity insulted the work of the many people on his team at CISA, who had put in long hours together over two years. (The long 2020 election was even longer for Chris Krebs than it was for the rest of us.) Krebs said his greatest regret was not that he was fired but that he never got to say goodbye to his team. Working together with others in common cause creates an esprit de corps, a sense of being in it together. Being fired like that hives you off, peels you away from the group. It might feel like an amputation.

Many of the photographs of the election work published in the *Detroit Free Press* and the *Washington Post* focused on the hands that were doing the work. The images recalled the last century's Work Projects Administration (WPA) images of hands put to work on behalf of the nation. All those hands counting and recounting all those ballots during the long election of 2020, working together, were part of the election infrastructure too: the other side of what Krebs's CISA worked on, also essential to the mainte-nance of democracy. Notably, the word *maintenance* is from the French word for "hands"—*les mains*. Maintaining democracy is a hands-on affair. Even in our world, where it seems like so much that was once solid has long since melted into air, there is work that needs doing by hand: it is infra-structural work, and it is often care work.

In the aftermath of the Capitol insurrection on January 6, 2021, the work that needed doing was to clean up the debris of a white riot, and mainte-nance workers of color were photographed holding the brooms and dust-pans with which they would sweep away the broken glass of a day (Figure 24.2). In one of these two images, a worker is backgrounded by paintings of great men, and for once it is clear—as it should have been other days as well—that it is they who are ennobled by him.

Visible in the workers' hands, the hands that counted the ballots and swept up the debris, was the care work that Silvia Federici says always disappears under capitalism. Hannah Arendt mentions it too. In her afore-mentioned critical discussion of the deskilling of work, two of her exam-ples are cleaning and cooking. These are care work, the kind of work that is not easily replaced by machines nor easily accelerated by new productiv-ity specialists (telehealth notwithstanding). Arendt subtly invites us to laugh with her about how men misunderstand such work when she observes wryly that one of Hercules's twelve heroic labors involved cleaning a sta-ble and then says, "It is only the mythological Augean stable that remains clean once the effort is made and the task achieved."[12] We could wryly note as well that there was in this case, as in so much maintenance work

FIGURE 24.2. A workman cleans up debris outside the office of Speaker of the House Nancy Pelosi on the day after violent protesters loyal to President Donald Trump stormed the U.S. Congress, at the Capitol in Washington, D.C., Thursday, January 7, 2021. AP Photo/J. Scott Applewhite.

to this day, a dispute about pay, with the stable owner, Eurystheus, refusing to honor his agreement with Hercules.

Notably, it was through the manipulation of nature that Hercules was able to achieve his task. He dug trenches to reroute two rivers so that they flowed through the stable and washed out the filth. Thus the heroic Hercules is an apt figure for the heroic hydropower projects of dam construction through which the United States, with its New Deal projects of the early to mid-twentieth century, monumentalized the country. The dam projects nationalized the natural world and naturalized the country's sovereignty. The men who did the work were memorialized by WPA photographers in heroic images that still feed a nostalgic—and masculinized—sense of American possibility that inspires but also haunts the Build Back Better motto of the Biden presidency (Figure 24.3).[13]

American democracy is not like the mythological Augean stable. It is more like the ordinary stables to which Arendt contrasts the myth. Her joke invites awareness that the objects of care need constant tending. Democracy is one such object. It depends not on the occasional divine or heroic intervention but on the daily attention of ordinary people. Our recent pandemic-driven societal recognition of care work as "essential" to a functioning society works to counter Herculean myths with the more democratically ennobling image of action in concert. But care work is still treated as "low" and not paid properly, and providers are often anonymized and rewarded for their labors with job insecurity and vulnerability.

Fortunately, in the long 2020 election, the long-promised but never-held "infrastructure week" finally arrived. And, because of the contestation and improprieties around the election, because its legitimacy was (and still is) questioned, and democracy, as such, was endangered, the curtain was drawn back, and everyone could see for herself the work of the count. What we saw were scenes of infrastructure. We saw the work and the hands, the collegiality and determination that metonymize democracy as such: the daily boring of hard boards and the esprit de corps that comes from working on something worthwhile together with others. The occasional outbreak of dancing at polling stations is part of American democracy, too, as joy can sometimes be part of work, and people broke out into a fuller chorus of dancing in the streets when, on Saturday, November 7, 2020, Joe Biden was finally declared the winner of the presidential election. It was an unseasonably sunny day in the District, as if the weather itself approved of the outcome.

"Somebody built the Pyramids. Pyramids, Empire State Building—these things don't just happen," says Mike, one of Studs Terkel's interviewees in his great book, *Working*. "There's hard work behind it. I would like to see a building, say, the Empire State, I would like to see one side of it a foot-wide strip from top to bottom with the name of every bricklayer, the name of every electrician, with all the names. So when a guy walked by, he could take his son and say 'see, that's me over there on the 45th floor. I put the steel beam in.' Everybody should have something to point to."

The idea that all people should have something to point to, something to which they contributed, is a democratic idea. And that foot-wide strip, for all sons, daughters, and gender-nonbinary offspring to see, is a democratic version of the marquees with which some real estate branders have seen fit to adorn buildings. It is also the case that *democracy* itself is something people can point to, with the same sense of pride Terkel's Mike wants to take in his work. Those who offered rides to the polls, donated to a campaign, canvassed a neighborhood, helped count the ballots, made calls, or served as a dignified poll watcher, are some of the many thousands

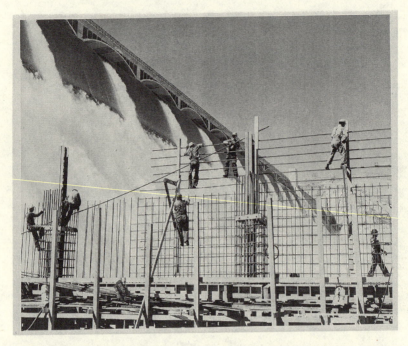

FIGURE 24.3. Grand Coulee dam construction. Library of Congress Prints and Photographs Division, Washington, D.C. https://lccn.loc.gov/2004667708.

of people who can point to Mike's proverbial "45th floor"—in this case, it is the 46th—and can say with pride, "I put that steel beam in." Of course, as Hannah Arendt notes in *The Human Condition,* the world wears away even the most sturdily built objects, if we neglect them. So we know we will have to do it all again, and again. Because, as the long 2020 makes evident, in a democracy, every week has to be infrastructure week.

NOTES

1. The term took an Orwellian turn in the 1990s with the welfare reform legislation that marked the new Clinton-engineered "centrism" of the Democratic Party. Women who had been on welfare would now have to work two or more jobs to *feed and house* their families but were left with no time to *mother* their children. This absurdity was owed in part to the fact that care work, as Silvia Federici has made clear, was somehow not dignified as work: neither dignified, nor work.

2. Marc Stears, *Demanding Democracy: American Progressives in Search of a New Politics* (Princeton, N.J.: Princeton University Press, 2013), 45.

3. Stears.

4. Hannah Arendt, *The Human Condition,* Enlarged ed. (Chicago: University of Chicago Press, 2018), 90.

5. Arendt.

6. Robert Dahl, *After the Revolution? Authority in a Good Society* (New Haven, Conn.: Yale University Press, 1970), 135, quoted in Cyrus Ernesto Zirakzadeh, "Theorizing about Workplace Democracy: Robert Dahl and the Cooperatives of Mondragón," *Journal of Theoretical Politics* 2, no. 1 (1990): 114–15.

7. Feminists said all the same things about marriage, an institution that allows for tyranny at home while expecting moral independence from women in the public sphere.

8. Russell Muirhead, "Meaningful Work and Politics: Why Does Money Have to Spoil Things?," *The Hedgehog Review* (blog), Fall 2012, https://hedgehogreview.com/issues/work-and-dignity/articles/meaningful-work-and-politics.

9. Ed Mazza, "Stacey Abrams Has a Blunt Reality Check on Georgia Secretary of State Brad Raffensperger," *Huffington Post,* January 4, 2021, https://www.huffpost.com/entry/stacey-abrams-brad-raffensperger-colbert_n_5ff3d58bc5b6e7974fd5be82; Julie Hollar, "Media Make 'Heroes' of Republicans Who Oppose Trump—and Also Democracy," *Salon,* March 6, 2021, https://www.salon.com/2021/03/06/media-make-heroes-of-republicans-who-oppose-trump--and-also-democracy_partner/.

10. No More Deaths, "Guilty Verdict in First #Cabeza9 Case," January 18, 2019, https://nomoredeaths.org/guilty-verdict-in-first-cabeza9-case/.

11. Gopal Ratnam, "Cybersecurity Chief Who Oversaw 'Most Secure Election' Fired by Trump," *Roll Call* (blog), November 17, 2020, https://www.rollcall.com/2020/11/17/cybersecurity-chief-who-oversaw-most-secure-election-fired-by-trump/.

12. Arendt, *Human Condition,* 101.

13. Nelson Lichtenstein, "Dreamers with Shovels: How the First New Deal Remade America," *American Prospect,* December 5, 2019, https://prospect.org/greennewdeal/dreamers-with-shovels-how-the-new-deal-remade-america/.

25 From Devastation to Wonder

SLOUGH SAYERS (JANELLE BAKER,
PAULLA EBRON, ROSA E. FICEK, KAREN HO,
RENYA K. RAMIREZ, ZOE TODD, ANNA TSING,
SARAH E. VAUGHN)

> To provide care in the wastelands is about gathering
> enough love to turn devastation into mourning and
> then maybe turn mourning into hope.
>
> —Erica Violet Lee, "In Defence of the
> Wastelands: A Survival Guide"

Across and beyond North America, the year 2020 was a time of plague, fire, and floods. Illness, displacement, houselessness, and unemployment followed. And yet devastation is not the only story: there has also been "wonder." By wonder, we mean attentive appreciation, which sometimes includes laughter and even joy. We also mean to include reflective thinking, as in "I wonder . . ." To complement, complicate, and deepen Euro-Western interpretations of a self-confident, future-looking value of "hope," wonder stays in the present, where we must build those relationships that allow us to continue. In contrast to the bureaucratic capture of the term *resilience,* wonder can flourish in the ruins shunned by the state and capital. "From devastation to wonder" is an exploration of social lives—and social research—in the midst of trouble.

"Wonder," in the first sense, opens our hearts even in the face of the unfamiliar. In the second sense, to "wonder" draws us back and forth between curiosity and doubt. Will we be able to cope with the terrors and opportunities of the future? We wonder. Will we be able to find a generous connection to stories and lives quite different from our own? It takes courage to tell—and really listen to—stories. We are moved to reflect not from a place of certitude but instead from a place of wonder. The devastation that marked this long 2020 is a starting point for many kinds of stories. In this chapter, we tell a few that have shaped and guided our thinking about what it means to create more livable environments for all. Together, we wonder.

The quotation with which we begin is taken from an article by Erica Violet Lee, a Nēhiyaw philosopher from inner-city Saskatoon. She reminds us to "tend to the devastation with destabilizing gentleness, carefulness, softness."[1] Since the European invasion of the Americas, Indigenous survivors have witnessed not only mass human deaths but also the death of millions of our plant, fish, and animal relatives. Today, both humans and nonhumans get sick and eventually die not just from Covid-19 but also from widespread toxins and poisons from pesticides, oil and gas, uranium, and mercury. While living in a human-caused wasteland, our human relatives continue to gather and pray with our plant and animal kin, bearing witness to the devastation and mourning the loss of life, including the clearcutting of the forests around them. This gathering generates love, connection, and energy, inspiring us to fight back against corporations, powerful nation-states, and other kinds of colonial, imperial, and capitalistic forces that could eventually kill us all. Gathering empowers us not only to survive but also to thrive, offering us motivation to organize and struggle against climate change and the poisoning of our land, rivers, oceans, and all living things. This community building helps us persist through hurricanes, pandemics, earthquakes, fires, and ecological devastation.

How can mobilizations for a livable environment and for racial justice work together in the midst of this devastation? The Slough Sayers are a group of women of color working and writing against Anthropocene devastation. For this chapter, we asked group members Rosa Ficek and Janelle Baker to write about their respective research: Rosa's in creating the Hurricane Maria Archive and Janelle's in collaborations with the Bigstone Cree Nation in determining the toxicity of foraged foods. Each of these projects shows how people work "from devastation to wonder," even as they exemplify research that both draws from and contributes to communities in the making. Fieldwork is oftentimes not only an act of storytelling and theorizing but also a mode of wonder. Rosa's description of communities in Puerto Rico still gasping from several waves of hurricane destruction and then thrown into the Covid-19 pandemic offers a particularly vivid view of the creativity with which people pick up their lives despite the complete absence of governmental responsibility to provide even the most basic infrastructure. Janelle's meditation on "returning to the land" among Bigstone Cree in Alberta, Canada, also takes us to those hinterlands of state responsibility where toxins spread irresponsibly—but people pick up the challenges of living with joy as well as with rage. Rosa and Janelle each introduces us to forms of research designed to make community aspirations possible: to collect the fragments of experience and memory in Puerto Rico and to catalog insults to human–nonhuman relations in Alberta. These studies show how important it is to bring issues of the environment and racial justice together, in a unified analysis, rather than letting such studies malinger in inherited segregations. Both cases, too, expand a U.S.-centric focus to consider the power of the United States from the outside as well as the inside.

"UNTHINKABLE THINGS" IN THE VOID
LEFT BY THE STATE; OR, RAGE AND JOY

When Puerto Rico went into lockdown for Covid-19, people were still responding to the earthquake cluster that had shaken the southern part of the island two months earlier—and still recovering, too, from Hurricanes Irma and María in 2017. State neglect during these other emergencies, and especially during the humanitarian crisis in the long months after María, a megastorm fed by warming ocean temperatures, made it clear that to survive the pandemic, people would have to rely on each other.

After Hurricanes Irma and María, Taller Salud, a feminist organization based in the town of Loiza and focused on women's health, worked together with the community to respond to the immediate emergency and longer recovery process in a way that recognized the violence of state abandonment but also the importance of radical joy. Much of their collective expertise can be seen in their "Community Protection Guide."[2] The illustrated recommendations provide step-by-step guidance for how to respond to storms and other emergencies by organizing community kitchens, cleanup brigades, and distribution centers, along with other ways to ensure collective access to food, water, health, and housing when public infrastructure and government agencies fail.

The Covid-19 pandemic encouraged new forms of collaboration among knowledge-makers wary of official information and strategies. Ciencia

Puerto Rico, a nonprofit organization that promotes science in Puerto Rico and civic engagement among Puerto Rican scientists, created a Covid-19 prevention tool kit that brings scientific knowledge about the virus into dialogue with the knowledge of community leaders who know firsthand how to help their communities during emergencies. Aquí Nos Cuidamos, translated as "here we take care of each other," is a collection of Spanish-language educational materials created with input from vulnerable communities as well as scientists familiar with Puerto Rican society. The images, documents, audio recordings, and videos can be shared through social media or text messages, or printed out and displayed, to promote public health and support the work of local leaders who organize and look after their communities.[3]

The "Community Protection Guide" for emergencies and the Covid-19 prevention tool kit emphasize the importance of local, place-based knowledge for collective survival, especially at the community level. Meanwhile, the state places responsibility for disaster preparation and response on individuals, encouraging a neoliberal kind of resilience that asks people to withstand—with financial responsibility and a positive attitude—the ever-deepening inequalities that seem inescapable. Economic policies under U.S. rule created dependency by dismantling sources of local livelihood and autonomy for the benefit of imperial capital accumulation.[4] Who would have thought that Puerto Rico could survive without the United States? And yet, this is exactly what happened in the months after Hurricane María, when people survived despite the botched official response, completely cut off from the rest of the world.

In *Silencing the Past,* Michel Rolph-Trouillot argues that the Haitian Revolution was unthinkable for contemporaries because it challenged the conceptual frameworks that colonizers used to understand the world. It defied what they knew to be true. Western philosophies about the Human prevented observers, and, later, historians, from even asking the right questions.[5]

What if unthinkable things are happening now in Puerto Rico? In the void left by the state, diverse practices of autonomous organizing, mutual aid, community sovereignty, and other kinds of popular democracy attend to the humanitarian crises of debt and climate change by challenging the neoliberal order that emphasizes individual salvation.[6] Sometimes this takes the form of the censuses that many community leaders across Puerto Rico conducted to identify neighbors with chronic illnesses, bedridden relatives, or small children so that the community could prioritize channeling assistance to those who needed it most after Hurricane María. Sometimes it looks like the diaspora fundraising and sending aid directly to communities and community-based organizations, bypassing big foundations. In other places, communities take control of their energy and water infrastructure. The decentralized networks for exchanging knowledge and resources that sustain *autogestión,* the horizontal and participatory forms of decision-making, and the principles of solidarity and mutual responsibility that guide these practices build alternatives to the dependency on external aid and external knowledge that the state expects of Puerto Rico.

What kinds of research are useful in this configuration of rage and joy? Rosa participated in designing collaborative research that gathered communities to bear witness to devastation and wonder about the connections between past, present, and future. Some of this also involved gathering fragments of experience before they would be lost.

María created new opportunities for extractive projects to exploit colonial dependencies. The devastation attracted a frenzy of disaster capitalists eager to privatize public infrastructure with the blessing of the local government.[7] Researchers also flocked to Puerto Rico, especially disaster specialists. Meanwhile, the University of Puerto Rico has endured massive cuts to its budget as part of broader efforts to reduce public spending.[8] Some U.S. universities received federal relief funds to host Puerto Rican students temporarily. In contrast, Puerto Rican professors recommended that U.S. universities figure out ways to support local students' access to food, water, Wi-Fi, power, and housing.[9] The researchers ask questions. They record stories. They repeat these stories in their publications. Some turn the stories into data. The publications enhance the status of the institutions sponsoring the research. The publications also help researchers advance their projects and careers. Local knowledge is appropriated and addressed to English-speaking audiences in the United States. Given how the extraction of knowledge has worked hand in hand with the extraction of resources, and given how Western philosophies about the Human who underpin this expert knowledge prevent observers from recognizing events that challenge white supremacist colonial orders, what kinds of questions should knowledge-makers ask, and how?

Taller Salud's "Community Protection Guide" and Ciencia Puerto Rico's Covid-19 prevention tool kit might be one place to begin learning about how to survive the violences of debt and climate change in Puerto Rico. These tools communicate knowledge generated from past experiences responding to emergencies without the state's help. They also anticipate a future when people must continue to rely on each other, similarly, without the state. At the same time, because they explore ways of surviving state abandonment, these tools invite wonder about futures where emergencies like the ones caused by Hurricane María or the Covid-19 pandemic are impossible because the political and economic dependencies that created those disasters no longer organize collective life. These disaster responses work to hold the state accountable at the same time that they assemble alternatives. Taller Salud demands justice in the multiyear Hurricane María recovery process while at the same time teaching other ways to collectively organize so that the disaster does not repeat itself even with the anticipation of bigger storms in the future. Ciencia Puerto Rico advocates for science-informed public policy at the same time that it builds essential public health infrastructure from the bottom up in rural communities and among other vulnerable groups.

Modeling research practices after community-led disaster response efforts could mean doing research that confronts institutional violences at the same time that it wonders about, and with, other kinds of knowledge-making and sharing practices. The digital archive that brings the "Community Protection Guide" and Covid-19 prevention tool kit to these pages is one effort along these lines, made possible by by a history of community-engaged and participatory research that generates knowledge together with communities to address local problems.[10] This project gathers materials documenting practices of autonomy, solidarity, and sovereignty through collaborative methods that work to redistribute expertise so that decisions about what to preserve, how to contextualize, and how to organize the materials are made collectively. Gathering and telling stories in this way holds space to bear witness to the devastation and, in the process, wonder about joy and other unthinkable things as communities rebuild and remake themselves.

Janelle responded to Rosa's description of life and research in Puerto Rico with her own inquiry into the conditions of living and studying—in northern Alberta, Canada. When the Slough Sayers convened to discuss the two essays, Janelle stressed how much Rosa's depiction reminded her to think about the pleasures of living, even without the state. In returning to the land, Bigstone Cree Nation members also returned to the pleasures of living with plants and animals as kin and neighbors. Janelle pointed out that there is almost an obligation to be joyous when living on the land. Laughter and teasing are a part of every encounter. Teasing leads to nicknames, which in turn keep funny stories circulating long after their original occurrence. Zoe Todd told of the jokes that were such an important part of spending time on the land, and learning about relationships on and off the land, among her Métis relatives and colleagues. The hilarity of stories, such as that of "elder brother farting," keeps everyone alert—and in a sense of wonder.

Rosa added that straightforward reporting is inadequate to get at the pleasures of life in devastation. Instead, her collaborative research has created online galleries and collections of interviews and essays. These provide fragments of the past and open up alternative futures in which—as one Puerto Rican gathering put it—rage and joy can be held together, simultaneously.

It was this conversation that brought our group to the theme of beauty within horror. Janelle's essay shows how communities make this work—and how researchers can work together with communities in amplifying this sensibility.

BEAUTY AND HORROR IN DEVASTATED LANDS

The boreal forest, in the northern part of the place now known as Alberta, Canada, has become an area of extreme extraction since the 1970s, with increasing devastation in recent decades.[11] Bigstone Cree Nation, a sâkawiyiniwak (Northern Bush Cree) community, whose territory rests on top of the eastern edges of the Athabasca oil sands deposit, embraces humor and wonder despite the increase in natural resource extraction from the region. There are several small settlements, on lakes and up dirt roads around and over the muskeg or peat bogs, where most community members, including children, speak their language, sakaw nehiyawewin. Throughout Bigstone Cree Nation, but especially in these "back lakes," people have a strong preference for, and identity linked to, eating forest food.[12] Grocery stores are sometimes hundreds of kilometers away, offering an equally unappealing choice between unaffordable spoiled fresh food of distant origin and packaged processed foods. Sâkawiyiniwak preferences for traditional foods run deeper, though, than simply being a better alternative to the poor quality and prices for recently introduced foods. To be considered a traditional, real, four-dimensional person, sakaw nehiyawak, a person must enter into the reciprocal life cycles between hunter, prey, and consumption.[13]

Reincarnation and ancestral connections with living beings situate humans in kinship relations with all life. Sâkawiyiniwak show respect to their more-than-human kin through offerings, speech, and butchering practices and by the distribution of foods and medicines to people who need them in the community.[14] When respectful protocols are followed, humans experience abundance, and when beings are disrespected, they no longer offer themselves for human consumption. This is why the lack of demonstrated respect to all life concerns Bigstone Cree Nation members during natural resource extraction. Large-scale commercial development disrupts an expectation of care, where people are meant to balance extraction with offering and to share the bounty with everyone.

Bigstone Cree Nation directs several environmental research and monitoring programs, which is where my research as an environmental anthropologist and ethnobiologist is situated. There is a deep irony in the very term *environmental monitoring,* though, which implies that First Nations members require some sort of technical training and permission from the government and companies to go out on their ancestral lands and observe their devastation, assessing whether gestures of mitigation are being followed. Realistically, going on the land for food with Elders and relations is a superior form of environmental monitoring. It is how and where wisdom, or expertise, on how to find, approach, harvest, and honor food is enacted and reaffirmed. Still, scientific proof is a means to gain recognition in a colonial-settler state, and so Bigstone Cree Nation members and I have designed a three-year study on moose *(Alces alces)* and water sampling for toxins and microbiological indicators of pollution. Previously, during my doctoral research, we sampled 150 food species for testing the effects from oil and gas contamination.[15] Results accrue slowly, despite the most recent wave of Anthropocene fallout spreading quickly. Indeed, those who go on the land for food can easily identify dramatic landscape changes and signs of pollution and climate change from their encounters with the living beings who offer themselves as gifts in the forms of food and medicine. The science is trickier in that it is costly and takes a large amount of data over long periods to be able to make any definitive claims. This means we wait for science to catch up to what living beings, including Bigstone Cree Nation members, already know. In the worst sense, it also means that the government and companies are insisting on "proof" of what community members already know to be true through embodied experiences.

The Covid-19 pandemic in this long 2020 affected these efforts in ways that pushed and pulled at the tensions and ironies of environmental monitoring. Indigenous peoples in Canada have clear memories and oral traditions of pandemics and associated devastation. Hummocks on hillsides throughout traditional territories from burial sites of entire extended families and villages attest to the earliest apocalyptic waves of the Anthropocene's reach to Indigenous lands, when smallpox and then the 1918 influenza pandemic blazed through.[16] Colonial control of life restricted access to the land and its bounty by prohibiting people from moving through the forest to seasonal camps and ceremonial gatherings, confining children to residential schools, and confining adults to reserves. Treaties promised people access to traditional food while simultaneously setting the stage for large-scale resource extraction and devastation of those foods. Despite constraints, many Elders have always found ways to honor relations with bush food, medicine, and one another, including knowing antiviral medicines during pandemics.

During the 2016 oil price crash, many Bigstone Cree Nation young men who worked in oil and gas and related industries were the first to be laid off from work. When I asked if they were coping well, they responded that they were happy to have the time to go moose hunting. Likewise, when Covid-19 first started spreading across Canada in 2020, many northern First Nations communities put up checkpoints at their reserve borders and only let residents enter, with mandatory quarantines. While in isolation, people went to the land and camped to gather bush food.[17] All living beings were able to slow down and breathe well. The wonder of sâkawiyiniwak food sovereignty resounded.

In spring 2020, Alberta's minister of environment and parks and minister of energy announced that they were suspending environmental reporting requirements across multiple sectors of the energy industry.[18] At the same time, the Alberta government deemed industrial activities, like oil sands operations and logging in northern Alberta, to be *essential services*. This means that consultation with First Nations about how projects would affect their treaty rights to hunt, fish, and trap halted. They had to lay off environmental monitors. Our research has continued as much as possible, but the increased presence of people harvesting food from the bush has meant that they are witnessing industrial activities in their traditional territory. For example, Elder Helen Noskiye, who is an active hunter and trapper, saw, and filmed, a power company's mulcher disturb a bear and her two cubs from a den. According to the Province of Alberta's Wildlife Act, section 36(1), "a person shall not wilfully molest, disturb or destroy a house, nest or den of prescribed wildlife."[19] But when Helen notified a local Fish and Wildlife officer of the infraction, he did not investigate the offence. Meanwhile, a logging company recently logged an ancestral trail and associated cultural sites that were clearly marked by signs.[20] This is a punishable offence of the province of Alberta's Historical Resources Act (2020), but the Alberta Heritage Section of the government told Bigstone Cree Nation that they do not have enforcement power, "like Fish and Wildlife."[21] Members of the Bigstone Cree Nation's lands department are planning to go on the land to check on other important cultural and heritage sites in spring 2021, as they worry that a lot of damage is being done during this period of no environmental or consultation requirements. Checking on the land, honoring the ancestors, and getting bush food are the true centerpieces of our research labeled as environmental monitoring.

CRITICAL LINKS AND CONNECTIONS
ACROSS MARGINALIZED COMMUNITIES

Though not usually recognized in the normative imaginary, marginalized communities, from African American to Indigenous communities, have long made critical links and connections between their own experiences of oppression and dispossession and the treatment of more-than-human worlds. They point out that the very lens of disposability and expropriation that dominant society has used to apprehend these communities is precisely how they have approached the environment as well.

It may come as a surprise that, in 1930, W. E. B. Du Bois, in a searing speech reflecting on the wonder and beauty of the Housatonic River in the Berkshires and its subsequent contamination by industry, powerfully stated, "Rivers have been made to slave for men and carry their burdens."[22] He critiqued his own town of Great Barrington, Vermont, which, like hundreds of other towns, not to mention the entire valley, has "turned its back upon the river. They have sought to get away from it. They have neglected it. They have used it as a sewer, a drain, a place for throwing their waste and their offal," instead of allowing rivers to manifest as natural and spiritual centers. He notices that the very treatment and neglect of rivers are perhaps a central measure of the very problematic underpinnings of a civilization that has also turned its back on Black folks.

Artist and photographer LaToya Ruby Frazier, no stranger to environmental racism as she grew up in Braddock, Pennsylvania, the site of a now-shuttered U.S. Steel plant that sloughed toxic chemical emissions into the Monongahela River, spent five months in Flint, Michigan, in the midst of the water crisis, to record the devastation. To co-create an artistic engagement with this crisis, Frazier embedded with three generations of an African American family in Flint and witnessed the following: "When I visited these women over this past winter and spring, to learn about how one family endured the water crisis, they stressed that to me. Flint was family. Family was Flint—until now. This is the story of how a town loses a family and a family loses a town."[23]

The town was family, and for generations, African Americans stuck with Flint, despite the racism, segregation, deindustrialization, corporate disinvestment, and liquidation—until now. Their relationship to a place was one of relationality, community, and kinship until the city turned its back in the final, poisoning straw that pushed this Flint family to migrate south, to start a new life on a farm in Mississippi.

Critical environmental scholar David Pellow argues that it is impossible to understand "racist violence, and the way we think, talk, and enact it, without paying attention to the relationship between humans and nonhumans."[24] Drawing inspiration from the Black Lives Matter movement (and we would also add the Combahee River Collective) with the crucial notion that "none of us are free until all of us are free," Pellow links this solidarity to the more-than-human world, to Frazer's Flint and Du Bois's Housatonic River. Rejecting "human dominionism" and hackneyed dichotomies, Pellow connects the movements for "racial indispensability" and "socioeconomic indispensability," linking human with nonhuman oppression, racism with speciesism, and the devaluation of BIPOC lives with the devastation of nature.[25]

In the midst of devastation, if there is wonder, there is also kinship. Wonder, in both senses, takes us across gulfs of difference to open the possibility of new forms of kinship—kinship with other kinds of beings and kinship with other kinds of human communities. Melinda Cooper has argued that the intersection between neoliberalism and social conservatism produces a particularly selfish and exclusive kind of "family values."[26] The constricting walls of such family values make us forget that we are kin with plants and animals and that we are kin, too, with other people whose histories, stories, and ways of staying afloat are quite different from ours. These two kinds of kinship are essential to moving into the challenges of our times. Kinship creates paths for intimacy and understanding. Indeed, LaToya Frazier likens the elisions and forgetting of Black folks in the American Rust Belt to the jettisoning of the towns themselves and the rejection of more-than-human worlds. To revitalize the notion of family, we must remember, too, more-than-human kinship.[27]

The power of both Janelle Baker's and Rosa Ficek's research is in the way they both draw us into the materiality of community struggles as well as their discursive frames and semiotic commitments. To appreciate making wonder within devastation, we need close attention to more-than-human lives and livelihoods in the making of community that both researchers show us. Both testimonies show us how people ignored by or, worse, actively oppressed by their respective governments are wondering their way to different futures beyond the long 2020. In listening to their stories, we, too, are provoked to wonder.

NOTES

1. Violet Lee, "In Defence of the Wastelands: A Survival Guide," *Guts Magazine,* November 30, 2016, http://gutsmagazine.ca/wastelands/.

2. Taller Salud, "Conferencia de Prensa: Guía de Preparcación Comunitaria," press conference, Facebook, June 25, 2020.

3. Ciencia Puerto Rico, "#AquíNosCuidamosPR ante la COVID-19," press release, *Aquí Nos Cuidamos,* February 15, 2021, https://www.aquinoscuidamos.org/.

4. Cesar Ayala and Rafael Bernabe, *Puerto Rico in the American Century: A History since 1898* (Chapel Hill: University of North Carolina Press, 2009).

5. Michel-Rolph Trouillot, *Silenciando el pasado: el poder y la producción de la historia* (Granada, Spain: Comares, 2017), 69.

6. Adriana Garriga-López, "Puerto Rico: The Future in Question," *Shima* 13, no. 2 (2019): 174–92; Beatriz Llenín Figueroa, "Puerto Rico como archipiélago-experimento de emancipación contra el poder: hacia nuestros futuros decoloniales y archipiélagicos," *Visitas al patio* 14 (2019): 111–30; Mariolga Reyes Cruz, "Por quiénes esperamos," *80 grados,* February 2, 2018, https://www.80grados.net/.

7. Yarimar Bonilla and Marisol LeBrón, eds., *Aftershocks of Disaster: Puerto Rico before and after the Storm* (Chicago: Haymarket Books, 2019).

8. Rima Brusi, Yarimar Bonilla, and Isar Godreau, "When Disaster Capitalism Comes for the University of Puerto Rico," *The Nation,* September 20, 2018, https://www.thenation.com/article/archive/when-disaster-capitalism-comes-for-the-university-of-puerto-rico/.

9. Isar Godreau, Yarimar Bonilla, and Don E. Walicek, "How to Help the University of Puerto Rico—and How Not To," *Chronicle of Higher Education,* November 27, 2017, https://www.chronicle.com/article/how-to-help-the-university-of-puerto-rico-and-how-not-to/.

10. Isra Godreau, Mariluz Franco Ortiz, Hilda Lloréns, María Reinat Pumarejo, Inés Canabal Torres, and Jessica A. Gaspar Concepción, *Arrancando mitos de raíz: guía para una enseñanza antirracista de la herencia africana en Puerto Rico* (Cabo Rojo: Editora Educación Emergente, 2015); Patricia Noboa Ortega and América Soto Arzat, "Psychoanalysis and Research for Communities," special issue "La Libertad," *Cruce* (2018): 11–21.

11. Janelle M. Baker and Clinton N. Westman, "Extracting Knowledge: Social Science, Environmental Impact Assessment, and Indigenous Consultation in the Oil Sands of Alberta, Canada," *Extractive Industries and Society* 5, no. 1 (2018): 144–53.

12. Janelle Marie Baker, "Do Berries Listen? Berries as Indicators, Ancestors, and Agents in Canada's Oil Sands Region," *Ethnos* 86, no. 10 (2020): 273–94.

13. Robert Brightman, *Grateful Prey: Rock Cree Human–Animal Relationships* (Berkeley: University of California Press, 1993).

14. Baker, "Do Berries Listen?"; Baker and Fort McKay Berry Group, "Cranberries Are Medicine: Monitoring, Sharing, and Consuming Cranberries in Fort McKay," in *Wisdom Engaged: Traditional Knowledge for Northern Community Well-Being,* ed. Leslie Main Johnson, 117–41 (Edmonton: University of Alberta Press, 2019).

15. Nasrin Golzadeh, Benjamin Barst, Janelle Baker, Josie Auger, and Melissa McKinney, "Alkylated Polycyclic Aromatic Hydrocarbons Are the Largest Contributor to Polycyclic Aromatic Compound Concentrations in Traditional Foods of the Bigstone Cree Nation in Alberta, Canada," *Environmental Pollution* 275 (2021): 116625; Nasrin Golzadeh, Benjamin Barst, Nilandri Basu, Janelle Baker, Josie Auger, and Melissa McKinney, "Evaluating the Concentrations of Total Mercury, Methylmercury, Selenium, and Selenium: Mercury Molar Ratios in Traditional Foods of the Bigstone Cree in Alberta, Canada," *Chemosphere* 250 (2021): 126285.

16. Heather Davis and Zoe Todd, "On the Importance of a Date, or Decolonizing the Anthropocene," *ACME: An International E-Journal for Critical Geographies* 16, no. 4 (2017): 761–80.

17. Ina Vandebroek et al, "Reshaping the Future of Ethnobiology Research after the COVID-19 Pandemic," *Nature Plants* 6 (2020): 723–30.

18. Victoria Goodday, "Environmental Regulation and the COVID-19 Pandemic: A Review of Regulator Response in Canada," *University of Calgary: The School of Public Policy Publications SPP Briefing Paper* 14, no. 10 (2021).

19. Government of Alberta, *Wildlife Act,* Revised Statutes of Alberta Chapter W-10 (Edmonton: Queen's Printer, 2000).

20. Janelle Marie Baker, "Logging Company Clears Cree Ancestral Trail without Recourse," *The Conversation,* March 10, 2021, https://theconversation.com/logging-company-clears-cree-nation-ancestral-trail-without-recourse-154921.

21. Baker.

22. W. E. B. Du Bois, "Reflections on the Housatonic River," July 21, 1930, reproduced in *The Berkshire Edge,* April 3, 2016, https://theberkshireedge.com/.

23. LaToya Ruby Frazier, *LaToya Ruby Frazier: The Notion of Family* (New York: Aperture, 2016).

24. David N. Pellow, "Toward a Critical Environmental Justice Studies: Black Lives Matter as an Environmental Justice Challenge," *Du Bois Review* 13, no. 2 (2016): 221–36.

25. Pellow, 231.

26. Melinda Cooper, *Family Values: Between Neoliberalism and the New Social Conservatism* (Princeton, N.J.: Princeton University Press, 2017).

27. Frazier, *LaToya Ruby Frazier.*

Contributors

STACY ALAIMO is professor of English and core faculty member in environmental studies at the University of Oregon. She is author of *Undomesticated Ground: Recasting Nature as Feminist Space*; *Bodily Natures: Science, Environment, and the Material Self*; and *Exposed: Environmental Politics and Pleasures in Posthuman Times* (Minnesota, 2016). She coedited *Material Feminisms*; edited *Matter* in the Gender series of Macmillan Interdisciplinary Handbooks; and edited a special volume of *Configurations* titled Science Studies and the Blue Humanities.

ELISABETH ANKER is associate professor of American studies and political science at the George Washington University. She is author of *Ugly Freedoms* and *Orgies of Feeling: Melodrama and the Politics of Freedom*. She serves as coeditor of *Theory and Event*.

JANELLE BAKER is assistant professor in anthropology at Athabasca University in northern Alberta, Canada. She is the North America representative on the board of directors for the International Society of Ethnobiology and a coeditor of *Ethnobiology Letters*.

DANIEL A. BARBER is professor of architecture at University of Technology Sydney (UTS). His most recent books are *Modern Architecture and Climate: Design before Air Conditioning* and *A House in the Sun: Modern Architecture and Solar Energy in the Cold War*. He edits the *accumulation* series on *e-flux architecture* and is cofounder of *Current: Collective on Environment and Architectural History*. In 2022 he was awarded a Guggenheim Fellowship.

A D I A   B E N T O N is associate professor of anthropology and African studies at Northwestern University. She is author of *HIV Exceptionalism: Development through Disease in Sierra Leone* (Minnesota, 2015).

L E V I   R .   B R Y A N T is professor of philosophy at Collin College. He is author of *Difference and Givenness: Deleuze's Transcendental Empiricism and the Ontology of Immanence*; *The Democracy of Objects*; and *Onto-Cartograpy: An Ontology of Machines and Media*.

B E A T R I Z   C O L O M I N A is Howard Crosby Butler Professor of the History of Architecture and codirector of the Media and Modernity program at Princeton University. Her books include *Sexuality and Space*; *Privacy and Publicity: Modern Architecture as Mass Media*; *Domesticity at War*; *Clip/Stamp/Fold: The Radical Architecture of Little Magazines 196X–197X*; *Are We Human? Notes on an Archaeology of Design*; *X-Ray Architecture*; and *Radical Pedagogies*.

W I L L I A M   E .   C O N N O L L Y is Krieger-Eisenhower Professor at Johns Hopkins University, where he teaches political theory. His recent books include *Facing the Planetary*; *Aspirational Fascism*; *Climate Machines, Fascist Drives, and Truth*; and *Resounding Events: Adventures of an Academic from the Working Class*.

C A R Y   G A B R I E L   C O S T E L L O is director of LGBTQ+ studies and associate professor of sociology at the University of Wisconsin–Milwaukee.

M E G A N   C R A I G is a multimedia artist, essayist, and associate professor of philosophy at Stony Brook University. She is author of *Levinas and James: Toward a Pragmatic Phenomenology* and coeditor of *Richard J. Bernstein and the Expansion of American Philosophy: Thinking the Plural*.

W A I   C H E E   D I M O C K is a researcher at Harvard University's Center for the Environment. She is author of *Weak Planet*.

P A U L L A   E B R O N is associate professor in the Department of Anthropology at Stanford University. She is author of *Performing Africa*.

N I R M A L A   E R E V E L L E S is professor of social and cultural studies in education at the University of Alabama. She is author of *Disability and Difference in Global Contexts: Towards a Transformative Body Politic*.

RODERICK A. FERGUSON is William Robertson Coe Professor of Women's, Gender, and Sexuality Studies and American Studies at Yale University.

ROSA E. FICEK is professor at the Institute of Interdisciplinary Research at the University of Puerto Rico at Cayey.

STEFANIE FISHEL is lecturer in politics and international relations at the University of the Sunshine Coast in Queensland, principal researcher at the Planet Politics Institute, and visiting fellow and member of the Environment and Governance Research Group at UNSW, Canberra. She is author of *The Microbial State: The Body Politic and Global Thriving* (Minnesota, 2017).

JONATHAN FLATLEY is professor of English at Wayne State University in Detroit, Michigan. He is author of *Affective Mapping: Melancholia and the Politics of Modernism* and *Like Andy Warhol*.

JENNIFER GABRYS is chair in media, culture, and environment in the Department of Sociology at the University of Cambridge. She leads the Planetary Praxis research group and is principal investigator on the ERC-funded project "Smart Forests: Transforming Environments into Social-Political Technologies." She is author of *Citizens of Worlds: Open-Air Toolkits for Environmental Struggle* (Minnesota, 2022).

DAVID GISSEN is professor of architecture and urban history at the Parsons School of Design and the New School, New York. He is author of *The Architecture of Disability: Buildings, Cities, and Landscapes beyond Access* (Minnesota, 2022).

RICHARD GRUSIN is Distinguished Professor of English at the University of Wisconsin–Milwaukee. He is author of *Transcendentalist Hermeneutics: Institutional Authority and the Higher Criticism of the Bible*; *Culture, Technology, and the Creation of America's National Parks*; *Premediation: Affect and Mediality after 9/11*; and *Radical Mediation: Cinema, Estetica, e Tecnologie Digitali* and coauthor of *Remediation: Understanding New Media*. He is editor of *The Nonhuman Turn*, *Anthropocene Feminism*, *After Extinction*, and *Insecurity* and coeditor of *Ends of Cinema*, all from the University of Minnesota Press.

D E H L I A   H A N N A H is postdoctoral fellow at the Royal Danish Academy of Fine Arts and ARKEN Museum of Modern Art, Copenhagen, and a curator. She is author of *A Year without a Winter* and coeditor of *The Routledge Handbook of Art and Science and Technology Studies*.

K A R E N   H O is associate professor of anthropology at the University of Minnesota. She is author of *Liquidated: An Ethnography of Wall Street*.

B O N N I E   H O N I G is Nancy Duke Lewis Professor of Modern Culture and Media and Political Science at Brown University and (by courtesy) professor of religious studies and theater and performance studies. She is author of several books, including *Antigone, Interrupted*; *Public Things: Democracy in Disrepair*; *A Feminist Theory of Refusal*; and *Shell Shocked: Feminist Criticism after Trump*.

F R É D É R I C   K E C K is senior researcher at the Laboratory of Social Anthropology (CNRS Paris). He is author of *Avian Reservoirs: Virus Hunters and Birdwatchers in Chinese Sentinel Posts*.

E B E N   K I R K S E Y is associate professor of anthropology at the University of Oxford. He is author of *Freedom in Entangled Worlds*; *Emergent Ecologies*; and *The Mutant Project: Inside the Global Race to Genetically Modify Humans* and editor of *The Multispecies Salon*.

B E R N A R D   C .   P E R L E Y is Maliseet from Tobique First Nation, New Brunswick, Canada. He is director of the Institute for Critical Indigenous Studies at the University of British Columbia, Vancouver.

T O M   R A D E M A C H E R is an eighth-grade English teacher in the Minneapolis area. His books include *Raising Ollie: How My Nonbinary Art-Nerd Kid Changed (Nearly) Everything I Know* (Minnesota, 2021) and *It Won't Be Easy: An Exceedingly Honest (and Slightly Unprofessional) Love Letter to Teaching* (Minnesota, 2017), which was a finalist for a Minnesota Book Award. In 2014, he was honored as Minnesota's Teacher of the Year.

R E N Y A   K .   R A M I R E Z is an enrolled member of the Winnebago Tribe of Nebraska and professor of anthropology at the University of California, Santa Cruz.

M A U R E E N   R Y A N is research assistant professor of media arts and film and media studies at the University of South Carolina. She is author of *Lifestyle Media in American Culture: Gender, Class, and the Politics of Ordinariness* and coeditor of *Emergent Feminisms: Complicating a Postfeminist Media Culture*.

Z O E T O D D (Métis) is a practice-led artist-researcher who examines the relationships between Indigenous sovereignty and freshwater fish futures in Canada.

A N N A T S I N G is professor of anthropology at the University of California, Santa Cruz. She is author of several books, including *The Mushroom at the End of the World: On the Possibility of Life in Capitalist Ruins*, and coeditor of *Feral Atlas: The More-than-Human Anthropocene* and *Arts of Living on a Damaged Planet: Ghosts and Monsters of the Anthropocene* (Minnesota, 2017).

S A R A H E . V A U G H N is assistant professor of anthropology at the University of California, Berkeley. She is author of *Engineering Vulnerability: In Pursuit of Climate Adaptation*.

R E B E C C A W A N Z O is professor and chair of the Department of Women, Gender, and Sexuality Studies at Washington University in St. Louis. She is author of *The Suffering Will Not Be Televised: African American Women and Sentimental Political Storytelling* and *The Content of Our Caricature: African American Comic Art and Political Belonging*.

M C K E N Z I E W A R K teaches at the New School for Social Research and Eugene Lang College in New York City. She is author of *A Hacker Manifesto, Gamer Theory, 50 Years of Recuperation of the Situationist International*, and *The Beach beneath the Street*.

Index

BLM. *See* Black Lives Matter

body, x, 249n32, 256n7; and architecture, xv, 108, 111, 116–117 (*see also* architecture); and the body politic, xvi, 78n2, 162–64, 165n1; collective body of protestors, 223–25; and Covid-19, 71, 84, 162 (*see also* Covid-19); and disability, 68; as part of a binary, 4, 19; of trans individuals, 251–55 (*see also* trans); and the unconscious, 61

breath, xii, xv–xvi, 9, 144–45, 149, 151n20, 152–53, 282; and architecture, 109, 111, 127, 130 (*see also* architecture); difficulty breathing with COVID-19, 66, 146, 194, 196; "I can't breathe," 70, 79n10, 146 (*see also* Floyd, George); and inequality, 147–48, 162; and social distancing, 156–58 (*see also* social distancing)

Burnet, Frank M., xiv, 48–49, 51, 52

capitalism, xi, xiii, xix–xix, xxn8, 10–11, 131, 201n24, 265, 269; as barrier to institutional readiness, 96, 218, 285n8; global and transnational capitalism, 62, 67, 69, 71, 76; and Christianity, 101n1; and climate change, 90, 93, 159n11; and colonialism, 198

Carson, Rachel, xiv, 46–48, 51

Chan, Alina, 36

Chauvin, Derek, ix, 32, 84, 92–93, 229

cities, x, 5; Hong Kong, 158n1, 217; and inequality, 126n14, 196; Jakarta, 153; London, 147; Los Angeles, 84, 126n14; New York City, 122; Paris, 118, 153, 217, 225; and post-truth, 56 (*see also* post-truth); and protests, 89, 92–93 (*see also* Black Lives Matter); and sickness, 106–8, 112; and solarization, 121–23; and ventilation, 114, 129, 144, 146–48; and wilderness, 20, 153; Wuhan, 34–35, 42, 187–88, 199, 200

climate change, xi, xvi, 9–10, 90, 92, 94, 95, 97, 120, 159n6, 159n8, 213, 258; against, 213, 258, 275, 278, 281; and air, 152–54, 157–58; and the Anthropocene, 7, 18, 36, 44n31, 152 (*see also* Anthropocene); and architecture, 121 (*see also* architecture); and capitalism, 90; denial of, 91, 98, 155–56; struggles and disability, 78 (*see also* disability); and wildfires, 148;

Clinton, Hillary, 54

Combahee River Collective, 284

contact tracing, xvii, 39, 229–35

coronavirus. *See* Covid-19

Covid-19, ix–x, xiii–xvi, xix, 4–5, 10, 82, 89, 150n7, 166, 168–85, 188, 203n54, 236, 279, 285n3, 286n17, 286n18; and animal testing, 12n5; and anti-trans activism, 245; and architecture, 105–6 (*see also* architecture); and Black Lives Matter, 216, 229 (*see also* Black Lives Matter); and breathing, 145, 150n5, 153, 155–58, 159n3, 194–96, 199n4, 201n32, 201n33 (*see also* breath); and China, 201n36; and climate change, 142, 152, 154, 156, 159n6, 159n12, 282 (*see also* climate change); death toll, 196, 201n37, 258, 275; depictions of, 200n17; and disability, 80n35; and food, 202n43; and freedom, 161; and history of other pandemics, 38, 68, 73, 94; and isolation, 24, 29, 32n11, 32n18, 164; and LGBTQ+, 242, 248n21; and lockdowns, 79n7, 237, 276; and long Covid, 196, 201n38; and masks, 207–8; and Native American populations, 38, 40, 43n20, 43n27, 44n34, 44n37, 44n38; and nursing homes, 69; and pollution, 149n1; and prevention, 277–79; and racism, 6–7, 80n25, 146, 150n7, 196, 198; and storytelling, 34 (*see also* narrative); and testing, 242; theories of origin for, 36, 42n5, 42n7, 42n8, 169–71, 199n5; transmission of,

Index